# Science, Technology, and Ecopolitics in the USSR

*Miron Rezun*

 PRAEGER

Westport, Connecticut
London

**Library of Congress Cataloging-in-Publication Data**

Rezun, Miron.
    Science, technology, and ecopolitics in the USSR / Miron Rezun.
        p.   cm.
    Includes bibliographical references and index.
    ISBN 0–275–95383–1 (alk. paper)
        1.  Science—Russia (Federation)    2.  Technology—Russia
    (Federation)    3.  Environmental policy—Russia (Federation)
    I.  Title.
    Q127.R9R49    1996
    306.4′5′0947—dc20          95–22010

British Library Cataloguing in Publication Data is available.

Library of Congress Catalog Card Number: 95–22010
ISBN: 0–275–95383–1

First published in 1996

Praeger Publishers, 88 Post Road West, Westport, CT 06881
An imprint of Greenwood Publishing Group, Inc.

Printed in the United States of America

The paper used in this book complies with the
Permanent Paper Standard issued by the National
Information Standards Organization (Z39.48–1984).

10 9 8 7 6 5 4 3 2

*To the memory of my mother, Lea*

# Contents

# Preface

This book is the fruit of a decade of intermittent investigations into Soviet Russia's mission to become a mighty scientific and technological power. The failure of that mission coincided with the decline and then the demise of the USSR. One of the major causes of that decline was precisely the failure of the technological quest. This is at least what many experts believe. The theme is an interesting one, inasmuch as the USSR had made great strides and kept up with the West. Russia could very well rise again, taking up where it left off.

This is a topic that is fabulously rich in data and congenial for discussion of a dialectical kind. Covered here are the themes of science, technology, the environment, and general culture. Many books have appeared in the last few years that depict the disastrous effects of economic growth on the environment and the appearance of Green parties; many studies offer a normative, holistic approach to the economics of growth and progress. In the year 1995 alone both *Newsweek* and *Time* magazines ran elaborate cover stories on the growing commitment to technology, thus fuelling the current debate about "cyberdemocracy" and "cyberinequality." My task, however, is to show that the Soviet Union and its peoples had a very large scientific establishment, replete with institutions, research institutes, science cities, great men and women of wisdom and foresight, and wonderful advances in technology--but that, in many respects, while there was great progress in some areas of technology and research, the final outcome was a total and dismal failure.

Moreover, the people of the former Soviet Union were literally left physically and mentally sick. So much pesticide and herbicide had been sprayed on the crops that harvesters were being poisoned by the fumes. In some extreme cases, it has been documented that one could flick a cigarette butt into a river meandering past a big factory in a large industrial mega-city, and find that the river would explode because it was blanketed with thick layers of oil. Ill-advised dam construction and inappropriate irrigation projects caused the level of the Aral Sea, the fourth largest sea in the world, to drop forty feet. One suspects that in twenty years or so the Aral will probably disappear altogether. Reports have it that resorts along the Black Sea have now banned swimming after warnings that the waters are contaminated with dysentery and typhoid germs. In its drive for gross output--*Valovaya Produktsiya*--and the desire to attain or surpass the economic and technical standards of the West, there was so much neglect that it fouled up both industry and ecology. A lot of what has happened in the USSR, of course, has happened elsewhere in the world. It is still happening in China and North America on a grand scale, although with more devastating effects in the East than in the West.

There are so many paradoxes in the Russian experience. Individual Russian scientists in past centuries made enormous breakthroughs in chemistry and physics, in scientific theories. Yet when the printing press--a practical tool--was first introduced in Russia, the Tsar declared it the property of the state, and the state monopoly of print lasted for 250 years. It is often said that when Leon Trotsky proposed to Stalin that a modern telephone system be built in the USSR, Stalin replied, "I can imagine no greater instrument of counter-revolution in our time." Today, Russia has the lowest per capita distribution of telephones--ten out of every 100 citizens--among the industrialized nations. A public telephone directory for the city of Moscow is only now coming into being.

Yet Russia is an industrialized nation. Despite the neglect and inefficiency, the USSR did manage to pull itself up by its bootstraps. Otherwise, there would not have been so many experts in the West who, year after year, were keen to follow every advancement, every techno-logical breakthrough, every strategic move for the benefit of the Western security services. The Soviet Union was, after all, a mighty military power.

I can remember attending AAASS (American Association for the Advancement of Slavic Studies) meetings in places as far apart as Bavaria's Garmisch-Parten Kirchen, in Boston, and Hawaii, where there were incalculable debates, seminars, and workshops on the position of the Soviet military and the state-of-the-art Soviet civilian technology. Lieutenant Colonel David Wellman studied this subject on behalf of the National Defense University in Washington, D.C. Before him was Dr. Seymour Goodman, the foremost U.S. expert on Soviet computers from the University of Arizona, working under contract for the CIA. Others are William McHenry of Georgetown University, a one-time student of Professor Goodman's; Richard Judy, who worked for the Hudson Institute and other great specialists such as Carl Hammer and, of course, the Dean of Soviet Science Studies at MIT himself, Professor Loren Graham. Europe's leading authorities on this subject have been in Germany, chiefly at the research and analysis division of Radio Liberty/Radio Free Europe in Munich, under the supervision of the Soviet expatriate Victor Yasmann. In Germany, too, the Germans followed Soviet technological innovations very closely; many institutes were involved, and not always associated with those bearing names like Max Planck. Most of these, like the one in the town of Ebenhausen outside of Munich, received generous funding from the West German Christian Democratic Party and possibly even from the *Bundesnachrichtendienst*.

I remember going to Paris on many occasions to consult the American embassy's COCOM annex, which adamantly refused to reveal a critical list of technologies and materials, privy only to NATO. To this very day the CAD/CAM capability of the West is closely guarded by the major commercial hardware producers and is the object of trade embargoes advanced by the U.S. Department of Defense in the interest of national security.

There is much in this book that shows that Russia's industrial base could easily take off again, that the Cold War, dead now, might begin anew. The scientific minds of men and women in the post-Communist epoch do not die. Indeed, if there is a shift to either the extreme right or the extreme left again, Russia's scientific genius will be resurrected. And to make my narrative of events and the analyses of the problems as readable and digestible as possible, I have kept most of the technical terminology in laymen's terms. Clearly, my study covers the covert world of espionage-skulduggery, of purloined secrets, of resource wars that may or may not have existed but were regularly and exaggeratedly reported by the Western press, anti-Soviet scholars, and Western businesses.

I explore how the West was being outstripped in space, and generally how the Soviet Union passed through a long period of travail in computer technology, while continually tottering on the edge of a precipice. I try to answer such cultural questions as to whether Russians have a work ethic, whether they really have a technical bent, and where they are headed today. Some light is shed on the symbiotic relationship of technology and Marxist dialectics; I examine how rigid theoretical thinking can sometimes become and how, sooner or later, everyone will probably come to the realization that market economics is far superior to central planning, now that socialism and Communism and Marxism have been utterly discredited as realities of life.

In the epilogue to this book, I introduce the readers to similar problems caused by science and technology in the West, specifically in North America, where I live, by a short examination of the ongoing academic debate between the pro- and anti-technology camps. Western technomania in the private and public sectors has become such a compelling issue among University scholars that I examine the perspectives of the academic Left, particularly those pertaining to the postmodernist, Marxist, and feminist schools of critical theory.

I feel a deep sense of gratitude to many people who, over the years, read early drafts of the manuscript and offered valuable suggestions toward its improvement. Among them are Stephen Turner, a historian of science at my university; Garry Allen, who has for years now taught innovative courses on politics and technology in my department; and many Russian friends, too numerous to mention here, in Russia, the U.S., and in Israel, who have read and made critical comments. Paula Dawson, one of my students, is to be thanked for having helped my inquiry into the problems of the environment. As always, I owe much to the research assistance of Angela Williams, who helped me in every way to finalize this project. I also wish to thank Mark Kane and Jean Lynch of Greenwood Publishing Group for all of their help in finalizing the manuscript. To all of these people I owe much. I am indebted to Queen's University's Centre for Resource Studies in Canada for making it possible to travel to Russia's Arctic Circle, where I was able to conduct interviews on strategic minerals. Last but not least, I would also like to extend my appreciation to Stanford University and particularly to the Hoover Institution Library for inviting me in 1989 to come and spend a fruitful summer of research financed by the Olin Foundation. Whatever is left out--or the reader still finds wanting in the book--is entirely my fault.

*Chapter 1*

# The Importance of Science and Technology in Soviet Society

## WHAT IS SCIENCE AND TECHNOLOGY?

Charles Darwin's epoch-making publication, *The Origin of Species* (1858), sparked nothing less than a scientific revolution. The book was shocking when it first came out. It challenged all contemporary religious beliefs and became a milestone in the new scientific thought. It was a pity, though, that post-Darwinian society in England and elsewhere, should have made such a farce of Darwin's basic theories, for the zoological and biological differences that Darwin propounded were distorted by social scientists as cultural changes called "social Darwinism." Publicists and political thinkers of the day, for instance, were ever ready to pervert his theory of evolution with biases that reinterpreted and redefined what Darwin really meant by "the survival of the fittest."

This new science fell in well with the Industrial Revolution. The Protestant movement in Europe had become synonymous with the rise of capitalism and the individual work ethic. Protestantism effectively split the Christian Church, creating new social classes and more complex socioeconomic relations. Yet the impact was a positive one in terms of human advancement; it gave rise to and encouraged greater economic competition. Economic competition in turn encouraged free enterprise, fostering the spirit of the market and technological advancement--never mind that it had produced "raw capitalism," with all the horrors of economic and social inequality. We needn't go into these lurid details; the human suffering of the Industrial Revolution beggars description.

Science and technology have thus long been regarded as a central core in the whole evolutionary process of the human species. In this sense, even in the worst of times, scientific knowledge was regarded as critical to the whole equation of modernization and human development.

Just as there is a link between Darwinism and fascism, there is a distinct correlation between Darwin and Marxism, or Communism. These philosophies in turn have much to do with Judeo-Christian teleology. The latter is the belief that all phenomena are determined by an overall design or purpose. When Darwin's ideas about evolution spread in the second half of the nineteenth century, Judeo-Christian teleology dovetailed nicely with Darwinism. Rigid cultural evolutionists foresaw a predetermined historical destiny. Communism was looked upon by the evolutionists as a reality and as the vision of a future utopia. Western and American societies also believe in a cultural evolution that reinforces belief in a "one directional, convergent destiny for mankind."[1] Central to this determinism is the belief in progress, and the instrument to achieve such progress is technology. Consider just how technologically minded the Calvinists were when they extolled the great virtues of wealth and banking. Technical progress plays the same role in the twentieth century that gold played in the fifteenth and sixteenth centuries.

In many ways the central theme of the history of the twentieth century may be seen as the way in which science and technology have preponderantly affected Western civilization. Science and technology have much to do with growth and industry, business and commerce, medicine and labor productivity, and military might. Science and technology were the yardstick for measuring the degree of poverty and the distribution of wealth. Technological breakthroughs and their spinoffs resulted to a certain extent in the age-old struggle between classes, even in conflicts between nations. The belief that there is something evolutionary and progressive about the concept of science and technology would also imply that there is something devolutionary and regressive about it as well.

If science is knowledge writ large (though many will dispute this notion), or designating a body of knowledge, then technology must be assumed to be the technical ways of doing things, relating to the instruments, machines, and tools. Technology is, as it were, the practical application of scientific knowledge. And nowhere is this application more evident than in the research and development that produce the technological advances oriented often toward military-related purposes, but ultimately giving rise to spinoffs that are increasingly beneficial to the economy and to society as a whole. Most observers concur that in the post-World War II era, over half of all scientists and engineers in the world had been working for the military establishment, directly or indirectly funded by grants from departments of defense, inventing or developing ever more sophisticated means of destruction.[2]

This whole equation must also account for the human factor, since science and technology in isolation would make no sense. We must get a feel of the society that uses it, produces it, and improves upon it, if we are to consider it evolutionary. It should logically follow that societies and nations that have mastered technology are, by definition, economically and militarily more powerful and influential than those that have not.[3] Such nations also enjoy relatively high standards of living.

But if humanity is to be taken seriously, we must be mindful of the Faustian bargain struck with technology. One nation might want to steal it from another. Technology may also appear to be devolutionary and regressive; it easily becomes the means and conduit for mass destruction. Frequently it is anti-ecological, antisocial, unhealthy, and inhuman. For others it represents the only means of cleaning our air, purifying our water, or maintaining the longevity of our flora and fauna. In the past century, technologies increasingly determined the nature of our value system and influenced our economic and social relations more than at any other age.

## HIGH TECHNOLOGY

The first Industrial Revolution was triggered by a steam engine to the benefit of transportation and by the introduction of the spinning jenny to the benefit of textiles. This innovative trend worked its way into the economy over the course of several decades. The revolution was primarily associated with England, a country that had already risen to global prominence through its mastery of sea power. England maintained that dominance as long as the Industrial Revolution supported its economic and commercial (mercantilist) strength relative to the continental powers. But England's relative strength slowly eroded as railroad technology developed with the spread of the Industrial Revolution. Thus the advantages of being a coastal sea power began to wither away. When railroads became the sinews of economic penetration and military expansion, Germany was able to compete successfully with England for supremacy in Europe and the world. By the beginning of the twentieth century, Germany on the continent was able to surpass England as the major European power.

The second Industrial Revolution was characterized by such innovations as the internal combustion engine, electricity, the telegraph, the telephone, radio, television, and other amenities that revolutionized old methods of production and manufacturing, attended, of course, by significant economic, social, and political consequences.

In our own age it is customary to refer to this ongoing evolution as "high technology," since we are in the midst of a third Industrial Revolution spearheaded by the advent of the computer and the microprocessor.

Indeed, the "high technology" of the third Industrial Revolution (some call it a post-industrial phenomenon) is transforming at breakneck speed whole industries and creating new ones, not only in the production of goods but of services as well. These are primarily in the field of information technology: materials science, fiber optics, biotechnology, systems analysis, CAD-CAM (Computer-Aided Design and Computer-Aided Manufacturing) artificial intelligence, robotics and so on, with far-reaching consequences in communications, transportation, and standard of living. Economic leadership in the world unfailingly went to those countries that were able to master and lead the way in high technology: Japan, Western Europe, and the United States.

## SOVIET STAGNATION

The ideologies of the modern world, liberalism and Marxism, have wholeheartedly embraced science and technology as a progressive, evolutionary force, with varying degrees of success. In East and West, modern technology is generally thought to work wonders; individuals and institutions have come to believe that every problem has a technological solution. The Soviet Union, hardly an exception to this rule, was invariably called until very recently--by Soviet leaders and Westerners--a "technotopia." One observer of the Soviet scene described it as

a political regime promising its citizens a technological leap to a qualitatively better existence. Science and technology underlie the regime's ideology, guaranteeing scientific explanations of history and society, solutions to economic and social difficulties, and even a transformation of humankind into a new Soviet species.[4]

That the Soviet Union had transformed Russia and much of its Asian periphery from a backward, agrarian nation to a literate one was a stupendous feat. The fact that the USSR successfully harnessed modern technology to its own military-industrial complex was an achievement to be marvelled at. But the USSR only stayed a military superpower because it spent at least 20 percent of its GNP on defense, compared with America's 7 percent. Some estimates even claimed that as much as 30 percent or 35 percent of the Soviet GNP went toward the military while the Soviet GNP stood at roughly half of the American, with far slower rates of economic growth.

Toward the end of the Brezhnev era, it was widely felt that the Soviet nation was in a deep state of economic decay, its people suffering from moral and social alienation, living daily double lives, one for themselves and one for the state. Corruption was pervasive. Inflation was artificially suppressed. The problem of daily shortages of consumer goods and food had become the stuff of daily witticisms. Bureaucrats--about 18 million of them--have until now wielded enormous power. Innovation and incentive were so low that there was hardly any encouragement of new product and process technologies. Since the entrepreneurial spirit was never a characteristic of Soviet communism (except for products bought and sold on the black market), a single individual could not privately market a product for personal profit, or take out and market a patent on an invention. In addition, there was constant declining productivity of resources, both human and material. The main problem was the system of central planning that developed under Stalin in the late 1920s and 1930s. The Soviet command economy would have collapsed by the early 1970s had it not been for the fact that Soviet oil production had more than doubled in the wake of the world price rise after the Arab oil embargo of 1973. Oil revenue generated about $200 billion in hard currency and staved off total disaster. But the world price of oil declined a decade later. And even if natural resources were (and still are) plentiful--ores and energy in particular--it was extremely costly to extract them in view of the weakness of technological applications. The productivity of the whole economy, that is, the real rate of growth, declined to about zero for the better part of the 1980s. The quality of life of the Soviet people and their general standard of living deteriorated accordingly. The very concept of a Soviet "technotopia" became irrelevant.

As subsequent chapters will discuss in much greater detail, the Soviet planned (or administrative) economy was not capable of keeping up with the industrialized nations. Thus the Soviet claim to prominent world leadership came into question. The USSR was even being outclassed economically by the emerging nations of the Pacific Rim: Taiwan, South Korea, Hong Kong, and Singapore.

A few caveats must be mentioned first. Firstly, Soviet science carried with it a great deal of Marxist-Leninist ideological "baggage" that is essential to an understanding of science and technology in the Soviet Union. Within the Marxist scheme of things, science was always seen as the means through which the true Communist state is realized.[5] Secondly, much information, particularly on the state of contemporary Soviet science, was either unavailable or inaccurate. Many of the most interesting works on the subject of Soviet science were written by Soviet dissidents and Russian expatriates. Zhores Medvedev and Mark Popovsky are two who have written seminal works. The opinions of others were collected by Western specialists in surveys sponsored by Harvard, Columbia, and other American and Western universities. Soviet sources have tended to be overly laudatory of Soviet achievements.

Our third caveat is in many respects an outgrowth of the second. Soviet writers themselves are at a loss to understand the nature of the "scientific-technological revolution" (STR).[6] This term was used by Soviet writers and policymakers for decades to explain that the USSR was also going through a third Industrial Revolution. Although there is much speculation in Soviet circles on the subject, most of the analysts confidently predicted that the Soviet STR was going to cause the decline of capitalism and the triumph of Communism. Milder versions of this theme continued until the era of *perestroika* and then, suddenly, a complete reversal of this position prevailed.

## THE RUSSIAN EXPERIENCE

The history of science in the Soviet Union, like so many other areas of the nation's social, economic, and political fabric, began when science and a scientific establishment were literally imported from Western Europe as part of Peter the Great's attempt to bring Russia into the eighteenth century.[7] In 1724, the Russian Academy of Sciences was established with the object of utilizing science for the betterment of Russia. Although Peter's utilitarian intentions for science in his homeland were unquestionably ahead of his time, the imported academicians, who were generally natural philosophers schooled in the French tradition, quickly lapsed into their traditional approach to the study of nature: the pursuit of knowledge for knowledge's sake. This approach to science was a permanent feature in the Russian tradition.

One of the main components of Soviet science--indeed, one of its most original innovations--was set up before the Bolsheviks seized power. During its short-lived tenure, the provisional Russian government under Kerensky in 1917 created several research institutes, a trend that was continued by their revolutionary successors. According to a contemporary Soviet analyst, the creation of research institutes was very much an innovation in the structure of international science.[8] Paradoxically, the period during which a virtual civil war gripped the country (1917-21) was called the "Golden Age" of Soviet science. A dramatic expansion of scientific institutes took place in an atmosphere of little political interference. (Note that this was not the case in the humanities, where the effects of ideological re-education were quite significant.) Among the notable triumphs of Soviet science was the rise of Soviet biology to world prominence, especially through the work of Nikolai Vavilov, among others.[9]

The initial policies pursued by the Bolsheviks were very sensible. They expected science to unleash untapped creative powers and the inventiveness of the people to unprecedented heights, calling for a technical revolution that was destined to change bourgeois society. Lenin instituted not only the New Economic Policy (NEP) of restricted private enterprise--to the exclusion only of the commanding heights of industry, the utilities, and communications--but also the GOERLO, or electrification plan. He often equated electrification with the building of communism, since electrification in a backward country had profound economic and social implications. He was once quoted as saying that Communism meant "the electrification of the entire country and Soviet power." Lenin considered capitalism to be evil; he wanted to channel it toward state capitalism as the "intermediary link between small production and socialism, as a means, a path, a method of increasing the productive forces."[10]

Scientific policy under the NEP was directed by GLAVNAUKA, a special department of the People's Commissariat of Education. GLAVNAUKA handed out government research contracts and authorized foreign travel for scientists. Led by A.V. Lunacharsky, Director of GLAVNAUKA, the number of scientific papers multiplied. Scholarly journals proliferated, and stupendous advances were made in genetics, biochemistry, physiology, biology, physics, chemistry, and geophysics.

## STALIN

The end of the civil war in 1921 led to the development of a new political climate that brought the Golden Age to an abrupt end. Largely through the influence of Stalin, Soviet science became subject to the same sort of politicization that had been thrust upon the humanities in the previous decade. Beginning in 1928, the Communist Party attempted to persuade the Academy of Sciences to admit members of the Communist Party. When this failed, the academy was reorganized. The new academy, included the humanities, which, having already been reformed, gave the party significant influence within this prestigious organization. This period was also characterized by other major problems in the Soviet Union, notably the failure of agriculture to feed the nation. Although this failure was officially blamed on foreign saboteurs and bourgeois influences, in reality it appears that Stalin's ineffective and unrealistic policies, coupled with the years of civil war, brought Soviet agriculture to the verge of collapse.

Stalin considered himself an authority in many scientific fields, including biology, evolution, linguistics, and the social sciences. In the natural sciences, all research had to be based on the principles of dialectical materialism, which held that matter is in constant motion and proceeds through ever greater stages of development. Human society was thought to develop that way as well. It was under Stalin's wing that men like Trofim Lysenko rose to prominence by maintaining that genetics was useless in the study of natural growth.

Lysenko believed in the inheritance of acquired characteristics and denied the existence of genes and chromosomes as units of heredity, which essentially denied the role DNA plays in inheritance. This dialectical materialist philosophy fit in very nicely with the totalitarian Marxist state, a philosophy that was at odds not only with the study of genetics, the laws of physics and chemistry, but with all forms of idealism, metaphysics, and religions. The Lysenko group had the full support of Stalin, who endorsed the idea that deterministic principles of environment were the mainstays of growth and development. Hundreds of Soviet scientists who did not fall in with this dogma were purged and usually perished or saw their careers ruined. Foreign scientists who had come to the land of socialism to escape fascism or the bourgeois decadence of their own countries quickly became disillusioned.

One of the foreigners was a New Yorker, H. J. Muller. Invited to come to Moscow by the Soviet geneticist Nikolai Vavilov (who later died in a Soviet labor camp), Muller changed his mind about the Soviet system and left. Back in the U.S., he continued his research and was awarded the Nobel Prize in 1946.

The impact of Lysenkoism and the bogus interpretation given to dialectical materialism cannot be exaggerated. A fraud and a charlatan, Lysenko was never interested in pure biochemistry; he wanted to apply his untested and spurious beliefs to improve farming methods. The Lysenkoites believed that the soaking of seeds, or vernalization, could convert winter wheat into spring wheat. Soviet agriculture made almost no use of established techniques of mutation and hybridization in the improvement of livestock and crops. To the extent that this modern socialist state was making dramatic headway in improved literacy, employment, and general social conditions, it was reasonable to assume that a better form of man would be produced if only the environment could be made to improve. No one in those days, especially in the USSR, would have thought that the very decadent theories that were denounced would one day permit unorthodox experimentation with "designer genes" and genetic engineering. Quite ironically, the Soviet Lysenkoites believed that if man could be improved in a new socialist environment, then it would be possible in the long run to do away with hereditary afflictions such as mental retardation, heart disease, diabetes, and others. What about political dissent? Was this an affliction of the body or the mind? The Soviets must have taken this quite seriously. Lysenko died in 1976, with his ideas invalidated--but political deviants and dissidents were still placed in psychiatric wards long afterward. It was only after 1964, when Lysenko was thoroughly discredited in the USSR, that the Austrian monk Gregor Mendel's theories on heredity were published again and used in scientific experiments.

From the perspective of Soviet science, this failure is particularly important because it marks the first occasion that Soviet science was called upon to solve a specific problem. Amidst this rise in expectations, the credible work of men such as Vavilov was overshadowed and eventually destroyed by men like Lysenko.

In applied science, the "discovery" of plots of industrial sabotage brought political repression into the scientific and technological camp. The impetus for this development appears to have been the large number of Western engineers who entered the Soviet Union as part of the industrialization effort, a development that owed much to the effects of the Great Depression in the West. The attempts of these engineers to assist the USSR in building a new society in part led to the closing of Soviet society in general, and the scientific community in particular.

Soviet scientists were restricted from foreign travel. When the Western engineers and scientists were expelled or left the USSR, Stalinist authorities enforced the draconian restrictions on all foreign contacts.

The stagnation brought about by the isolation of the Soviet scientific community was quickly overshadowed by perhaps the single most devastating event for Soviet science: the Great Terror. The latter half of the 1930s saw a great many scientific and technical persons arrested and imprisoned. Most scientific research ground to a halt, while "Stalinist" technicians maintained industry. The renowned Soviet historian, Zhores Medvedev, states that no new technology was produced by Soviet applied scientists during this period.[11] When World War II began, however, Stalin realized that the Soviet Union could not stand up to Nazi Germany without technical innovations in the rapidly diminishing Soviet war machine. Consequently, many scientists and technologists, Tupolev and Korolev being perhaps the most outstanding, were organized in prison factories where essential war materiel could be produced.[12] The historical significance of the Gulag, or prison camp system, lies in two areas. First, prison work camps served to bring together, although under difficult conditions, the key figures in many technological areas. Virtually all Soviet aeronautics scientists could be found working under Tupolev; the founding fathers of Soviet rocketry could be found with Korolev; and the core of the Soviet nuclear physics program was associated with Kurchatov. Second, the prison work camp can be seen as a forerunner of the specialized academic and industrial city, a development that perhaps owes as much to Stalin's slave labor system as it does to Kerensky's vision of specialized research institutes.

One of the most important guiding principles in the Soviet tradition is that collective work is always preferable to individual effort. This is contrary to the tradition of Western liberal capitalism. It is more productive to concentrate efforts on one problem rather than several. This principle became especially important to Soviet science. Beginning in World War II, Soviet scientists were increasingly concentrated in "science cities" to enable them to work in a truly scientific atmosphere with no outside distractions. The first such cities were really concentration camps, called *sharashki*, during the war. Physicists became part of the first scientific state farm system, concentrated in atomic research cities known only by post office numbers. These cities were usually surrounded by prison camps under Stalin and later by construction battalions. Thus, for example, biologists came to settle in the Bacteriological City in Kirov, where experiments with biological weapons took place in the middle of this crowded city.

Akademgorodok, in Siberia, became one of the first modern science cities. Another was Zelenograd, on the Moscow periphery. The original plan for these science cities was to build them away from large towns and cities. However, due to chronic shortages of food and transport, this became impossible.[13] Authorities used the lure of enhanced living space and cultural life to attract leading scientists. This life was not without its problems, though. Shortages of food and a rigid class structure within the cities (in which senior scientists gained tremendous privileges which the younger scientists were denied) led to a decrease in trust between the classes. Eventually, the quality of work took a turn for the worse. Many people enroled in science programs in these cities merely to gain material advantages. Social life became virtually nonexistent; many scientists turned to drink and adultery to escape. Boredom, leading to suicide, was quite common. Life was not bereft of the political informants who constantly lurked in the background. Although these cities produced many a scientific breakthrough, they had a destructive effect on the individuals.[14]

## THE POSTWAR PERIOD

The immediate postwar years (1946-53) saw the decline and death of Stalin as well as the beginning of Soviet attempts to catch up with the West. Because of this political imperative, the areas of supersonic aircraft, atomic physics, and rocketry were given preferential treatment. In biology and chemistry, political interference brought Lysenkoism to new heights, as well as other brands of scientific sensationalism.[15] The idea of Lysenkoism was not overthrown until 1964 by the Soviet Academy of Sciences. Medvedev sums up this period by stating, "Considering the general picture of scientific progress during the period 1945-53, it is very difficult, however, to find something outside the military-oriented areas of nuclear science, rocketry, and aircraft technology."[16] Politically, the intellectual wave of terror showed no signs of abating, and many scientists of suspect nationalities were placed in special prison research centers. In one of Alexander Solzhenitsyn's books, *The First Circle*, we are introduced to such a research circle of political prisoners working on science projects--the so-called *Sharashka*.

Before leaving the Stalin era, it may be useful to outline the traditional structure of Soviet science and technology.[17]

1. The main branch is the Academy of Sciences of the USSR and the regional and specialized academies that historically form the nucleus of Soviet science. The heavy theoretical content of science (in comparison with Western nations) is largely due to the fact that the planning of fundamental research is done by the academy's departments and subordinate institutes.[18]
2. The industrial ministries, with their associated institutes for research and development, have invariably been held in lower esteem, a status reflected by the pay structure and other perks of the two arms of Soviet science.
3. The higher educational system, which is the source of raw material for the academies and industrial ministries.

The post-Stalin years saw a new development in Soviet science--the growing sense of inferiority in the face of rapid Western advancements. Because of the nearly complete isolation of Soviet science, the scientific and technological void between Russia and the West was not evident before 1953. Correspondence, exchange of literature, personal contacts, scientific trips or any other contact with the Soviet scientist's Western colleagues was not permitted. The only literature to receive official sanction was scientific writings that attributed all of the most important scientific discoveries to Russian scientists.[19] Medvedev points out several trends that developed during Khrushchev's tenure:

1. Attempts to copy foreign scientific and technological advances became pronounced, a development that condemned the Soviet Union to lag behind the West in most technical fields.
2. The compulsory merger of the applied sciences with industry and agriculture was an attempt to bolster the output of these poor performers. The most significant development in terms of science was that the Academy of Sciences once again became concerned primarily with theoretical research, as its divisions of applied research were transferred to industry and agriculture.
3. The decentralization of pure and applied sciences into academic towns (the science cities referred to above). Most of these were located within 100 kilometers of Moscow, although the most famous, Akademgorodok, was in the suburb of Siberia's Novosibirsk.[20]
4. Breakthroughs in space and atomic science.
5. The beginnings of dissent within the scientific establishment, largely the result of the Cheliabinsk nuclear accident (1957) and a rocketry disaster in 1960.

The years between the ousting of Khrushchev and the birth of detente saw Soviet science embark on yet other courses. Immediately following

Khrushchev's dismissal, the undefined position of the party leadership, as manifested by the provisional nature of the Brezhnev-Kosygin-Podgorny leadership, resulted in greater autonomy for the Academy of Sciences. The effect of this was not necessarily liberalization within the scientific establishment, but an even greater emphasis on theoretical studies at the expense of useful applications. The practice of copying, or reverse engineering, technology gradually came to an end in this period. Instead of falling further behind with superceded technology, the USSR began to purchase entire systems from foreign manufacturers. Unfortunately for Soviet industry, there were substantial pitfalls inherent in this approach as well. First, importing entire systems from the West had a negative effect on the Soviet industrial infrastructure and the Soviet Union was still at the mercy of Western innovations. It was still impossible to surpass the West on the technological front, for the West was setting the standards. Moreover, Soviet technologists had implicitly admitted that they could not duplicate Western innovations through their own devices.

This predicament was in no way improved by the effects of restrictions on foreign travel, exchange of information, and concerns over secrecy, which were now more manifest than ever in Soviet science.[21] Intellectually, the initial thaw in the early to mid-1960s was reversed when Soviet authorities cracked down on dissent, beginning in 1968, as part of their response to the causes of the Czechoslovak rebellion. Several institutes in the fields of chemistry, physics and biology were rendered impotent as a result.

Detente brought about a new spirit to Soviet science, a development many observers believe was induced by a feeling of military equality with the U.S. and by the success of military science and technology.[22] During this period (1972-77) the tendency to develop domestically every type of equipment that existed in the outside world had started to decline, mainly because of the sheer magnitude of the task. As a result of their lessons of 1968, new regulations were introduced that were designed to prevent potential or actual political dissidents from achieving prominence or a high rank in science or in any other field of intellectual activity. Perhaps the most significant development during the era of detente was the rise to power of the State Committee on Science and Technology. Established in 1965, the committee is primarily responsible for planning applied research and owes its existence to the fact that the Department of Engineering Sciences was transferred from the Academy of Sciences to the Industrial Ministries as part of Khrushchev's reforms.[23] It is ironic that the Academy of Sciences should find itself faced with a competitor that owes its existence to the academy's desire to become as purely academic an organization as possible.

The final years of the Brezhnev tenure saw several disturbing trends in Soviet science and technology, problems that the Gorbachev administration unhappily inherited. In his 1982 article, "Science in the Brezhnev Era," Professor Loren Graham of MIT made several predictions for the post-Brezhnev era. First, the period of tremendous expansion of Soviet research and development has ended. The emphasis for the near future will be on qualitative improvement. Second, pressure will continue for improvements in industrial productivity through more technical innovation. Third, bureaucratic competition between the State Committee on Science and Technology and the Academy of Sciences will continue. Finally, Graham concluded, "The problems of industrial productivity and health are the most serious ones faced by Soviet science and technology, and it seems doubtful that there can be radical improvement in the near future."[24] In general, perhaps the most interesting aspect of the Brezhnev period was the shift in emphasis, once again, to "useful" research, and the response of the Academy of Sciences to the problems of industry and its need for effective technology.

Thus, Soviet science was connected to the government directly through clearly defined lines of organization. Moreover, the producing elements of Soviet science are the academy laboratories, ministry laboratories, and the universities. Professor Graham concluded that

it is probably no exaggeration to say that the Academy of Sciences of the U.S.S.R. is the most important single scientific institution in the world, since in those countries which equal or surpass the Soviet Union in quality of science or overall scientific effort, fundamental research is dispersed throughout a variety of autonomous universities and institutions, both public and private.[25]

In a later publication, *Science, Philosophy and Human Behaviour in the Soviet Union,* Loren Graham examined the role of dialectical materialism in Soviet science. In this book he urged the reader to separate the philosophy of dialectical materialism from its misuse by Stalin and others.[26] Although Western scientists have dismissed it as totalitarian in nature, Soviet scientists have found it to be important for their work. Recent years have seen the rise of an ontological school of dialectical materialists who hold that matter is destined to evolve toward humans, who are the master of nature.[27] Graham described the intellectual in-fighting taking place in the Soviet Union on such issues as genetics, nature versus nurture, computers, physics, cosmology, and cybernetics (one field that has been left out of this work, unfortunately, is space science).

In response to these assessments by Graham, the noted American scientist and host of a long-running U.S. science program, Carl Sagan, argued that the state's enforcement of the universality of such ideas has led to the bowing and scraping of Russian scientists to orthodoxy, a deflection of scientific talent into nonscientific fields and a suppression of free debate.[28] Sagan quickly reminded us that the idea of a state ideology hampering scientific progress was also prevalent in the United States.

From a Western perspective, the political component of Soviet science was perhaps the most unusual aspect of the Soviet attitude toward science. The degree to which politics is shaping science was difficult to gauge, although some authors, Popovsky among them, believe it is considerable. Popovsky quotes from part of an article in the *Medical Gazette* (1968) concerning the type of persons who might become a scientist and what attributes they should possess: "The Soviet scientist . . . must not only defend the principles of Soviet science, but must be able to demonstrate its superiority over bourgeois science. This is especially important at the present time, when international links were developing so rapidly."[29]

Generally speaking, then, the Soviet scientific technological system was far from perfect. At the risk of oversimplification, there emerged two major problems with Soviet science: the twin problems of absorption and adaptation of existing technology, and the problem of creating new technologies. In the first case, it could be argued that a prime reason that the Soviet Union had great difficulty in absorbing new technology and adapting it to its needs is that the industrial ministries and academies insisted on using *Western* technology in a *Western* fashion. The principal reason for the lack of sufficiency (in Soviet science) is that the Soviets allowed the West to set standards for achievement. The Soviets allowed themselves to be slaves to goals set by the West and Western standards and not their own objectives. An inevitable pressure then emerged to turn toward the West for imported technology.[30] Although many theorists on the nature of technology argue that technology is inherently neutral and may be exported from one culture to another with no ill effects upon the receiving culture, this conclusion is difficult to support in the case of the USSR. It is often stated that the Soviet Union was not really a Western nation, but a Slavic one, ostensibly "Asiatic." The fact that it was and still is an Eastern nation, with a history, psychology, and tradition quite different from those of Western nations, would suggest that to import entire technological systems from the West and then expect similar performance is fallacious. All technologies are shaped by the culture that produces them, and technology in turn helps shape their cultures.

Marshall Goldman, in his book *Gorbachev's Challenge--Economic Reform in the Age of High Technology*, stated that the Soviets were not able to rely upon reverse engineering as a way of compensating as technology became more advanced. Not only was it becoming difficult to track hundreds and thousands of connections, but it had become harder to understand how they all fit together. The Japanese seemed to be at the top of this field, Goldman wrote, since "the Confucian oriented cultures that stress study, hard work, and diligence may be particularly suited to doing the fine detail work required in microelectronics."[31]

To pursue this argument further, there may be another explanation for Japan's prominence in this field. Although technological sophistication was essential to the Soviet Union's economic and political survival, technological backwardness was essential to the Soviet Union's system of government.[32] Japan is the least bureaucratic, the least secretive, and the most flexible industrialized superpower--and this has led to a decentralized, open planning system.[33]

Michiyuki Uenohara points to the higher education level of the Japanese. Japan lacks most of the resources needed to support industry; therefore, its only resource is its highly educated people. Since World War II and the loss of its military, technology came to the forefront and led to Japan's desire for higher education and cooperation between government and industry.

When viewed in this light, it is not difficult to understand why many old-style Soviet Communists are wary of Western technology transfer. To these slavophiles, who are seen in the West as present-day Luddites, Western technology and work methods are dangerous commodities. Few Russians ever get to see how things are done in the West, so some have no notion that standards can be any higher. Many Russians do not believe that Western technology will be able reshape Russia, or Ukraine for that matter, in a Western image, so why even try? To carry on with Gorbachev's *perestroika* would be like changing the face of the Soviet Union--for the worse. There always appeared to be the principal philosophical difference between the reformers (exemplified by Gorbachev and, to a more radical extent, Boris Yeltsin) and the conservative Russian nationalists and hard-line Communists. The reformers believed that the initiative-sapping central planners had to go. They argued that Russians could and would learn to work better, achieve independent thinking, and benefit from an increased technological presence in society. The conservatives tended to doubt the "benefits" would be for the better.

This debate on changing the Russian culture and the national character is an open one. Central to this debate is the Russian work ethic. It was a sociologist from Novosibirsk, Tatyana Zaslavskaya, who first drew attention to the importance of what she called "the human factor." Gorbachev constantly referred to this theme in most of his speeches about raising standards of productivity. Russians, he argued, had to learn to take responsibility rather than orders. Zaslavskaya, who was one of Gorbachev's advisers, had been writing for years in letters and in scholarly journals that the Soviet system was producing the wrong person for a modern economy. Advanced technology demanded extreme responsibility, while Russians are for the most part lethargic and lackadaisical. The disaster at Chernobyl, after all, was due to human error.

The second problem, the creation of new technologies, is not necessarily the most vexing at present but certainly deserves closer scrutiny. At the very least, it must be embarrassing, and, at most, quite disturbing, to have to explain why the USSR had produced few useful technological systems, or, as in the Japanese example, "built a better mousetrap," since the October Revolution. Although their record in the field of theoretical science is much better, Soviet scientists had shown a disturbing capability to become sidetracked down the scientific equivalent of a blind alley, as their experience with genetics indicates. Aside from this bizarre episode in the history of Soviet science, there were numerous Soviet triumphs in chemistry, metallurgy, and mathematics before the revolution, and in nuclear physics in the present day.

In the field of applied sciences, it is well known, mainly because all parties freely admit it, that the USSR has had little success in transforming homemade ideas into useful processes and products. Many in the West would attribute this problem to the lack of individual initiative, which has played so prominent a role in the history of Western science. (In fact, histories of Western science often seem to be dominated by the "Great Man" school.) However, the history of *worldwide* science and technology since World War II appears to indicate that there are other routes to realizing technology, the best example being the spectacular success of the Manhattan Project, or the building of the atomic bombs that were dropped on Hiroshima and Nagasaki. This approach to science was, as previously mentioned, pioneered by Russia prior to the Revolution and has been particularly successful for the Soviet military.

This leads us to conclude that there are at least two aspects of Soviet science that have been recognized as strengths and that are often absent in Western approaches. The first of these advantages is focus--the degree to which research personnel and technologists can be brought to bear on a project. Virtually all successes in Soviet technology since the Revolution bear this trait of goal-directed research to some degree, the best examples being Soviet aviation, its nuclear power and weapons programs, and the successful Soviet space effort.

The space program was perhaps the best example. The program continued uninterrupted since its inception in 1957, in stark contrast to the American effort. It is interesting to note that modern science in general has become much more dependent on government and industrial assistance; the myth of the backyard experimenter has for the most part become just that.[34] As with so many other things regarding the Soviet Union, we are once more confronted with a paradox: the USSR may have been on the verge of abandoning its few systemic strengths in an attempt to keep up with the West, while disregarding the fact that the West had progressed to the degree it had by unwittingly adopting the advantages of Soviet science as its own.

## *THE REFORM MOVEMENT*

The Soviet Academy of Sciences underwent a number of reforms under Gorbachev. In the past, this institution was controlled by older, more narrow-minded, faithful party members. Within the last few years of the USSR's existence, a new rule established a mandatory retirement age of sixty-five for directors of scientific labs, research institutions, and academy departments. There has been an increase in the independence of its various scientific departments from the central organization. Perhaps the largest scientific establishment in the world, the USSR Academy of Sciences included over 2,800 research institutes, with new institutes often being created. Gorbachev called for a shake-up in the way this organization was run in order to increase its contribution to the modernization of the Soviet economy.[35]

Certainly, there have been instances of stupendous achievements in the seventy-year history of this nation. In the land that gave us Mendeleyev, father of the periodic table of the elements, and Pavlov, still an authority on behavioral science, we now find the world's largest aircraft, the ANTONOV 225. The MI-26 (Hind) helicopter enjoys the distinction of being the world's largest vertical lift aircraft. The USSR once boasted of producing punch presses, blast furnaces, hydroelectric dams, unique welding techniques, plasma scalpels, intramuscular electro-stimulation devices, large-scale seismology experiments using revolutionary deep-drilling techniques, new processes in metallurgy, and the beauty of the Moscow metro with its marble and mosaics. But, despite this, there were those other deep-seated problems that plagued the system and had to be addressed in a rapidly moving high-tech age. The subsequent chapters of this book will examine the ways the USSR tried to cope with them, and failed.

We can perceive at least four dominant themes in the history of Soviet science and technology. First, science has always been the domain of the central government; the Western conception of science as being an expression of individualism has thus been absent from the very beginning. Second, since the Revolution, the Communist Party has strived to bring Soviet science into a tighter orbit around the party. Since this inevitably implies academicians losing power to the party, the Academy of Sciences has always utilized its opportunities to gain more autonomy. Third, emphasis (or perhaps tolerance) has swung from pure science to applied science and back again on several occasions. This is very much the result of the Cartesian tradition, which began in France and eventually spread throughout continental Europe, and holds that science is the means through which humans attain enlightenment. (Cartesian science is thus the prototypical "ivory tower" approach and perceives itself as being no more threatening than opera.) Significantly, this attitude stands in complete contrast to the current British, North American, and Japanese attitude which sees science as primarily utilitarian. The Baconian tradition, paradoxically enough, was one of the reasons that Peter "brought" science to Russia, but was quickly discarded as the Cartesian tradition dominated. Thus, the USSR finds itself once again importing an alien philosophy in an attempt to impose a Western style technology upon itself. Finally, Soviet science was almost entirely a reaction to the achievements of Western science. With the exception of the Sputnik launch in 1957, the Venus probes, and laser technology (with an orientation toward space), the USSR showed great reluctance to strike out on its own scientifically since the Bolshevik Revolution. When it did, the result was often a Lysenko-type quagmire, which saw reputable scientists' reputations ruined and charlatans gaining the upper hand. Another aspect of this problem has much to do with the early attitude of the party, which saw itself as standing alone against the world. The Soviet Union thus took it upon itself to provide a Communist alternative to every feature of the West. It was not until the late 1970s that Soviet officials and intellectuals realized that that attempt was hopeless.

The result of the Soviet experience with pure and applied science has been, at the very least, unique. Despite severe systemic flaws that have the effect of smothering the potential of the vast array of scientists, there are several advantages that are only now becoming apparent. It would appear that there are lessons for both the East and West when examining their respective scientific and technological achievements. One is reminded, perhaps disturbingly, of the race between the tortoise and the hare; if both parties continue blindly without paying heed to the actions of the other, the outcome is all too familiar.

## NOTES

1. Chris de Bressen, *Understanding Technological Change* (London: Black Rose Books, 1987), p. 159.

2. David Suzuki, *Inventing the Future* (Toronto: Stoddart Publishing, 1989), pp. 87-101. See also Fritjof Capra, *The Turning Point: Science, Society and the Rising Culture* (New York: Bantam Books, 1983); and Robert Ornstein and Paul Ehrlich, *New World, New Mind: Moving Toward Conscious Evolution* (New York: Doubleday, 1989).

3. That military technology is the main determinant of power is usually attributed to a school of thought led by William H. McNeill. See his book, *The Pursuit of Power* (Oxford: Basil Blackwell, 1983).

4. H. Balzar, *Soviet Science on the Edge of Reform* (Boulder, Colo.: Westview, 1989), p. 4.

5. One of the more interesting examples of this is Marx's writings on such developments as robotics and the like, which can be found in his *Grundrisse*, translated by David McLellan (New York: Harper and Row, 1971), pp. 583-92.

6. Some of the earlier Soviet literature that was devoted to the STR is discussed by Erik Hoffmann in "Soviet Views of the Scientific Technological Revolution," *World Politics*, July 1978, pp. 622-27.

7. The history of pre-revolutionary Russian science has been gleaned from *The Soviet Union* by Vadim Medish (2nd edn., Englewood Cliffs, N.J.: Prentice-Hall, 1984), pp. 174-76.

8. Zhores Medvedev, *Soviet Science* (New York: W. W. Norton, 1978), p. 4. See also Mark Popovsky, *The Vavilov Affair* (Hamden, Conn.: Archon Books, 1984).

9. Because he tends to represent the embodiment of all that was "good" in Russian science, at least to many dissident writers, Vavilov figures prominently in any discussion of Russian science during the Revolution.

10. See V. I. Lenin, "The Tax in Kind (June 1921)" in *Lenin on Politics and Revolution*, ed. J. Conmer (New York: Pegasus, 1968).

11. Medvedev, *Soviet Science*, p. 34.

12. Unfortunately, many valuable scientists had died before they could be "rescued."

13. Mark Popovsky, *Manipulated Science--The Crisis of Science and Scientists in the Soviet Union Today*, translated by Paul S. Falla (New York: Doubleday and Company, 1979), p. 159.

14. Ibid., p. 179.

15. Russia, like America, has always had a penchant for all forms of sensationalism, be it religious, as with Rasputin, political, as under Stalin, or, as in the case of Lysenko, a pseudo-science based on scientific Marxism.

16. Medvedev, *Soviet Science*, p. 56.

17. Loren Graham, "Science in the Brezhnev Era," *Bulletin of the Atomic Scientists*, February 1982, p. 24. Dr. Graham is a professor at MIT and one of the leading American writers on Soviet science.

18. John P. Young and Jeanne P. Taylor, "Science and Technology Policy in the U.S.S.R.: Impact of the Changing Character of Soviet Science and Technology in its Administration," *Policy Studies Journal*, December 1976, p. 214.

19. Medvedev, *Soviet Science*, p. 60.

20. Akademgorodok became a haven for renegade fields of study such as mathematical linguistics, econometrics, and cybernetics. Mark B. Adams, "Biology After Stalin: A Case Study," *Survey*, Winter 1977, p. 67.

21. According to Mark Popovsky, "it has been estimated that a present day scholar gets 70% of his information from direct contacts with his colleagues. The free exchange of information is a vital feature of

contemporary international science, and the lack of it is what bedevils science in the Soviet Union." Popovsky, *Manipulated Science*, p. 102.

22. Halloway ascribes the sophistication of military science and technology to two factors: The increasing complexity of military weaponry requires a more refined scientific input, and the scientific community in turn is proposing weapons that were not imagined by the military. John Thomas and Ursula Kruse-Vaucienne, "Soviet Science and Technology," *Survey*, Winter 1977, p. 24.

23. Graham, "Science," p. 25.

24. Ibid., p. 27.

25. Ibid., p. 11.

26. Carl Sagan, review of *Science, Philosophy, and Human Behavior in the Soviet Union* by Loren Graham, *The New York Times Book Review*, September 27, 1987, p. 34.

27. Ibid.

28. Ibid.

29. Mark Popovsky, *Manipulated Science*, p. 53. Quoted from *Medical Gazette*, August 9, 1968, p. 3.

30. Thomas and Kruse-Vaucienne, "Soviet Science," p. 25.

31. Marshall I. Goldman, *Gorbachev's Challenge--Economic Reform in the Age of High Technology* (New York: W. W. Norton, 1987), p. 33.

32. Robert Reich, review of *The Soviet Economy: Problems and Prospects* by Padma Desai and *Gorbachev's Challenge: Economic Reform in the Age of High Technology* by Marshall Goldman, *The New Republic*, August 3, 1987, p. 33.

33. Ibid., pp. 34, 36.

34. The myth of the backyard experimenter was prominent in Communist China under Mao, witness his backyard blast furnace and electrification programs.

35. David Dickson, "Shake-Up Announced for Soviet Academy," *Science*, 27 March 1987, p. 1565.

# Chapter 2

# Cloak and Dagger

Since the dawn of history, a technological advantage has invariably made the difference in a nation conquering another or being conquered. The technology advantage was never more critical than in biblical times, when Saul set out to become the first king of Israel. At that time the Israelites were still divided into fiercely independent tribes throughout Canaan. By 1050 BC that entire region was controlled by the Philistines, who had learned the art of smelting iron somewhere in Asia Minor and were able to maintain their domination by imposing a monopoly on metallurgy. Any armed resistance was doomed to fail because the Israelites, who knew only copper and bronze, had no access to the sharper, more durable iron weapons. The Israelites were not allowed to have their own forges, and the Hebrew farmers were forced to buy their plow points and other metal implements from Philistine smiths who demanded prohibitive prices.

David, the future king of Israel, stole from the Philistines the coveted art of iron-making, turned ploughshares into swords, and conquered all his enemies. Israel as a nation grew as a result of this technical prowess. It would be a blatant misnomer to call this technology transfer, a term implying legal methods of transfer. If David stole it, it was illegal and covert. The precise term used today would be "reverse engineering".

The chariot was a later and equally important technological innovation that revolutionized warfare. It was followed by the saddle and the stirrup, which were used by a single horseman who was capable of riding and shooting (lance and arrow) at the same time. Wars were fought and won by gunpowder and muskets, the use of the catapult and the Gatling gun, and the knowledge of these technologies became a closely guarded secret. Despite the French inventions like the *mitrailleuse* and the *chassepot* breech-loading gun, the Franco-Prussian War of 1870 was actually won by the Germans due to their superior, long-range field artillery made by Krupp steel. In our own century, a perfected form of command and control technology (C2) helped the Japanese to defeat the Russian fleet at the battle of Tsushima in 1905, primarily because of the Japanese wireless. Today, we have communications technology added to C2 to make it C3. The technologies now being developed--space weapons, robotics, lasers, MIRVed MX and particle beams, and remote command and control systems with the help of computers, such as the smart bombs used in the Gulf War--will further this trend. The history of war is full of such examples.

The beginning of the atomic age was dominated by the fact that only the United States had nuclear weapons and the means to deliver them in the aftermath of Nagasaki and Hiroshima. The U.S. monopoly of nuclear weapons ended in August 1949, when the USSR exploded a nuclear device.[1] This event was a milestone on the USSR's path to becoming a superpower; indeed, it set the stage for a world with two superpowers. It also set the stage for the arms race, nuclear proliferation, and many changes in military doctrine and strategy. It became one of the two great turning points in U.S.-Soviet relations. In fact, one can even say that tactics and strategy, even basic military doctrine, are of less consequence in today's technological age. No one understood this better than the early Marxists themselves, Engels, Marx, and Lenin, all of whom believed that warfare and political power could be transformed by industry and technological change: "The Soviet Union seeks broad technological self-sufficiency for a number of political, economic, and military reasons--national and ideological prestige, the lack of enough hard currency for large-volume, long-term purchases of products from the West, the need to guarantee spare parts for military systems, etc."[2]

In regard to strategic arms development, most Soviet weapons and technological innovations have developed in response to U.S. programs, despite the technological limitations of the Soviet economy. To keep up, the Soviet Union has had to duplicate or purloin any new technique. Just as there began a race for better and improved nuclear weapons because of a weapons gap in favor of the Americans, so, too, there was always a gap in weapons delivery systems. Again, the Soviets had proven themselves to be good copiers. One calls to mind the day in 1944 that three U.S. B-29 superfortresses landed in Soviet Siberia after bombing raids against Manchuria and Japan. The aircraft were copied by the Soviets in remarkable time; this was how the *TU-4 Bull*, the first Soviet aircraft capable of carrying an atomic load, was produced and used as a strategic bomber of the *Aviatsiya Dal'nogo Deistviya*, or the Soviet Long-Range Aviation.[3] This very limited Soviet nuclear strike capability, and the subsequent Soviet explosion of a nuclear device, spurred additional U.S. strategic weapons development. The Americans detonated the first thermonuclear device--the precursor of the hydrogen bomb--on November 1, 1952. The Russians simply followed suit less than a year later with their first thermonuclear bomb.

But atomic warheads and delivery systems were not the only focus of superpower rivalry. It was widely acknowledged that the continued application of scientific know-how would accelerate the pace of weapons improvement that began in the late 1930s. Every new and successful invention meant that some secret weapon or weapons design might make the difference in a final showdown. Therefore, scientists, technologists, design engineers, and efficiency experts in the postwar era did their utmost to improve existing weapons and to invent new ones on an unprecedented scale.[4] One of the most recent Russian defectors to the West, a former officer of the Soviet GRU (Military Intelligence) revealed not-so-startling news around the time Gorbachev came to power in the USSR. He said that even knowing the strategic plans of NATO for resisting a Soviet invasion across the north German plain is not that important--military technology has become the main espionage battle-field.[5]

Thus the arms race since 1945 has been a race in technology. What advantage one side may temporarily have had was soon copied and countered by the other. Military technology represented the expenditure of billions of dollars and the hiring of people to produce that knowledge. It was estimated that 40 percent of what nations spent on research and development went for weapons and about 25 percent of the world's scientists and engineers were working on military projects.

What was not known in the West about the Russians--just like the ignorance regarding the Soviets' own Manhattan Project--was the extent and the degree to which they would keep pace. It was not enough just to set up NATO in response to the presence of large Red Army forces in Eastern Europe. In 1949, when NATO was established, the non-Communist industrialized countries set up a collateral organization to review the flow of technologies to Communist countries. This organization, COCOM, (Coordinating Committee on Multilateral Export

Control) still exists. Today it is made up of all NATO countries plus Australia and Japan (with the exception of Iceland). With a staff of twenty, its headquarters is on the second floor of the U.S. Embassy Annex in Paris.

COCOM is a non-treaty-based organization that relies on a voluntary agreement of its members. It has no enforcement capability and must rely on each nation to create its own export regulations and laws. Three lists of items were set up to became subject to control: (1) the International Atomic Energy List (radioactive material); (2) International Munitions List; and (3) International Control List (dual-use items with commercial and military applications).[6] The system of import verifications has not proved foolproof. The Toshiba Corporation of Japan and the Kongsberg Vaapenfabrikk of Norway between 1980 and 1984 sold submarine technology to the USSR. When caught, both were punished by their governments. As the Soviet Union and various East European governments fell, COCOM restrictions were correspondingly loosened.

COCOM worked reasonably well in those early days when East-West trade was at a low ebb at the height of the Cold War. In any event, in the 1950s, the Soviets made tremendous headway in science, engineering, and weapons design. There was no longer any doubt as to their achievements in research and development of high technology from the very moment they stunned the world in October 1957 by launching a rocket powerful enough to put a tiny satellite, the Sputnik, into orbit around the earth. To the West, of course, it seemed that the Soviets had achieved this on their own, without any significant boost to their power from Western technology. The Western technocrat, engineer, or scientist involved in rocket propulsion knew better.

The U.S. government responded to this potential danger by heavily subsidizing research and development with a view to guaranteeing prosperity at home and security abroad. Fiscal limitations on education were reduced. There emerged a boom in the natural sciences, attended by another in the fields of aerospace and electronics. It set the Soviets back by more than a decade, and it appeared that the Russians would never develop the economic wherewithal with which to bridge the widening gap. Not since Lend-Lease aid during World War II and the Soviet capture of German rocket scientists was there a greater need for an infusion of Western technology and capacity. In the immediate postwar period, the Soviets were able to put to practical use all the technology, the plants, and the equipment they acquired from the areas they occupied in Germany. Documentary reports of the inter-Allied commissions in Germany estimated that at least two-thirds of the German aircraft and electrical industries, most of the rocket production industry, several automobile plants, several hundred ships, and a plethora of military hardware were "transferred en masse to the USSR."[7]

It just so happened that Stalin's death had given new life to the conviction that the Soviet economy might not be able to catch up and surpass the productivity levels of the West, that Russia would remain backward if it failed to transform its rigid, highly centralized economic structure. This realization had been latent since the end of the NEP (Lenin's New Economic Policy) and began to gain currency among Stalin's immediate political successors. Two schools of thought had emerged, one representing the traditionalists and the other the nontraditionalists. There was no significant difference between the two; they were both in favor of rapid modernization and industrialization, at best by crude mechanical means, with whatever automated systems could be used, painfully realizing that the West had already entered the electronic age. Both groups strongly felt that the transfer of Western technology was an absolute precondition to bridging the gap that separated them from the West. In fact, several high-tech projects were canceled in favor of transfers. The acquisition of technology and the creation of a scientific-technological revolution was rarely questioned in the Politburo. What the schools debated was how much transfer should take place, what form it should take, and what price should be paid for it. It was very much like the erstwhile dispute between Marshal Nikolai Ogarkov (formerly Soviet chief of staff) and the Military-Industrial Commission (*Voenno-promyshlennaia Kommissiya*, or VPK) on both technology-related matters and future military doctrine, which ended in Ogarkov's dismissal.[8] Since 1979, Ogarkov had argued that the new generation of Western "smart" weapons could wage war against the Soviet Union's mechanized deep-penetration tactics and would enable NATO to defend itself without ever resorting to nuclear force. When Ogarkov came back in the limelight after Gorbachev's rise to the top, most influential Soviet military leaders, including then-Marshal Akhromeyev, trumpeted Ogarkov's call for development of the Soviet Union's own high-tech arsenal. Gorbachev and his political colleagues were bracing themselves for another decade of massive military spending.

It is simply not enough to say that the Russian economy will always be buoyant because Russia, Ukraine, and Central Asia are endowed with all manner of inexhaustible resources: ferrous and non-ferrous metals, minerals and energy, huge expanses of timber and water. Over both short and longer time spans, Soviet statistics had already revealed a slowdown in Soviet industrial development, both quantitatively and qualitatively.[9] The former head of the Department of Economics and Investment at the USSR National Institute of Economics of the Construction Industry described the structural disequilibrium: "Soviet industry is becoming increasingly stagnant technologically. The transportation network cannot keep up with the needs of the economy."[10]

This state of affairs grew to the point that some authors regarded the acquisition of Western technology as an imperative for the very survival of the Soviet system.[11] These analysts were generally of the view that the endemic technological backwardness in industry and agriculture was reflected in low living standards, that there was a lack of experimentation, a lackadaisical attitude to the work ethic because of the absence of property rights, and a general lack of financial autonomy.

Yuri Andropov drew the attention of the Soviet leaders to these problems in a roundabout way. At his inaugural speech as first secretary on November 22, 1982, he underlined the declining growth of labor productivity, wasteful use of resources, transportation problems, and inefficiency.[12]

With no domestic innovation or any urge toward it, it has been exceedingly difficult for science to move beyond its theoretical foundations to practical applications. Consequently, imported Western technology had to compensate the Soviet system for some of its built-in defects.[13] The overall conclusion is familiar to us: Western technology has played an important role in promoting Soviet military programs, reducing military expenditures on research and development, and releasing additional domestic resources for military uses. However, not everyone will agree that imported or stolen Western technology helped to perpetuate Soviet "totalitarianism." Indeed, totalitarianism may be seen as a consequence of comparatively primitive modes of production characterized by a society with a weak technological base. It is my view that one of the major inner contradictions of the Soviet system--and the contradictions are so many--was this constant desire to obtain technical know-how without triggering a politically dangerous liberalization of the Soviet system towards a competitive market economy. It is a contradiction because if it had worked it would have been counterproductive and self-defeating. If technology is really the opiate of the intellectuals, most intellectuals hoped that technology would inevitably modernize and liberalize the Soviet economy. And that was already beginning to happen.

Nevertheless, one calls to mind Lenin's famous post-revolutionary prophecy that the "capitalists will sell us the rope on which we will one day hang them." Lenin implied that the rope would have to come from the West if and only if the Soviets could not make their own, and that would happen if the economy were to collapse.[14] In fact, Lenin had always believed that technology (modernization) and Communism were inseparable. Once, when asked what communism was all about, Lenin replied that it meant "the electrification of the entire country and Soviet power," implying that it had nothing to do with Marxist theory. This electrification of the country still remains the goal.

Much of modern technology, even in the West, has both military and civilian uses. When constructed in the civilian sector, its precision and efficiency warrant its utilization by the military. For instance, air traffic control systems can be employed for air defense and for vectoring fighter aircraft. The computer revolution in the United States ushered in a new technology that is applicable to military purposes. The semi-conductor technology used in computers can be applied to missile guidance systems, and the technology utilized in the manufacture of wide-body aircraft and high-bypass turbofan jet engines can be applied to the production of military aircraft.

As a result, a significant proportion of imported Western civilian technology was easily harnessed by the Soviet military-industrial complex. Computer technology alone--bought or stolen--contributed to Soviet advances in strategic weaponry, while Western-built factories in the USSR were easily convertible to military uses. Western technology was capable of giving Soviet research and development and the Soviet armed forces the industrial wherewithal, or the "support system"[15] necessary to free the USSR's domestic resources for military purposes. Although difficult to assess, roughly 25 percent to 40 percent of the USSR's GNP was earmarked for military purposes.[16] Some argue that it was twice as much in view of the expenditures concealed by the Soviet intelligence establishment.[17]

It is generally recognized that there were two very distinct industrial sectors in the Soviet Union, the military and the civilian. Of the two, the military was by far the largest, commanding 80 percent of the government's scientific research allocations.[18] Because of the secretive and esoteric nature of the USSR, and with the bureaucratisation of the economy, everything was geared to the military. For all practical purposes, the two sectors were not separated. Highly skilled personnel, heavy equipment, and the lion's share of research funds reverted to the military and to the defense sector. Secrecy was so paramount in this military-industrial complex that there was no apparent exchange of information on research and development between it and the tiny civilian one. This compartmentalization was one of the major hurdles to Soviet utilization of its full scientific and industrial potential.[19] The corollary of compartmentalization was redundancy and duplication, with the attendant problems of poor allocation of resources that, on the one hand, overemphasized research and theory and, on the other, underemphasized development and application, the true mainstay of technological innovation. Worse, as long as any piece of existing equipment produced a satisfactory output, there was little reason to change or improve it. Low depreciation rates and scarcity of equipment meant that it was a long time before it could be replaced, whether an updated version was considered essential or not. The result was that equipment became obsolescent, if not altogether obsolete. A Western analyst summarized the Soviet predicament thus:

The search for effective reforms of science and industry is a story of marginal successes and large failures. The essence of the failures is that it has proved virtually impossible to make scientific and industrial institutions more innovative without injecting a large dose of market competition into the economy.[20]

During the late 1960s and early 1970s there was a perceptible shift in the attitude of the Soviet leaders concerning their technological base, which they expected would expand under the effect of the scientific-technological revolution. The USSR was facing a decline in the rate of growth of the labor force as well as a decline in labor productivity and industrial output. The figures and statistics were never really revealed; propaganda and disinformation covered up the flaws. There was, by the beginning of 1970, a desperate need to import technology from abroad, not simply to improve performance in industry and agriculture but also to save millions of roubles in research and development costs. The Soviets feared that, as in the field of information technology, which was already commonplace in the West, continued deficiencies would adversely affect the military and the civilian sectors of the economy. The Soviet Union might never catch up.

With this purpose in mind, the Soviet government concluded a trade agreement with the United States in 1972 that allowed Moscow to buy high-tech goods, to enter into joint ventures, exchange information, send scientists to study at American institutions, lease patents and procure technology by whatever legal means it had at its disposal. Every possible scientific journal and every technical magazine ever published in the West was carefully studied in the USSR. These ranged from the perfectly innocuous *Popular Mechanics* to *Aviation Week* and *Space Technology*, the *Computer Trade Journal* and not excluding *Jane's Aircraft* and *Jane's Fighting Ships*.[21] The Soviet scientific establishment was able to glean at least 75 percent of what it did not know through these Western publications, or through the purchase of licenses and patents and turnkey plants. The other 25 percent had to be obtained by covert means.

All foreign technical imports were supervised by the State Committee on Science and Technology (GKNT), or *Gostekhnika*, as it was more commonly known in the West.[22] It coordinated all research and development activities and was the single most important adviser to the Soviet Council of Ministers in technology. Appointed by the Supreme Soviet, the Council of Ministers in turn supervised the day-to-day activities of the sixty-six ministers that made up the administration of the state apparatus. The GKNT worked closely with the State Planning Committee (GOSPLAN), the KGB, the GRU (Military Intelligence) and the Military Industrial Commission. The Industrial Commission served the whole military establishment and ensured that the military got the best of the technology acquisitions, especially where major defense-related ministries were concerned. Aside from the Ministry of Defense, which naturally had a great deal to say in this matter and fed abundant information to the GKNT (primarily when the defense establishment knew that a technology must be obtained by other than legal means), there were at least sixty foreign trade organizations operating in conjunction with the GKNT. When information could not be had by legal means or by the normal transfer channels, it was the GKNT that assigned technology targets to the KGB and the GRU.[23]

The most important of these foreign trade organizations were *Techmashimport* (Technical Machinery Import) and *Elektronorgtekhnika*, the Organization of Electronic Technology. The latter, which was also called ELORG dealt primarily in electronics and integrated microchip circuitry that constituted computer technology. *Techmashimport* was primarily concerned with optical systems and lasers, both of which were invaluable in the advancement of space technology.[24] Lasers and electronic components were not sought after as finished products with potential military applications, but rather as specific components that revealed the intricate production know-how. In its quest for these critical materials

GKNT showed an unqualified predilection for technology complexes (i.e., systems), as opposed to single technologies. Reports read before congressional committees in the U.S. suggest that the Soviet Union saved as much as $100 billion in military research and development costs. According to the CIA's congressional testimonies, which began in 1982, the *Gostekhnika* decided what to do when a certain technology was missing. This agency was responsible for determining how it was to be acquired and how it was to be integrated into the system; the KGB and GRU merely executed these decisions. The foreign trade organizations involved in the activities of the GKNT cooperated with the intelligence apparatus outside the USSR. Inevitably, they were used as covers bearing diplomatic standing for KGB and GRU operations represented as legal delegates and diplomats. Since the demise of detente in 1975, when the trade organizations were prevented from importing technology through normal legal channels, the links with the Soviet intelligence community were strengthened.

The intelligence organization that provided the skilled manpower and stage-managed these clandestine operations was the KGB's First Chief Directorate. Some maintain that it was done by the Politburo itself or the inner ruling circle.[25] There is sufficient evidence to suggest that there may have been direct links between the GKNT and the First Chief Directorate of the KGB.[26] The latter consisted of a number of sections divided into directorates and departments. By far, the most esoteric of these subdivisions was the Scientific and Technical Directorate, generally known as "Directorate T," whose sole function resided in the theft of technological secrets from the West. The chief task of Directorate T was to acquire data on space research and rocket designs, and to keep abreast of technical advances in areas such as robotics, cybernetics (of which more will be said in subsequent chapters), cryogenics, holography, and numerous other processes.[27] Central to its espionage activity were electronics and computers. Entrusted with that brief was a special department called "Line X," responsible for foreign agents and field operations in the industrial states of Western Europe and North America. Generally, these agents were highly specialized in their field, be it electronics, engineering, chemistry, and so on.

Directorate T, with its enormous scientific and technical expertise, became the most cost-effective component of the entire KGB establishment. In pure monetary terms, its contribution to the Soviet economy was invaluable. It covered the financial outlays that bankrolled the entire Soviet intelligence system. It was soon to become the fastest-growing operational sector of Soviet foreign intelligence; without it the Soviet Union would have been compelled to spend billions of dollars in research costs. The Directorate numbered roughly 500 operatives, for the most part graduates of Soviet universities and polytechnical schools, with hundreds more consultants and advisers from major industrial centers.

Conservative accounts put the number of KGB and GRU personnel operating in the United States at well above 1,000, reaching as high as 3,000 if one considers the number of direct informants. Industrial espionage among competing U.S. companies benefited the Soviet intelligence apparatus in a way that the Soviet leaders had not expected. In Silicon Valley south of San Francisco (silicon is the semiconductor material for memory chips, and most of the superelectronics industry is situated there), the competition for trade secrets was fierce. With thousands of engineers and workers employed there, a black market, and even a "gray market," for information had mushroomed among brokers and middlemen, most of whom had at one time or another been suborned by the Soviet Union. American intelligence reports recorded as many as sixty agent-diplomats working in the Soviet consulate in San Francisco, no doubt to be near Silicon Valley.[28]

Among the most porous countries that suffered from the theft of technology were France, West Germany, and Japan. France is regarded as one of the most developed laser and telecommunications centers in the world. French multinationals such as Thompson and Honeywell-Bull are among the world's prominent purveyors of high-tech equipment, and France, moreover, is richly endowed with a nuclear research infrastructure. France has always acquired high technology from the United States through trade licenses and borrowing patents. While it is not a member of NATO, France maintains close ties with the Atlantic Alliance. In intelligence circles around the world it is argued that until President Mitterrand's expulsion of forty-seven Soviet diplomats in February 1983--the second largest expulsion of Soviet staff after Britain's--France had been the easiest country to infiltrate, and the French SDECE (counterespionage) the most permeable of the Western secret services. It is estimated that 30 percent of French industry and military establishments had been penetrated by Soviet agents and that as late as 1983, 10,000 Soviet spies were operating in the country, controlled by 600 KGB officers.[29] According to one document, the Soviet Aeronautic Ministry acquired enough intelligence from the West in 1979 to upgrade the MiG-29 and the SU-27 with onboard digital computers, signaling systems, and better fuel management and armament systems.[30]

Japan is yet another site of Soviet covert operations. It is in its own right a world leader in integrated circuits, computer technology, and artificial intelligence,[31] but this nation benefits heavily, if not exclusively, from the import of U.S. military high technology. Japan, after all, must continue to licence U.S. weapons for production in Japan. The CIA once reported that the U.S. lost more secrets to KGB agents in Japan than in any other nation.[32] To this day, this belief is reflected in U.S. hesitancy to transfer high-technology and complex machinery to Japan, a reluctance that may also be born of commercial rivalries between the two countries.

The famous Toshiba affair provided some evidence for this statement. In 1987, the U.S. learned that one of Toshiba's subsidiaries had been shipping advanced machinery to the USSR, permitting Soviet submarines to navigate quietly enough to escape U.S. naval detection. Japan and the U.S. had signed a bilateral agreement concerning supercomputers. While the Soviets planned and completed the construction of large U.S.-style naval aircraft carriers capable of accommodating high-performance combat fighters, catapult technology has so far been alien to Soviet naval engineers. Most of these acquisitions were made in Japan. From Japan the Soviets also acquired the technology to build floating dry-docks that are capable of providing out-of-the-water repairs to the largest ships in the Soviet fleet, including Kiev-class aircraft carriers and the Typhoon and Oscar classes of missile-carrying nuclear-powered submarines.[33]

Just as there have always been thieves, so there have always been smugglers. Both become more sophisticated as law enforcement measures become more complex, and as the stakes get higher. This is true of drug smugglers, bootleggers, gun-runners, and the unauthorized exporters of high technology and weapons. Although the stakes are by far the highest for this last type of smuggler, as two blocs vie for military and technical supremacy, the smugglers of high technology have an easier life and possibly a higher success rate than all the others. In 1985, U.S. Customs detected and stopped $105 million in high-tech merchandise illegally bound for the Communist bloc. This was just the tip of the iceberg.[34] This $105 million figure surpassed the $83 million in legitimate high-tech trade in 1979 and the $19,318,000 it cost the U.S. to enforce the export laws in 1982.[35] As a result of these smugglers' efforts, the Soviets claimed that 70 percent of the computer microchips made in the Soviet Union were made on Western equipment, most of it shipped there illegally.[36] As the development of VHSIC (very high speed integrated circuits) continued, the most advanced chips--no larger than a thumbnail--were proscribed goods vital to national security in all Western countries. In the mid-1980s, the most advanced chip was said to be capable of over 360,000 memory functions, and was used in missile guidance systems and MIRVs. The chips were a prize coveted by the Russians and easily made the difference in military C3 (command, control and communications) combat operations, an advantage in today's electronic warfare.[37]

The Soviet Union and the Eastern bloc resorted to traditional methods of spying by recruiting suitable individuals. Many made a career out of supplying the Soviets with high technology.[38] Men like Richard Mueller and Werner Bruckhausen acted as the principal Soviet middlemen, establishing for the KGB more than sixty front companies in a large number of Western countries. Their names and exploits were known to the American authorities and to COCOM in Paris. Both Bruckhausen and Mueller were dealers in restricted contraband; both Germans were indicted by a U.S. federal court as early as 1977 for illegal trade activities and smuggling. But because illegal trade activities did not constitute an extraditable offense, the two men remained at large. They were never caught again.

Smuggling was very simple. A smuggler wrote one destination on the export licence and shipped the goods to another, often directly without ever passing through the stated destination. Then came an idea called an "end-use-certificate," which had to be filled in before the goods could be exported; this required the ultimate use of the cargo as well as its final destination. In addition, further transfer of the goods was not possible without the permission of the country of origin. Of course, it was assumed that the certificates would be truthfully filled in, but it was not long before officials realized that if a man would smuggle, he might also lie, and further checks were introduced into the system. Many countries demanded import certificates from the recipient country as proof of delivery, but this did not control retransfer. The French then came up with an ingenious system called the "caution-money system" in which the exporter would post a bond with the French government of up to 100 percent of the value of the export. If French consular officials in the recipient country later found the goods being used as foreseen, the bond or caution-money was returned. This system probably discouraged frequent users because of close government supervision, but for the one-time smuggler, it only increased the cost of doing business.

A more common method of smuggling involved orders placed by a third party, who reshipped them to the Communist bloc. One case using this method involved Werner Bruckhausen and three of his associates. Over a period of time they shipped two Data-General Computer systems, three Watkins Johnson microwave receivers and electronic surveillance hardware, and a Xincon semi-conductor memory test system via Austria, Germany, or Switzerland to the Soviet bloc.[39] The neutral countries of Switzerland, Austria, and Finland were the ideal locations for the third party and, as such, were the most important sources of illegally obtained high-tech goods for the Communist bloc.

Being neutral, these countries traded with both blocs, and the Russians used this to their advantage. Switzerland was made even more attractive to smugglers by its secretive banking and tax laws, and Austria's controls over East-bound high-tech goods were lax enough to prompt Fred Ikle, U.S. Undersecretary of Defense, to threaten Austria with restrictions on sensitive American industrial goods unless export controls were tightened.[40]

The U.S. also responded to this problem by becoming the only COCOM member to require a re-export licence.[41] In order to export American goods of strategic value from Austria to Hungary, both an American and an Austrian licence were needed. But even here, smugglers found a way to circumvent the new law: They simply lengthened the chain between the source and the ultimate destination. The disappearance of two projection mask aligners (with a price of $250,000 each) made by Perkin-Elmer Corporation was a prime example of this *modus operandi*. It was just one of the many Soviet success stories in piracy involving middlemen, neutral countries, and licenses, all superbly stage-managed by the KGB.

The mask aligners, or Micraligns, were automobile-size machines used in the manufacture of microcircuitry for everything from digital watches to missile guidance systems. The U.S. Commerce Department put them on the proscribed list of technologies bound for Soviet-bloc countries. FAVAG S.A., of Neuchatel in Switzerland, placed an order with Perkin-Elmer. The latter duly notified U.S. Customs, the Commerce Department, and the FBI. After months of investigation by American security agencies, Perkin-Elmer was allowed to export the Micraligns to Switzerland. When requested, the export licence was granted. But when the machines arrived, FAVAG sold them to ELER Engineering, a firm based in Geneva. No export occurred; therefore, no licence was needed. But ELER had no offices in Geneva, only a lawyer representing its interests. In fact, this firm was actually run from Paris by Joe Lousky, and the Micraligns were somehow re-exported to Paris, where they suddenly vanished. They were probably shipped there soon after arriving in Switzerland, with ELER in Geneva acting as a front availing itself of the secret banking and tax laws. The machines are presumed to have ended up in Russia, but exactly who broke the law, and where, are unclear.[42]

The presence of East European agents in the United States and in other Western countries was another factor contributing to the success of the smugglers. The East Europeans worked hand-in-hand with the ubiquitous KGB. According to CIA analysts, the East European countries generally had a better image in the West than the Russians, and their intelligence officers were thus able to operate more freely. The Soviets of course allowed for this to happen; it offered them multiple channels for acquiring Western technology so that none of their defense-related industrial ministries became dependent on a single channel. The most active substitutes in the Soviet bloc were East Germany, Hungary, Czechoslovakia, and Poland.[43]

One case that was extremely well-documented in U.S. congressional hearings is that of Bell and Zacharski. According to a detailed report by the Senate's Permanent Subcommittee on Investigations, William Bell "was burdened with debts and back taxes, family tragedy, and a job with no future."[44] He met Marian Zacharski, a Polish national and the West Coast manager of the Polish-owned machine manufacturing firm POLAMCO, which was incorporated in Delaware and Illinois and with offices in Chicago, Detroit and Los Angeles. Bell was eventually bribed to work for POLAMCO and consequently for the Polish intelligence service, with its obvious links to the KGB.

According to the report, Bell set about photographing sensitive documents at Hughes Aircraft Co., where he worked as a radar project engineer. Among the classified papers Bell eventually handed over to the Poles were: the F-15 look-down/shoot-down radar system, the quiet radar system for the B-1 and Stealth bombers, and all-weather radar systems for tanks, an experimental system for the U.S. Navy, the Phoenix air-to-air missile, a shipboard surveillance radar, a towed-array submarine sonar system, the improved Hawk surface-to-air missile, and a NATO air defense system.[45] When finally caught, Bell was convicted of espionage and given an eight-year prison sentence; Zacharski was given a life sentence.

But many smugglers were never caught and, when they were, the smugglers were rarely prosecuted to the fullest extent of the law. In July 1980, for instance, the government of Canada dropped charges against Barry Gunn and Alexander Apaya, two arms smugglers who had violated U.S., not Canadian law. A leading Canadian magazine wrote that violation of export law is not an extraditable offense, and the "Canadian legal system is not a branch plant of the U.S. economy."[46] Clearly, if smugglers of high-tech and weaponry can be said to have a relatively easy life, with a high success rate and no penalties or light penalties if caught, things were much easier for the 20,000 Soviet and East-European agents in COCOM countries. Many of these agents possessed some function at an embassy or consulate and were therefore protected by diplomatic immunity. The worst that could happen to them was expulsion.

A different type of case involved the Swedish firm Datasaab, which, in 1977, obtained a Department of Commerce export licence to sell radar parts to the USSR. The Commerce Department granted the licence on the basis of ten restrictions limiting the capability of the radar system to ensure that it was only used to track civilian aircraft. Datasaab then proceeded to acquire state-of-the-art radar circuit boards under a separate Department of Commerce licence and shipped it to the Soviet Union for the sum of $75 million under counterfeit inspection papers. In the law suit that followed, Datasaab was fined $3.1 million and the Department of Commerce was taken to task for having been negligent in this case.[47] It marked the beginning of a dispute that was to rage for years between the Pentagon and the Department of Commerce.

One of the most imaginative coups was the Soviet Union's illegal penetration of international computer systems. In a world where computers talk to one another, Soviet agents successfully used the privately run International Institute for Applied Systems Analysis near Vienna to penetrate Western computer systems. The Vienna Institute has links to the Euronet satellite computer system in Western Europe, which, in turn, talks to computers in the United States. Indeed, computer penetration became the surest form of espionage of any type, because surveillance against unauthorized entry by a skillful programmer is well-nigh impossible.

In May 1980, the FBI apprehended a thirty-one-year-old Belgian businessman, Marc André De Geyter, at Kennedy Airport in New York after he successfully bribed American businessmen for state-of-the-art computer technology. FBI agents had been trailing De Geyter throughout the United States, investigating his every move and inquiring into his secret contacts and illicit business dealings. Documents had been found in his luggage indicating that his brief was to seek out a computer technology known as a source code, a new computerized method of storing billions of pieces of data, with the information indexed and encoded in such a way that no one else could break into it. De Geyter and his Brussels-based company, Services Accounting (probably a Soviet-sponsored front organization), signed a contract with Computer Engineering. Documentary evidence seemed to suggest that he attempted to bribe several employees of SOFTWARE AG, raising his bribe to as much as $500,000. Other documents linked him to *Techmashimport*, one of several international trading agencies in the USSR. In August 1980, De Geyter was given a light sentence of four months' detention for attempting to smuggle computer design out of the country without an export license and trying to bribe the acquisition of high-tech secrets.

Semiconductor technology used in computers has international implications closely connected with espionage skulduggery. In the Canadian capital, for instance, federal security officials were led to believe that there were foreign agents in Ottawa who were attempting to steal government secrets by tuning into the high-frequency radio signals leaking from computer hardware.[48] These signals, when picked up on standard radios, sound like typical interference, but when the interference is intercepted by sensitive receivers, recorded, and then sifted out by other computers, it may reveal a code.[49] This process was quite feasible because in Ottawa, thousands of computer terminals were being used every day. The Communications Security Establishment (CSE), a top-secret intelligence agency within Canada's Department of National Defense, had been charged with the task of protecting certain computers that process highly classified information (e.g., computer communications with other members of NATO).[50] The Canadian government even hinted that the spies with the sensitive computers might be agents of the USSR, either Canadians or Soviets themselves. The whole affair was shrouded in secrecy.

It should be noted that Canadian-U.S. air defense installations are almost entirely computerized, and the CSE's computer security measures--besides restricting access to a computer--include various means to shield equipment with copper to block emissions.[51] All these security measures involving computers bear the NATO code-name "Tempest."

Another international issue was the perennial problem of penetrating an enemy's secrets. This form of infiltration and sabotage is intimately connected with computer software. In France, Thierry Breton and Denis Beneich, the former a programmer and the latter a free-lance writer, came up with a fanciful but by no means implausible account of a high-tech war. They wrote a book with the felicitous title *Softwar--La guerre douce*.[52] The authors gave their own version of the East-West confrontation. Below is a brief account of how the silicon chip was a coveted prize of the USSR.

The Soviet Trade Ministry, according to this hypothetical scenario, negotiates to buy an American supercomputer dubbed CRAIG-1 from a French firm. The computer, the Russians affirm benignly, will be used to forecast the weather on the Siberian steppes. In fact, Moscow is secretly planning to use the computer to tap directly into Western data banks containing American military and technological secrets. The American government avails itself of this unique opportunity and, instead of blocking the sale, which is under American license, sends an MIT scientist to Paris to plant a "soft bomb," or programmed booby trap, in the machine's meteorologic software. The result is that whenever the U.S. National Weather Service begins to transmit messages to meteorologic centers across the world on any trivial matter, all the Soviet computers connected to the CRAIG-1 show up unintelligible data. There are many more software traps in the machine, which two Soviet programmers set out to locate after the initial deception.

There is no technical hurdle to planting soft bombs of this type into the software that is sold to prospective enemy clients. Charles P. Lecht, a high-technology consultant and writer who frequently testified before American congressional committees on the relative technological strengths of Eastern and Western countries, in effect admitted that he knew of several instances in which this had actually occurred.[53] It is not beyond the realm of possibility that the computers the Russian authorities have been trying to import by hook or by crook may very well be used to the advantage of the United States. The possibility is always there that one of these powerful computers might be tagged with a chip wired to monitor Russian operations themselves. Such a Trojan horse chip would cause the Russian computer to unwittingly relay home secret data without Russian security ever being the wiser.

Over a period of twenty-five months, during which the Reagan administration did all it could to restrict advanced computer exports to the USSR, there were an inordinate number of leaks to the USSR of the usual contraband variety.

The largest seizure of machines to date occurred in Hamburg, West

Germany, where U.S. and German customs agents unloaded several crates of U.S.-made computer equipment, including a giant VAX 11/782, a powerful computer that could be used for guiding missiles and keeping track of troop deployments. Manufactured by Digital Equipment Corporation, the stowaway VAX was valued at more than $2.5 million. In West Germany alone--not to mention Switzerland and Japan, where technology leaks were routinely greater than anywhere else--150 firms and an equal number of individuals were engaged in the clandestine shipment of sensitive computers to the Eastern bloc.[54] The VAX had been bought by an unidentified firm in New York State and shipped by air freight to South Africa. Certain individuals who were known to be heading front organizations, sometimes with Soviet funds, were suspected of having arranged to have the computers transported to the Soviet Union. In many instances the companies were Soviet companies and constantly changed their names so as not to appear conspicuous.

A "Star Wars" race began between the two superpowers when Ronald Reagan unveiled his Strategic Defense Initiative (SDI), a fierce competition that would be played out between these two main protagonists. At stake was the perfection and deployment of the laser, the radio-frequency weapon, and particle beams. Lasers generate beams so powerful that they can burn through hardened steel, as can particle beams. Soviet researchers had concentrated on laser technologies since the early 1960s, and impressive progress was made with particle beams. But Moscow feared it would be overtaken by a similar American program that had all the weight of Western technology, industrial infrastructure, and economic resources behind it. Any of America's pirated space technology could have been used to speed up Soviet development programs in progress, to reduce costs, reduce technological risks, or improve on Western designs. No other technological endeavor has enjoyed as much publicity as the American space program; the Soviets felt that they would soon match it.[55]

Most of the students the Soviet Union had been sending to the United States had advanced degrees in electrical engineering and physics. They were usually in their thirties, unlike younger American students going to the Soviet Union who held degrees in the humanities. Ladislav Bittman wrote in 1985 that "a veritable explosion of Soviet students, professors, and commercial delegations came to the United States in 1976 and 1977, all of whom were interested in one subject--lasers."

A good example of skulduggery in the vital sector of aerospace technology is offered by the Soviets' success in acquiring more than fifty high-energy laser mirrors from Spawr Optical Research. The acquisition was, of course, illegal. Spawr was one of the American firms that had been contracted to do laser optics polishing work for such companies as TRW and Rocketdyne and for various government organizations, such as the Los Alamos Scientific Laboratory, Redstone Arsenal, and the Naval Weapons Laboratory. Spawr had supplied the Air Force Weapons Laboratory at Kirtland Air Force Base with high-energy laser mirrors. The firm then wanted to sell the same amount of mirrors to the Soviets, but the Department of Commerce rejected Spawr's application. The firm secretly shipped the mirrors anyway. The middleman in this transaction was a German (probably Bruckhausen) who forged export documents in order to conceal the contents and destination of the export item. It was estimated that the mirrors saved the USSR millions of dollars and nearly 100 work-years of research and development. It was primarily due to this acquisition in 1977 that the Soviet Union was able to maintain its lead over the United States in ballistic missile defense and anti-satellite capabilities.[56]

It therefore seemed possible that the Soviets were not merely substituting Western research for Soviet research, but were using Western know-how to reinforce Russian technology. This posed a threat to the West, as it was generally agreed that the Soviets applied new technology to their already powerful military apparatus to make it even more efficient. The West undoubtedly underestimated the impact technology had on the modernization of the Soviet military forces. Western leaders awakened to the idea that, in a confrontation, technology that might be Western or Western-inspired would be used by the Soviets against the West.

The idea of forcing the Soviets to advance at their own pace without any Western help has been proposed or rejected by successive Western leaders, especially American presidents, depending on the prevailing climate of East-West relations. As a result, technology transfer became a highly politicized issue, and U.S. trade policy toward the USSR varied between great freedom to export and near-total bans on high-tech exports. Washington favored an almost total ban as a result of the Soviet invasion of Afghanistan, the problems in Poland, and the problems of Jewish dissidents trying to emigrate from the Soviet Union. Reagan used trade as a strategic weapon to impede the growth of Soviet economic and military power.

COCOM's importance waned during the years of detente, as more and more East-West trade was permitted, but the changing international climate has arrested this decline. It returned to its former importance after the Soviet invasion of Afghanistan and it was reactivated to reduce the growth of Soviet military might. The United States perceives COCOM as indispensable because Japan (not to mention Western Europe) is threatened by the Soviet Backfire bomber and by SS20 missiles. This resolve has hardened in England, a country which was threatened by Soviet nuclear weapons and in which thirty-one Soviet agents were expelled in September 1985, and in France, where a Socialist government expelled forty-seven Soviet diplomats in 1983. Recently, however, some countries have sought to eliminate COCOM.

In addition to COCOM, the U.S. has promulgated a series of export control measures. One is on nuclear items, which is controlled by the Nuclear Regulatory Commission and the Department of Energy under the Atomic Energy Act of 1954, as amended by the Nuclear Non-Proliferation Act of 1978. It also applies to munitions, which is controlled by the Department of State under the Arms Export Control Act of 1976. It also involves items with both military and civilian applications (dual-use), which to this day is controlled by the Department of Commerce under the Export Administration Act of 1979.

The last-named piece of legislation was actually passed in 1949 and was reaffirmed in 1969. But during the period of detente, relations between the U.S. (and other COCOM members) and the Warsaw Pact countries became less acrimonious. Eastern Europe ceased to be regarded as a monolithic bloc. There was a Sino-Soviet split; Hungary was pursuing its own economic policies; Romania was pursuing an independent foreign policy; Poland was experimenting with social pluralism. Various East European countries had become members of GATT and the IMF, and some were granted MFN treatment by the U.S. The Export Administration Act was amended in 1974 to give the Department of Defense (DOD) certain rights to review proposed exports, while the Department of Commerce received jurisdiction over all unclassified technical data and commodities. The Export Administration Act thus constitutes the most important legislation on export controls. Commerce obtains advice from the departments of defense and state and other agencies. Any controversial item is considered by the Operating Committee (OC). This interagency networking is made up of representatives from the departments of commerce, defense, state, energy, and treasury, as well as from NASA and the CIA.

During the era of economic detente in the 1970s, substantially increased amounts of Western goods and technology were exported to

Communist nations, much of it on credit. The impetus to East-West trade was based upon the assumption that sales promotion would not only improve the Western balance of trade but also moderate Soviet political views.[57] This was the spirit in which the Helsinki charter was framed. But at the same time, excessive restrictions on technology exports to the Soviet Union could have had a negative impact on the ongoing debate among Soviet leaders regarding autarkic and interdependent approaches to the problem of technological process. Few experts in the West would say that the West was able to exercise much influence on internal Soviet politics.

Soviet decision-making was based at least in part on the leadership's perceptions of the outside world. If the West restricted exports to the USSR of strategic and defense-related goods, that policy buttressed the arguments of the Russian conservatives (the traditional faction) who had always been averse to doing business with the West.[58]

On the other hand, it was obvious that an increase in commercial intercourse with the East did not hinder Soviet military expansion. By capitalizing on the influx of advanced Western technologies, the Soviet Union launched a relentless, unprecedented build-up of its armed forces, far beyond any legitimate security interests. The Soviet invasion of Afghanistan is a good case in point. It is generally known now that the giant Kama River truck plant, built with American technology, produced trucks that were used by the Soviet Army in Afghanistan. Heavy vehicle-construction plants and plant support facilities provided the Soviets a quantum leap in load durability.

The U.S. Department of Commerce had a Commodity Control List of items that were subject to export controls. That list was drawn up around October 1980. But ever since the problems arose between the Department of Commerce--representing the business community--and the Department of Defense involved in national security, the list has been supplemented with new items, with the Department of Defense holding the upper hand. Commerce has listed 100,000 items, but the revised list, the Military Critical Technologies List (MCTL), is much larger and entirely classified. Only its general criteria are known to the public. Apparently the Soviets were not supposed to know that certain things exist, so that they would not be tempted to smuggle what they did not know about. According to Robert Schmidt, Vice chairman of the American company Control Data, aspirin at one point was one of the items on the list, which led to questions about the list's effectiveness and its secrecy.

In addition to the Commerce Department's sometimes vigilant surveillance of the export licenses, and the identification of strategic goods and technologies through the Critical Technologies List, Section 51 of the Export Administration Act foresees the replacement of the current COCOM strategic goods list by the longer, American List of Critical Technologies. The U.S. must, however, tread carefully here, because any one of the COCOM countries conducts more high-technology trade with Russia than does the U.S. For years Washington has been trying to impose barriers when U.S. high-tech sales to Russia are about one-tenth those of France, Germany, and Japan combined. Just as American farmers reacted unfavorably to the U.S. wheat embargo, West-European high-tech firms rejected trade restrictions with Moscow. To counter this, the U.S. boycotted goods of companies that violate COCOM rules, and refused these companies' products entry into the U.S. But there is no consensus in the U.S. or in Western Europe/Japan as to ways to protect Western secrets from any potential enemy. At the height of the Iran-Iraq War, most Western nations supported Iraq and sold Saddam Hussein priceless weapons and high-tech gadgetry. Both American and European/Japanese businesses in the 1980s seemed torn between a desire to trade with Russia (possibly cementing better East-West ties) and a fear that the Soviets would ultimately use any acquired technology to destroy the West, or counter Western goals.

The United States worked on proposals that would expand COCOM control lists into previously uncovered priority industries. These include gas turbine engines, large floating drydocks, certain metallurgical processes, electronic grade silicon, printed circuit board technology, space launch vehicles and spacecraft, robotics, ceramic materials for engines, certain advanced composites, communications switching, computer hardware, and software technology and know-how. This process continued into the triennial COCOM list review, when a general reappraisal of everything on the control lists took place.

Most countries require a licence to export arms, but the definition of arms can prove quite difficult because weapons are almost always in the forefront of technology. For instance, until very recently, Sweden did not consider civilian aircraft as possible arms. The Japanese consider as military goods only those used exclusively in combat.[59] Unfortunately, if there is uncertainty among COCOM members as to what constitutes a weapon, there is also a good deal of variation among member countries as to what constitutes "goods of strategic value" and what responsibilities each country believes it has in terms of the re-export of its own exported technology. The spirit of cooperation may be there, but dedication and organization are weak.

On April 16, 1985, the U.S. House of Representatives approved a four-year extension of the Export Administration Act that was designed to increase penalties for illegally exporting U.S. technology and goods in an effort to reduce the flow of sensitive equipment to unfriendly nations. The $167 million bill, approved by voice vote after little debate, went to the Senate. The Export Act had expired earlier when House and Senate conferees became deadlocked over whether extension legislation should include greater Defense Department review of technology export licenses and trade sanctions against South Africa for its policy of apartheid.

Now more than 200 categories of goods and technologies are listed in the MCTL. They are all subject to export license requirements for national security reasons, foreign policy considerations, or concerns about possible supply shortages. The House-passed bill provided new enforcement powers for the Commerce Department and the U.S. Customs Service. Such programs as the Customs Service's Operation Exodus increased substantially the American government's ability to staunch illegal exports. But this new sense of urgency did not necessarily bring about greater cooperation from U.S. exporters. The record shows that in many cases private companies paid lip service to the strict policy in place.

It is quite ludicrous when one imagines that Operation Exodus was implemented with a view to inspect and investigate strategic technology export shipments and the parties involved in them. All these efforts were accomplished by means of integrated task forces throughout the United States, replete with U.S. Customs inspectors, special agents with wide seek-and-search powers, and various other officers. These efforts were coordinated and supported by a national Command Center in Washington, D.C., and that center coordinated with the U.S. departments of commerce, defense, state, and other agencies concerned with illegal strategic technology movements.[60] Yet despite all this, the leaks and clandestine shipments and even government-sponsored transfers to a country like Iraq continued unabated. The Soviets, too, continued buying and pilfering.

Everyone knows by now that the ordinary citizen in the United States has far more access to information than any man or woman in any other country of the world. For years now the United States has adhered to its Freedom of Information Act. Communications technology has also spawned an all-pervasive information age, in which no document, however critical, can remain outside the public purview for long, or fall into the hands of an enemy. Since the U.S. Department of Defense has much more to say in these matters than any other government agency, the U.S. Congress passed the Defense Authorization Act in the late 1980s, reaffirming it in the early 1990s after the Gulf war, providing the Defense Secretary with the authority to withhold from public disclosure any technical data with military or space application that is under Defense Department control and would therefore be subject to export control.

As a result of the Defense Authorization Act, the Pentagon had a statutory basis for denying Freedom of Information requests for sensitive technology that, although unclassified, would have required an export license or otherwise be subject to export control.

The Soviet and Eastern European agents and their associates performed their tasks very efficiently at great cost to the West, and to the fantastic advantage of what was then the Communist bloc. Now-adays, whether the Russians spy, smuggle, steal, or take advantage of lax Western controls on computer distribution or freedom of the press in Japan, the U.S., the other COCOM countries, or in neutral countries such as Switzerland or Austria, one thing is certain. Industrial espionage, outright theft, or purchase from U.S. allies or neutral countries, is believed to have given the Russians a high-tech capability they might not otherwise have acquired. From Silicon Valley in California alone, the theft or illegal sale of Western technology allowed Moscow to save billions of dollars in research costs and accelerated the arms race.

The number of legal and semi-legal loopholes for smugglers, combined with the prospect of light or no punishment if caught as a result of international laws or diplomatic immunity status, together with divergent interests within COCOM, make the dream of any kind of real embargo on U.S. or even U.S.-inspired technology bound for an unfriendly nation a highly utopian one. In military terms, any illicit flow to a resurgent and radical Russia could have a debilitating effect on Western security. Before its final disintegration and demise, the Soviet Union made such great qualitative improvements in its armed forces that an equal amount of qualitative improvement in technology, derived from Western military and commercial technologies, could once again easily destabilize the military balance.

As one thoughtful observer pointed out, it is not always wise to let others do the development work for too long. In an era when technological change came slowly and generated less change than the computer and microprocessor industries did, it was advantageous to let others do the costly mistakes and innovation. The Soviets had only to import it, or steal it, and save time but they ran the danger of getting caught in what was called "a systems trap."

Marshall Goldman wrote:

It is as if the rest of the world had accommodated itself to an AC electrical system while the Soviets were still on DC. Conversion to the AC system requires a complete overhaul, not just the installation of a few AC appliances. The "systems trap" helps explain why the Soviets have had a hard time keeping up with the computer information revolution.[61]

As for these repeated cloak and dagger antics, we are reminded of the famous dictum, "cheaters never prosper." Let us now look at the area where the Soviets lagged dismally behind--computer technology.

## NOTES

1. The atomic bomb project in the Soviet Union is described in a well-documented survey of several U.S. intelligence agencies, "How Russia Became a Nuclear Power."

2. S. E. Goodman, "Advanced Technology: How Will the USSR Adjust?" In *Soviet Politics in the 1980s*, ed. Helmut Sonnenfeldt (Boulder, Colo.: Westview Press, 1985), p. 184.

3. Norman Polmar, *Strategic Weapons* (Washington: National Strategy Information Center, 1982), p. 23. The B-29s were impounded and never returned to the United States.

4. William H. McNeill, *The Pursuit of Power* (Oxford: Basil Blackwell, 1983), p. 357.

5. See "A Defector Warns: "What Fools," *Time*, May 27, 1985, p. 33.

6. David B. Mattews, "Controlling the Exportation of Strategically-Sensitive Technology: The Extraterritorial Jurisdiction of the Multilateral Export Control Enhancement Amendments Act of 1988." In *Columbia Journal of Transnational Law*, Vol. 28 (747): 1990, p. 754.

7. Office of Technology Assessment, *Technology and East-West Trade* (Montclair, N.J.: Allanheld, Osmun/Gower, 1981), p. 208.

8. See Nikolai Ogarkov's references to automated systems and to the winnability of a nuclear war. N. V. Ogarkov, *Vsegda V Gotovnosti K Zashchite Otechestva* (Always in Readiness for the Defense of the

Fatherland) (Moscow: Voyenizdat, 1982). With Gorbachev's rise to power, Ogarkov made a steady comeback. See article on Ogarkov in *Washington Times*, July 19, 1985.

9. See *Narodnoye Khozyaystvo SSR* from 1964 through 1982, Moskva, Statistika, Narkhoz--1982, pp. 111, 379.

10. Boris Rumer, "Structural Imbalance in the Soviet Economy," *Problems of Communism*, July-August 1984, p. 24.

11. Philip Vander Elst, *Capitalist Technology for Soviet Survival* (Washington, D.C.: Institute of Economic Affairs, 1981).

12. *Pravda*, November 23, 1982.

13. Besides the Vander Elst work, see also the well-documented work by Antony Sutton, *Western Technology and Soviet Economic Development, 1917-1965* (Palo Alto, Cal.: Hoover Institution, 1973). Both are already out of date.

14. The statement was made sometime in 1921 during the implementation of the NEP.

15. Vander Elst, *Capitalist Technology*, p. 49.

16. Brian Grozier, *Strategy of Survival* (London: Temple Smith, 1978), p. 41.

17. Viktor Suvorov, *Soviet Military Intelligence* (London: Hamish Hamilton, 1984).

18. Harvey Mose, Leon Goure, and Vladimir Prokofieff, *Science and Technology as an Instrument of Soviet Policy* (Miami: University of Miami Press), p. 14.

19. See Miron Rezun, "The Politics of Computers in the USSR," *Queen's Quarterly*, Vol. 93 (4): Winter 1986, 16 pages.

20. Bruce Parrot, *Politics and Technology in the Soviet Union* (Cambridge: MIT Press, 1983), p. 299.

21. *Scientific American*, for instance, now has a Russian-language edition called *V Mire Nauki*, literally "in the world of science."

22. The acronym is Russian; it stands for *Gosudarstvennyi Komitet Nauki i Tekhnologii*.

23. The best up-to-date account of how the various ministries of Soviet trade are linked to the Soviet intelligence establishment is contained in H. Rositzke, *The KGB: The Eyes of Russia* (New York: Doubleday, 1981). See also John Barron's *The KGB*, 1st edn. (New York: Reader's Digest Press, 1974); and Christopher Andrew and Oleg Gordievsky, *The KGB: The Inside Story of its Foreign Operations from Lenin to Gorbachev* (London: Hodder and Stoughton, 1990).

24. *Vneshnaia Torgovlyia* (Foreign Trade), Moscow, January 1979,

pp. 49-51.

25. Edgar Ulsamer, *Air Force Magazine*, December 1984, p. 532. See also Andrew and Gordievsky, *The KGB.*

26. L. Melvern, N. Anning, and D. Hebditch, *Techno-Bandits: How the Soviets are Stealing America's High-Tech Future* (Boston: Houghton Mifflin, 1984), pp. 68-69.

27. See my paper on this subject, "The Politics of Computers in the USSR," *Queen's Quarterly*, Vol. 93 (4): Winter 1986.

28. CIA, *Soviet Acquisition of Western Technology* (Langley, Virginia: Central Intelligence Agency, 1984).

29. Tad Szulc, "Why the Russians are Trying Harder to Steal our Secrets," *Washington Post Parade Magazine*, November 7, 1982, p. 17. Information has also been obtained from my student, Jane Boulden, "East-West Trade and Technology Transfer," research essay, unpublished, 1985.

30. *Pacific Defence Reporter*, November 1985, p. 52.

31. "The Dangers of Sharing American Technology," *Business Week*, March 14, 1983.

32. Ibid., p. 114.

33. CIA, *Soviet Acquisition of Western Technology*. See statement made by Secretary Perle before a congressional hearing.

34. William Lawther, "Operation Exodus Nets a Catch," *Maclean's*, January 17, 1983, p. 21.

35. *United States Congressional Code and Administrative News*, Vol. 3, 1981 (St. Paul: West Publishing Company: 1983), pp. 2786-97.

36. Frederick Painton, "Crackdown on Spies," *Time*, April 18, 1983, pp. 34-6.

37. Ibid.

38. See Melvern, Anning, and Hebditch, *Techno-Bandits*, chaps. 9-13.

39. Murray Seeger, "Tightening up the High-Tech Trade," in *Fortune*, December 28, 1981, entire article.

40. Painton, "Crackdown on Spies," pp. 34-36.

41. *U.S. Congressional Code*, Vol. 1, p. 1157.

42. Ibid.

43. In addition to Arkady Shevchenko (*Breaking with Moscow* (New York: Ballantine Books, 1985)) and Oleg Gordievsky (*KGB: The Inside Story* (London: Hodder and Stoughton, 1990)), one of the highest-ranking intelligence officials of the Soviet bloc to defect to the West was Ion M. Pacepa, deputy director of the Rumanian Intelligence Service and personal adviser on security matters to Nicolae Ceausescu. His fascinat-

ing account of the theft of Western technology is in *Current Analysis* (Washington, D.C.: Institute of Strategic Trade: September 1984), Vol. 5 (1-2).

44. U.S. Senate, *Transfer of United States High Technology to the Soviet Union and Soviet Bloc Nations*, 9th Congress, 2nd session, Hearings, May 1982, pp. 181-93.

45. Ibid.

46. Peter Carlyle, "The Litter of the Law," *MacLean's*, July 28, 1980, p. 10.

47. Boulden, "East-West Trade," p. 21.

48. Jeff Sallot, "Ottawa Tries to Protect Computers Against Spies with Sensitive Radios," *Globe and Mail*, October 14, 1984, pp. A1-2.

49. Ibid.

50. Ibid.

51. Ibid.

52. Written in French, *Softwar* (Paris: Editions Secuil, 1986) became an immediate bestseller, with over 100,000 copies in print. The book appeared in English and Japanese, and was adapted into a movie.

53. Charles P. Lecht was director of Lecht Sciences Inc., a New York City software company. See Richard Lacayo, "Racing to Win the Heavens," *Time*, October 15, 1984, pp. 84-9.

54. According to then CIA Director William Casey, in a report delivered before the Joint Economic Committee, Subcommittee on International Trade, Finance and Security Economics, Central Intelligence Agency Briefing.

55. Soviet research was conducted by the country's leading scientists and engineers. Mr. Nikolai Basov went on record in January 1985, stating that the Soviet Union would match the American SDI program. He and Alexander Prokhorov, both Nobel laureates, headed the Soviet research effort.

56. Theodor Wai Wu, assistant U.S. Attorney General, Criminal Division, Central District of California, in a statement before the Senate Permanent Committee on Investigations, May 5, 1982, in *Transfer of United States Technology*, pp. 510, 517-24.

57. For an interesting view of American policies, see Gerhard Mally, "Technology Transfer Controls," *Atlantic Community Quarterly*, Fall 1982, pp. 233-38.

58. Bruce Parrot, *Politics and Technology in the Soviet Union* (Cambridge, Mass.: MIT Press, 1983).

59. "The Dangers of Sharing American Technology," p. 114.

60. Department of the Treasury, U.S. Customs Service reports, 1982-85, 1985-89.

61. Marshall Goldman, *Gorbachev's Challenge: Economic Reform in the Age of High Technology* (New York: W. W. Norton and Company, 1987), p. 114.

*Chapter 3*

# The Politics of Computers

Why was the advent of the computer so instrumental in the dissolution of the Soviet Union? The computer, after all, is only a dumb machine, whereas the whole technology system has important social and economic implications.

The computer age and the computer revolution are Western phenomena. The United States in particular has pioneered this new technology; all others are emulators and copiers. At the heart of computer technology is the silicon microchip, which is an essential component for the well-being of the modern economy and the advancement of military technology. New chips have become faster than the previous ones, and there is almost nothing that semiconductor chip technology cannot do, from important military applications to weather forecasting to operating robots on an assembly line, to being able to think much the same way as human beings do--in short, everything from guiding missiles to artificial intelligence. Moreover, fundamental advances in materials science will soon produce a photonic technology transmitting information over glass fibre-optic cables that many scientists believe will one day replace electronics. The photonic computer will operate a thousand times faster than an electronic one.

California's Silicon Valley is the product of the technological age that spawned both the modern computer and other high-tech inventions. Silicon Valley straddles a ten-mile-wide peninsula between San Francisco Bay and the Pacific Ocean. Located here are the research centers, the factories, and the laboratories that have produced most of the computer hardware since World War II. The galaxy of brands accounts for some of the most successful corporations of our time: Amdahl, Fairchild, Hewlett-Packard, Tandem, Apple, Atari, Cromemco, the Stanford Research Institute, and National Semiconductor. Silicon Valley, moreover, is in no way restricted to its California site. Firms such as Digital Equipment Corporation and Data Control in Massachusetts, and IBM is in the state of New York. These locations in the U.S. are the most important places for research and development.

In Europe, too, several countries have agreed to pool their resources in advanced computer research in an attempt to avoid eventual domination by the U.S. or Japan. The European program known as ESPRIT--European Strategic Research Programme on Information Technology--was started in 1983 with an initial target budget of $1.3 billion over a five-year period. It was later extended over a ten-year period.

The most critical facet of a computer is the software, which is a set of programs or instructions that tell computers what to do. There are two types of software: systems and applications software, with the latter used extensively in guiding missiles and in SDI research.[1] As for systems software, most of its creators and manufacturers have been American. Brand names such as CP/M, MS-DOS, and UNIX are all familiar to the Western computer enthusiast. All of this hardware and software is copyrighted by its manufacturers, and it is an offense under patent law to duplicate or purloin such technology.

How and to what extent had the Eastern bloc countries kept up with this new technology? Was the Soviet system also involved in an information age? Was Soviet society and its economy, which was not a market system, receptive to the computer? If not, what were the obstacles in the Soviet system? Why has that system not generated American-style technology?

When I first went to the Soviet Union I did not know the proper translation of many technical terms in the Russian language. When there for the first time, I learned the expression *vychislitel'naia mashina*, which in Russian means computer, or literally "calculating machine." I noticed, too, that the Soviets were taking computer education very seriously. Every time I went back to the USSR I could not help noticing how remarkably the Soviets had progressed in computer technology and, at the same time, I wondered why it was that they had remained behind for so long.

## THE DILEMMA OF DIALECTICS VS. CYBERNETICS

In part the answer to this question can be found through a brief discussion of dialectics and cybernetics. The Soviets have always had a Marxist approach to scientific and social phenomena. The science of computing, generally known as "cybernetics," as expounded by Norbert Wiener, John von Neumann and others, was derided during the Stalin era as a bourgeois pseudo-science because of its refusal to emphasize the exact prediction of future states and conditions. Marxism is a materialist doctrine that sees phenomena as deterministic processes. The development of contradictions is inevitable in this Marxist scheme, and, if that is so, then there is no such thing as self-regulation in the pure, classical sense. A cybernetic system, however, does not operate under centralized control; it works rather on the basis of a constant flow of communication. In a feedback process, this communication makes adjustments to a system that is disorderly (entropic) until it reaches a point of equilibrium. In the Stalinist era, particularly during the 1930s and 1940s, such concepts of probability, rather than of inevitability, were derided as decadent and bourgeois. Only inevitable processes were considered the mainstay of Marxist materialist dialectics as it emerged on the heels of the quantitative and reductionist science of the previous centuries.

The paradox of the Stalin era lay in the disregard of cybernetics as a control mechanism by a leadership that could not help but regard it as too "subjectivist" a theory. The Stalinists contended that dialectical materialism sees objective reality as consisting of matter and energy in various forms; to them, information, the basis of cybernetics, which was neither matter nor energy, could not be objective. The same view was voiced abroad by non-Soviet Marxists up until the early 1950s. Another paradox was in the attitude that the discipline, with its application of computers to problem-solving, might one day replace Marxism as the ideology of the Soviet Union. As a result, the cybernetic approach was not considered a legitimate one. This was, after all, a period of severe ideological interference in Soviet science, as was exemplified in the field of genetics by the towering personality of Lysenko. When cybernetics was openly attacked in the press and in scholarly journals, it was in response to a growing interest in it by the scientific community; it was necessary to repudiate its undialectical approach. For example, the *Literary Gazette* called it a "science of obscurantists" as late as 1953. Many Soviet Marxists simply took issue with the view that a machine can think or duplicate organic life, arguing that consciousness and cognition are properties of man alone. It was often argued in Soviet writings that men would be replaced by robots, unemployment would rise and "bomber pilots who object to bombing helpless civilians would be replaced by unthinking metallic monsters."[2]

Opponents of cybernetics repeatedly drew a distinction between the human brain and a sophisticated computer. They called attention to the fact that computers work on a binary system (either 0 or 1) and, as a consequence of this linear language, there is no transition between "yes" and "no." How then could computers properly deal with dialectical questions when there are no possibilities for a dialectical logic? This situation became all the more paradoxical in view of the fact that cybernetics does not contravene the basic assumptions of dialectical materialism. Linearities themselves are not the characteristic feature of computing, and there is no evidence to prove that a feedback loop is undialectical.

The adialectical dialectics of Stalinism discredited this science. A careful reading of Marx will confirm that he had never been against the theory of probability. Marx's random notes on mathematics bear testimony to his flexibility on this subject. Engels himself acknowledged the objective nature of chance.[3] Probability theory was thus never un-Marxian, though it was anti-Stalinist. In any case, in publications, conferences, and symposia the Soviets were proven then and now to be most formidable in that particular branch of mathematics.

What caused the Soviets to change their attitude toward cybernetics by 1954? In the spring of 1954 the Central Committee promoted a policy of much greater leniency on ideological issues in the sciences. With the criticism of Lysenko's pseudo-theories on genetics it was agreed that the time had come for a more sober reassessment of cybernetics. But in the final analysis it was the military establishment that triggered the need for cybernetics and computer technology. After World War II, some Soviet observers had in fact de-emphasized the use of computers in military operations because they felt that wars were basically fought and won on national pride and morale. To others it seemed ludicrous to think that one could work on the H-bomb without the then available computing machines. Knowledgeable Soviet scientist knew perfectly well that rocket and guidance systems technology could not exist without cybernetic computing systems. By 1955, it became obvious to Soviet military planners that there were problems with delivery systems. Vehicles carrying the bomb had become more important than the bomb itself.

The political climate of the mid-1950s favored the legitimization of cybernetics. It took the form of a lengthy philosophical discussion in the pages of the journal *Voprosy Filosofii* (Problems of Philosophy), in which the main theme was that there was no inherent contradiction between Marxism and cybernetics. On 19 November 1954, an academician Ernst Kol'man, delivered a major speech to the Academy of Social Sciences of the CPSU in which he stressed that the USSR was in danger of overlooking a technological revolution by discrediting cybernetics.[4] He argued that the new computing machines were comparable to the decimal numeral system and to the invention of printing. Yurii Kolbanovski, another author, referred to the "withering away of the state" as a cybernetic phenomenon, a movement in history when society became "self-regulating."[5] Scholars such as Aksel Berg, Ernst Kol'man, Ilia Novik, Georgy Shaliutin, and A. N. Kolmogorov made a distinction between cybernetics as the science of control and communication in complex systems and Marxism as the science of the laws of nature, society, and thought.

But the real dilemma was not philosophical; it was one of infrastructure and of the delayed development of the Soviet economy. During the 1960s, Ernst Kol'man was assigned the task of rehabilitating cybernetics. By 1965, cybernetics had established itself; it received the stamp of official approval in 1961 with the adoption of the new program of the CPSU at the 22nd Party Congress in Moscow.[6]

## THE DILEMMA OF MECHANICAL VS. ELECTRONIC

Since the end of World War II, the Soviet Union kept pace with the U.S. and its allies in military technology. The Russians may not always have been the first in this competition (the exception being their launch of Sputnik in 1957), but they were successful in duplicating everything in the military field: the tanks, the planes of World War II, atomic energy technology, and MIRVed warheads in rocketry. All of these technologies, none of which were civilian-related or consumer-oriented, could be broadly defined as heavy-industry technologies. The Soviet Union placed great emphasis on achieving automation through mechanical rather than electronic processes. Thus, the whole of the Soviet system, shaped by the very nature of Soviet society, placed a premium on production rather than on innovation and marketing. As Lenin once said, "Quantity has a quality of its own."

The Soviet Union gave full priority to heavy industry, hoping to reconstruct the war-devastated economy on that basis alone, to the exclusion of everything else, including the agricultural sector. The entire economy was centrally planned, with norms and quotas in the productive process becoming more important than the private needs of individuals.

With relatively little money and industrial tradition, the Soviets began to acquire from others what they could not produce by themselves. Their technological base was rudimentary, even after the completion of the first Five-Year Plan.

The best way to illustrate the primitive mechanical side of Soviet technology as opposed to the electronic methods used in the West would be to look at a simple device like the abacus, or counting frame. The Chinese invented it some 2,500 years ago; it became the best and is still the most widely used computing device. It was a common sight in the whole of the USSR, not just in the less developed Asiatic republics. We could see the abacus at the grocer's, in the downtown cafes, in banks, and in schools. Electronic cash registers were a rarity, there were few calculators, and one seldom saw an electronic scale except in a government office. Manual methods were preferred. I was told several years ago by a Soviet economist that Russians like to invent things but that the mere idea of invention was something one could not plan. Fostering the inventiveness of the people by giving a special bonus to the individual did not work in the same way as in the West. Both the individual and the institution would amass unpredictable profits that could distort central planning by creating unplanned demands on resources. The prevalent Soviet view regarding any machine was, "If it works leave it alone," and the prevailing Western attitude has always been, "If it works, it must be obsolete." The problem this entailed is best described in an informative book published some time ago by three British authors who referred to the dilemmas of Soviet technology in terms of an "abacus syndrome."[7]

Faced with the problems of a centralized economic system, was it possible for the USSR to eventually catch up with the West? How could that be possible if the USSR was still in the grips of a mechanical age, an age of pulleys and punch-card tabulating machines? How indeed would that have been possible if the Soviets still encountered problems with microchip-manufacturing systems? And how could that come about if Soviet labor was still inadequately trained in the rudiments of a computer education? To have a computer-oriented society, was it not a desirable precondition to have a market economy? If so, was it at all possible for the Soviets to adapt Marx and Lenin to the marketplace?

### EARLY HISTORY OF SOVIET COMPUTERS

It was a foregone conclusion that the Soviets could not continue using the abacus. No doubt they had learned about the ENIAC vacuum-tube-powered computer in the United States. During World War II Soviet intelligence had been privy to the clandestine Colossus computer the British had developed to crack German Enigma codes. At war's end, a Soviet professor of mathematics and physics, Mikhail A. Lavrentyev, set up a program at the Ukrainian Academy of Sciences to design and construct the first Soviet computer. In the environs of Kiev, the Ukrainian capital, Lavrentyev set about organizing a research team that included Aksel Berg, a former admiral-engineer who had already become an active and influential member of the Soviet Academy of Sciences. After Stalin's death he was appointed chairman of the Council of Cybernetics. The first Soviet computer lacked large numbers of vacuum tubes, and these were obtained through Berg's intervention from the manufacturers of radio systems. The Ukrainian computer, the MESM, was thus completed in 1951, shortly after the first UNIVAC-1 prototypes were successfully developed in the United States.

No doubt the Soviet leadership gave its fledgling computer and electronics industry much less attention than its nuclear and space research programs. The country simply did not have the money and material resources for both. Lavrentyev's Kiev laboratory soon became the Kiev Institute for Cybernetics and Computer Sciences. Lavrentyev's assistant, S. A. Lebedev, then set up the Moscow-based Institute of Precise Mechanics and Computer Engineering, which in 1952 went on to develop the first BESM-1, an expanded and refined version of the Kiev computer. No doubt, too, these early computers had purely military applications. They were probably used to design the hydrogen bombs, to calculate the trajectory of spacecraft and, of course, to guide the world's first artificial earth satellite, the famous Sputnik. Research continued with the establishment of the Institute of Electronic Control Computers and the Institute of Mechanics and Instrument Design. These institutions were supervised jointly by the Academy of Sciences and the Radio Ministry. The infant Soviet computer industry was thus born, although it never reached the scale and magnitude that it had in the United States. Computer production remained predominantly in the hands of the Radio Ministry, at least until 1965, when the Ministry of Electronics was created at about the same time that the United States had announced its third-generation computers with the unveiling of the IBM System/360.

## ZELENOGRAD: THE USSR'S SILICON VALLEY

Zelenograd, or Green City, was planned from the start to become the USSR's high-tech capital. It was a typical Russian science city, very much like Akademgorodok or Norilsk. The difference was that it was within easy reach of Moscow, in itself a noteworthy characteristic. The site was an ideal one for quick transit and communication with the Soviet capital. It was close to the Leningrad highway out of Moscow and was a stop on the *electrichka* fast-transit railway.

Zelenograd was never intended to be a backwater science town like Dubna or Novosibirsk's Akademgorodok. From the very outset it bristled with all the trappings of a modern metropolitan suburb. Parking and traffic were always congested; there were copious displays in the center of the town; cafes abounded; and all workers carried the Moscow *propiska*, an internal passport allowing them to live either in Moscow or Zelenograd. The town did not really come into its own until the early 1970s, when chip technology had become extremely important, particularly in Soviet defense planning. Zelenograd emerged as a sort of nerve center for both a domestic microprocessing industry and legally imported or, as was increasingly the case, purloined foreign technology. Very soon an intricate network using constant feedback was established to connect Zelenograd with the other main electronics centers of the Soviet Union, notably the capitals of the other Republics, from Tbilisi in Georgia to Minsk in Byelorussia.

The man who masterminded the construction of the Zelenograd complex was the prime mover in the development of the Soviet semiconductor industry. Phillip Stavros, a Canadian of Greek origin, had graduated with a degree in engineering from the University of Toronto in 1941. It was not unusual for students in that era to feel partial to the Soviet Union in view of the Nazi threat. Stavros joined the Canadian Communist Party. When the Gouzenko case[8] erupted in Ottawa, the young electronics engineer probably decided to change his name and leave the country. With the experience he had acquired in working for firms like Westinghouse and Western Union, Stavros became an asset when he made his way to the Soviet Union sometime in 1955 after several years in Czechoslovakia. On his arrival in the USSR he was immediately given the task of overseeing one of the laboratories at a secret military research institute. An expert on computers and electronics, he was answerable only to the VPK (*Voenno-Promyshlennaia Kommissiya*, or the Military-Industrial Commission), linking the party, the armed forces, and Soviet industry. In a report he presented to a conference in late 1958 on the electronics industry, Stavros made a strong case for expediting research and development in microelectronics, and his secret laboratory soon expanded with the support of the military into a large office called the Leningrad Design Bureau, employing hundreds of workers. His main research focused on the development of a semiconductor production plant just outside of Moscow, which years later became the town and complex of Zelenograd. One émigré scientist, whose eyewitness report was collected by Harvard University's Mark Kuchment, describes the project:

All development of the project on the center of microelectronics was undertaken by a group of five to ten people under the direction of Stavros. Our project was not based on wishful thinking. It was meticulous throughout. We were young and enthusiastic. Stavros knew all the people who counted, enjoyed high authority, and had *carte blanche* from Khrushchev. Khrushchev visited our place in 1962 and saw for himself what possibilities the development of microelectronics could open.[9]

### THE RYAD MAINFRAME--MADE IN THE USSR

Under Stavros' stewardship, both the Leningrad Design Bureau and the newly created Centre for Microelectronics at Zelenograd began producing the RYAD (or Series) line of mainframe computers. The applications were to be military, with some controlled use in the civilian sector. The first Soviet-made integrated circuits began to appear in 1963, and the Leningrad Design Bureau was the first to use them in 1964 in the ELEKTRONIKA 200. The ELEKTRONIKA 200 was the forerunner of the subsequent three ELEKTRONIKA groups of microcomputers, built along the lines of Digital's PDP series, from which most of the hardware and software was copied. Since the Soviet Union never had to worry about the problems of infringement of patents, it could not be sued in accordance with any copyright laws--unless, of course, the Soviets decided to market a product abroad, which in the early development of Soviet computers was clearly inconceivable.

Heavily influenced by the design and construction of the IBM System/360, which was introduced in 1964, and the more advanced IBM System/370, the Soviet Union produced a remarkable range of RYAD-1 and RYAD-2 series. Until the advent of the RYAD, Soviet computers suffered from slow speeds and a lack of peripherals for data storage as well as printing and communications capabilities. They possessed poor software inventories and lacked sufficiently large main memories. The

RYAD system was a direct copy of the S/360, which at that time was the West's state-of-the-art computer technology. The new Soviet venture was designed to improve operational capabilities over a broad range of primarily military applications. It was far from perfect; nonetheless, it represented an enormous improvement on the more or less indigenous designs. What was more important was that it was supposed to be a concerted effort by the Warsaw Pact countries, and was accompanied by a proposal for a COMECON computer network. The Russians and the East Europeans called the new machines and network the *Edinennaia Sistema* (Unified System) or ES.

Throughout the 1970s, the participating Warsaw Pact countries expanded and modernized their productive capacity, although they maintained a proven Western design and used Western software. Each East European country was given its own part in co-ordinating ES development. To Hungary went the task of developing computer software; East Germany, which had produced its own ROBOTRON of the 1960s, improved the deficiencies in the magnetic disk storage devices, and so on. Several of the machines in the model ES-2 RYAD series were shown at the Tenth Anniversary Exhibit in Moscow in 1979. Of the seven models, Hungary built the ES-1010, Czechoslovakia the ES-1021, Poland the ES-1030. These mainframes were not without serious problems. There were delays in acquiring reliable, larger disk stores. There was a lack of modems connecting computers with phone lines, which made it difficult for computers to communicate via modem in the Soviet Union. Computer communication was still done by telex or telegraph lines. Spare parts were not readily available. Such equipment would have to rely on a network of distribution that is in its infancy because of the nature of this centralized industry. What is worse is that the computer working environment was deficient in its non-computing equipment infrastructure: that is, air conditioning, tapes, disk packs, paper, and data communications. A story was told of several computers that were installed in a factory with a hole in the roof; when it rained, the computers were ruined. No better graphic example of the Soviet "abacus syndrome" was needed.

The RYAD effort does not exhaust the gamut of Soviet activity in the computer field. A Soviet study of modeling and automation relating to C3 (military command, control, and communications) referred to the advent of large Soviet supercomputers of the ELBRUS-1 and ELBRUS-2 types, with operating speeds of 10 million to 100 million operations per second.[10] What the Soviets did not admit was that components of this technology were copies of Western designs. Novosti Press carried an article by two Soviet computer experts who boasted that "the country has, virtually alone, developed and is expanding the manufacture of its own computers. What is more, unlike Western European countries, it does not depend on American computer design or on American electronic components." In the same article the authors predicted that by 1987 Soviet industry would be in a position to make millions of microprocessors and tens of thousands of minicomputers and personal computers. They could not have been further from the truth, however. This led to important questions: Could Soviet society trigger a computer revolution and accommodate the information age? Could computerization in the USSR be decreed, like everything else?

## STRUCTURAL PROBLEMS

Secretive, wary of subversion, the USSR tenaciously guarded all important information. Although it possessed the largest scientific establishment in the world, Soviet science was both isolated and compartmentalized. Research suffered from communication lags. The practical effects (and defects) of various difficulties in transferring information and products between different branches of industry were indicated in a *Pravda* article on January 14th, 1972: "Because of the imperfect ties between branches and enterprises, the latter frequently must invent and construct that which has already been created in the scientific organizations and plants of other ministries."

Soviet scientists and researchers learned what was going on in their fields of study only after scientists in foreign countries were able to apply findings by other Soviets in the same field of research. Not all scientific journals were free of censorship. The system prohibited individual control over communications technologies. Even private checking accounts were nonexistent, and person-to-person credit arrangements were difficult to carry out. The country's telephone system was of a low quality, and modern-type communication involved special lines or a "search" system in which one out of a possible twenty circuits was good enough for high-speed communication. Where there was a relatively well-developed abstracting and indexing service, these services were not computerized to the same degree as in the West.

The Soviet Union embarked on a full-scale revolution in computers. While there were numerous indications that a significant improvement in research and development could have been accomplished, the main problem confronting Soviet society, however, was the capacity to absorb computers. Asking an abacus-based society to use computers seems tantamount to handing a medieval archer a modern machine gun. Needless to say, the rapidity with which a society absorbs a new technology is a crucial factor in determining the rate at which that technology will develop.

The Soviet system had built-in structural problems. During the early stages of computer development the main emphasis was on large, mainframe computers. Officials at Gosplan, the Soviet State Planning Agency, used them for everything from storing important data to calculating some 72,000 prices each year as part of the national economic plan or forecasting the weather on the Siberian taiga. The mainframe computer, institutionally controlled--be it for defense, the secret service, or economic planning--was an ideologically legitimate piece of hardware. It fit into the inner institutional framework and hardly extended beyond that to the public at large. Central planning and control were the major obstacles.

Evgenii Kachaturov said several years ago before an Academy Congress that it was necessary to restructure the system of information, to adapt it to new problems, and to intensify the training of the appropriate cadres. The key word here is "information." The subject of information again points up the weaknesses in the general culture's receptivity to computers. For example, to operate a computer, we must have reliable, accurate data. The axiom common to every computer specialist is "garbage in, garbage out." Yet anyone who has ever done research on the USSR knows that much of the economic, demographic, and even sociological data available was incomplete, biased, and inflated. Often they were intended to be misinformative and misleading. Students of Russian history know that not all the information from archival repositories was published. In fact, mortality rates were not published in the USSR since 1975. No statistics on unemployment or the inflation rate were given, although these indicators could be measured in the national economy. Grain production figures--those that existed-- were a state secret since 1981. Production managers, moreover, were loath to disclose true data, even to the authorities, lest they reveal corruption and managerial ineptitude. From my own experiences in studying Soviet Central Asia and Transcaspia, I have come across deliberate distortions in cartography. For security reasons, items, places, and topography appearing on maps are simply not there, or their precise location is inaccurate. Incomplete or false reporting led to certain rewards, much the same as with false income tax returns in the United

States. This decreased the efficiency of the whole system, and made the application of computers cumbersome.

Since the Soviet system was centralized, with no private ownership of business, it would not be able to perform in a Western-type business environment, which is decidedly uncentralized and, for the most part, in private hands. Concern over information and security notwithstanding, sooner or later the Soviets would have to foster such a business environment if they wished to modernize and improve their economy and compete with the West in the international marketplace since competition fuels rapid development in order for companies to remain in business. Time and again Soviet leaders and planners were confronted with the same contradictions. Any future modernization process appeared to involve a systemic decentralization and the increased use of microcomputers. The two are opposite sides of the same coin. Widespread use of microcomputers would permit managers and officials to collect and store information for their own records, to prepare balance sheets, and so on. In turn this would pressure the ministries and planning agencies to allow decisions to be decentralized as well. Information about the economy was crucial to party and bureaucratic control of economic decisions. The party *apparatchiki* regarded the computer as a threat to their power. But just as government departments in the West restricted access to computer information, so, too, did Soviet authorities supervise the use of their microcomputers.

Not all Soviet officials were averse to computers. Middle-grade managers were fascinated by them. Unlike the photocopier, which was only an administrative aid, the microcomputer played a direct role in the whole production process. As computer time becomes increasingly cheaper, industries that do not use the new technology will become less able to compete with those that do. That led to the inability of the USSR to sell finished goods to the West. Soviet economic planners were thus faced with an unavoidable quandary: Either pursue economic reform or lose political control.

Starting with Andropov but more so in the Gorbachev administration, many Soviet economists acknowledged that the advanced capitalist state possessed the building blocks for effective planning. First, they pointed to the fact that computer technology, combined with the systems management concept, promoted increased productivity and reduced needless duplication. Second, they admitted that a sophisticated computer base was needed to increase the capacity of the government enterprise to generate, store, analyze, and respond to vast quantities of diverse information. Third, they agreed that computers in industry provided for an improved information flow and allowed the use of better data generated by the policy sciences, such as regional economic planning and systems analysis. They would have liked to apply them to their own planned economy.[11] However, these commentaries said nothing about how in the USSR astute managers normally concealed extra stocks to beat the sudden shortages of raw materials that afflicted a tightly planned economy. Surely computerized inventories would have made it much harder to hide such deliberate mistakes.

To be sure, the most effective use of computers for a variety of applications required decentralized systems. If allowed at the local level in the Soviet Union, microcomputers could have been used alone or within a larger system (connected to a mainframe) for access to centralized data banks.

## SOFTWARE--THE ULTIMATE DILEMMA

Another problem connected with computers in the USSR was the production of software. As I pointed out above, this is the most interesting component of the computer. Most of the software sold today in North America still goes into mainframe computers used by large corporations or the government. But in the Soviet Union all software programming was directed by the government. Here in the West many observers have argued that software programming may be likened to a cottage industry. Cottage industries in the Soviet Union were illegal until 1988. Most software was produced by institutes and production facilities in specially constructed science towns like Zelenograd, or Akademgorodok in Siberia or Norilsk inside the Arctic Circle, or in KGB headquarters. Thousands of researchers were employed at these centers. In the United States, giant corporations like IBM buy their software from companies that make the programs or from private individuals. The largest of these software companies is called Microsoft, in a small town near Seattle.

The market in North America is extremely competitive, replete with advertisements and countless magazines on computing. The environment it caters to is consumer-dominated, and billions of dollars have been reaped by individuals and by software companies that sell their programs to the public. A popular "hacker" culture grew in the early 1980s, reminiscent of the ham radio enthusiasts and grease-monkeys of the 1950s and 1960s. I have already discussed the value of Silicon Valley in California, where about 200 high-technology firms were set up, most of which are computer-related. It would have been impossible to do the same thing in the Soviet Union. The dilemma of the USSR was that it was unable to replicate the same environment, the same culture, without contravening the most fundamental and durable principles of its socioeconomic order--state enterprise and no private ownership of industry.

The limitations that existed in Soviet hardware led to limitations in their software capability as well. Their policy of replicating Western computer systems proved to be more damaging in the production of software than in hardware,[12] since it led to a lack of programmer experience because the Soviets did not develop the systems themselves. A language barrier was also created because Western computer languages are dominated by English commands. None of the Soviet computer languages were used internationally and few were used even in the USSR. As well, the Soviets tended to design systems that relied on human input as the primary means of enhancing the scope of an automated system.[13] Software quality therefore tended to be low.

The current system was composed of inefficient computer codes processed on less-than-capable hardware. The Soviets' zeal in developing software for computer-based information systems had been marred by the bureaucracy's faulty incentives process. The system gave recognition for the number of systems initiated and tasks completed rather than for the completion of systems as a whole.[14] The result was a system in which quantity counted for more than quality. The bureaucrats also feared the false sense of security and power that a sophisticated software would have given its users. They were so security conscious that they would have prefered a backward software system to a system in which the Soviet citizen might have had access to things that they considered secret.

## TELECOMMUNICATIONS

Telecommunications within the Soviet Union were more fragmented than those in the United States and were generally backward. There were several general and special purpose telephone and telegraph networks, some of which were only partly connected. There were only ten telephones per 100 citizens (10 million to 15 million people were on waiting lists). The Soviet authorities hoped to have one telephone for every three persons by the year 2000. In 1985, only 23 percent of the urban population had telephones, and only 7 percent of the rural population had them.[15] Of these only 65 percent had direct long distance dialing. As such, there was a heavy reliance on the few public telephones that existed. Telephones also seemed to be distributed in a hierarchical manner. The system ran under CAMA (centralized automated message accounting), which recorded individual calls, including the called and calling numbers and thus led to a wariness of citizens who used the telephone. In addition to these types of communications, an extensive domestic satellite system also existed. However, telephone and other telecommunications formed only a small part of the satellite network.

The general network could not support data communications at any great speed. This pointed to the need to upgrade telecommunications lines in order to handle computer traffic. However, the Soviet Union was seeking to develop a variety of other systems for transmitting data (such as leased telephone lines) under an umbrella of programs for an All-Union State Network of Computers (GSVTs) and the Unified Automated Communications System (EASS). This led to the development, in 1977, of an All-Union System of Data Transmission (OGSPD), meant to become the backbone network for most data communications. However, it was threatened by the creation of independent ministry networks.[16] It was also retarded by the low priority given to serving the general population, by low investment, and by the fact that the Ministry of Communications was having difficulty in obtaining necessary equipment.[17] The EASS began construction of its second and third stages of development, which included electronic mail, facsimile, video conferencing, computer networking, and so on. Computers are able to communicate over long distances by telephone, dedicated lines, microwave, fiber optics, or satellite communications and, in local areas, over direct lines.[18] Monomode fiber optics would greatly increase transmission capacity for telecommunications on land and across oceans. Guided wave optics replaced electronic devices as the telephone system became an integrated digital network that, in effect, would be the world's largest computer. All of this fell under the rubric of networking that provided enhanced levels of computer communications.

## NETWORKING

Computer networking in the West was influenced by linking small computers to each other and to mainframes through the use of telephones and modems. Networking in the Soviet Union was meant to be used for modernization. At the enterprise level, networks were used for production control, leading to computer-integrated manufacturing.[19] At lower levels this was represented by robots, programmable controllers, and so on. However, few flexible systems were introduced and there were no local area networks for internal transmission.

Networks were also used to connect external organizations hierarchically. Through them, enterprises could report directly to a variety of other bodies. In 1971, the GSVTs were incorporated to create the OGAS (All-Union System for the Collection and Processing of Information for the Accounting, Planning and Management of the National Economy, or *Obshchegosudarstvennaia avtomatizirovannaia sistema*). The key element of the OGAS was the automated systems of management, which conveyed information from remote offices or factories to Gosplan, Moscow's central planning agency. At the top of the hierarchy of computer-based management information systems was the automated management system ASU (*Avtomatizirovannaia sistema upravleniia*), which stretched from a state committee, to ministry and department and regional systems to the enterprise and association system and which introduced new management methods to all levels of the economy.[20] ASUs did not provide computer services to the large numbers of organizations that needed them; therefore, a second front of computerization was opened based on collective use. These branch computer centers handled calculations for enterprises, although their development proceeded slowly. There were three levels to the process. The first did summary balances for the economy, the second calculated dealings in major areas such as labor and finance, and the third were subsystems devoted to planning for specific ministries. Because of the small number of enterprise-level ASUs, few ministries built networks.

The lack of personal computers in the Soviet Union prevented individuals from having access to such services as electronic mail. One important development in networking for the flow of information was Akademset', a network for the Academy of Sciences. The All-Union Scientific Research Institute for Applied Automated Systems (VNIIPAS) allowed some access to Western networks and data bases. This center was pressing ahead with some forms of remote access to information. As networking and personal computers became more prolific, it seemed that Soviet systems would become interested in breaking out of controlled networks and joining the rest of the world in its information revolution.

## THE REFORM MOVEMENT

In the early days of the revolution that brought him to power, Lenin defined Communism as Soviet power and electrification. If he were alive today, he would undoubtedly add computer technology to that list. The importance to the Soviet Union of gaining computer technology in a world increasingly dominated by the need for information and sophisticated networks with which to transfer this information was paramount if it wished to remain a world superpower. The authorities came to fear such advances. They believed that telecommunications, word processors, and computers would incite unorthodox ideas and inspire dissent. Allowing computers to set targets was tantamount to surrendering the power of the central economic planners to a machine, and this was ideologically unacceptable. The Soviet government thus faced a dilemma. It had to risk either a loss of control over information or the prospect of becoming a second-rate economic power.[21] The solution seemed obvious. The Soviet Union could not risk losing its position and therefore had to become part of this new information age.

All resources diminish with time except information. During the 1970s, the volume of scientific information doubled every five to seven years. During the 1980s, it doubled every twenty months and by the 1990s it will double every year. Therefore, it had to become the priority of the Soviet Union to provide ways to process this growing amount of data. The more quality information that was produced and the faster this could be assimilated, the higher the standard of living would be. In the West, the production of information became one of the world's most profitable and steadily growing industries. The Soviet Union had the potential to join in this industry.

The West and the USSR, however, had differing goals for computers. William McHenry writes of the West:

The personal computer and modem, under individual control and connected to an external information source, is the quintessential symbol of the information society in the West and Japan, and is the key to achieving many of the goals associated with it: instantaneous communication, previously unknown communications patterns and styles, dissemination of information, and increased decentralization and democracy.[22]

Soviet goals, however, were different. These included: attaining gains in productivity and modernizing the industrial base; maintaining and improving economic planning and control mechanisms; the support of military and internal security needs; and presenting an image of a progressive society to the people of the USSR and the outside world.[23]

Gorbachev made the development and use of computers one of the most important aspects of his modernization program. However, in order for the USSR to become computer-viable, there had to be major changes in six areas:

1. Research and Development. The Soviet Union had to move out of its heavy reliance on Western technology into national self-sufficiency. A step in that direction was accomplished through the creation, in 1985, of the Department of Informatics, Computer Technology, and Automation (a division of the Academy of Sciences).
2. Production Capability. Production of computer technology had to be hastened and the problems of planning rigidities and departmentalization corrected.
3. Applications. Computer applications were limited largely due to mainframe operations. However, wider applications are being developed, especially in areas such as robotics.
4. Networking. (Discussed above.)
5. Databases. The Soviet Union has become quite advanced in setting up data-banks across all disciplines.
6. Training. This involves millions of men and women. School courses had to be implemented to train high school students in the use and development of computer systems.[24]

Against the background of the computer revolution, the Soviet authorities had decided that they could have and should have slowly permitted the use of personal computers. Accordingly, in September 1984, the government solemnly announced that it was intending to launch a fifteen-year program to teach elementary and high school students the use of the Soviet-made personal computer, AGAT. Starting in early 1985, the schools received an estimated 1,131 AGATs and, at the end of the fifteen-year plan, the training course was expected to turn out one million students per year who would have been trained to work with and become knowledgeable about computers. These efforts were somewhat belated, but neither a shortage of teachers nor a dearth of reliable computers and word processors appeared to stand in the way of the Soviet government's eagerness to prepare Soviet youth for the computer age.

The Soviets first introduced the AGAT at a Moscow trade fair in July 1983. It was produced by ELORG (*Elektonorgtekhnika*), the celebrated Moscow-based government organization responsible for the purchase, manufacture, and marketing of electronic instruments and computers throughout the Soviet Union.

An American medical doctor, Leo Bores, who was president of Sun Bear software, a small firm specializing in medical software, traveled to

the Soviet Union and gave the following eyewitness account of the
AGAT:

Direct copies of early model IBM 1410s and 370s are known to be in use in
Russia, many controlled by old-fashioned paper-tape readers and punchers.
Except for an occasional Hewlett-Packard and a rare DEC (and perhaps a VAX
hidden away in the Ural mountains) computer systems in Soviet institutions are
outdated but serviceable.[25]

The only other thing one can say about the AGAT was that it was the
Soviet Union's first microcomputer. As such, it was a bad copy of the
Apple, with 64K bytes of RAM (random-access, read-write memory),
priced--because of the cost it took to produce it in the USSR--at roughly
$17,000, which included software. There was some speculation as to
whether the Soviets intended to market their product abroad. Ruling out
the Western market, there was, however, a tremendous demand for
computer hardware in Eastern Europe, where Hungary led COMECON
in developing computer software. As a government agency, ELORG
could have cut the price of the machine if only to create a market for it
in the COMECON countries. Most likely, however (at least in the initial
stages), the AGATs would be used in Soviet schools and institutions. If
the computer was eventually to be sold for home use, that event in itself
would have been a milestone on the road toward the liberalization of
Soviet society. Yet considering its prohibitive price, that likelihood
appeared to be far off. After all, the average Soviet citizen would have
probably preferred consumer goods such as washing machines and
refrigerators, and even more mundane office equipment like calculating
machines and typewriters. Men and women who did not have to plan
their investments or worry about how to reduce their income tax simply
had no need for computers.

If microcomputers were permitted in homes, they would have to be
under a system of decentralized control. First, the microcomputers would
not have been accompanied by printers. If any printing had to be done,
as was usually the case with word processors, it would have taken place
in a government institution, where it could be printed and stored as
classified information. The alternative was that the microcomputers
would have been connected to central mainframe computers that in turn
recorded every single manuscript. And if the local computer were
unhooked from the mainframe central network, it would not have operated at all. This was a sinister way of going about it. The KGB would
have been in a position to compile files on all the computers in the

country, resurrecting the Orwellian specter of intrusion into the private lives of citizens. Soviet commentators themselves dubbed this, by way of ideological justification, "the collective use of personal computers." There was a great deal of talk about creating a computer superministry to oversee the computerization drive.

The Soviet government finished negotiating the purchase of large numbers of Western-made personal computers, including models made by Apple and IBM. This was possible because of the more liberalized high-technology trade rules that went into effect in 1985 after several years of draconian COCOM surveillance. Moreover, the U.S. Department of Commerce had also relaxed controls on exports in response to pressure from 250 U.S. computer companies. The since-abolished Soviet Ministry of Trade placed additional orders in Japan, Britain, France, and West Germany. Control Data, which had previously sold computers to the USSR, would probably be the first to sell the Soviets a version of the Plato system, expanded into an online network of services stored in a mainframe, to which a personal computer equipped with modems and Control Data's own software could be tied.

With the proliferation of personal computers or microcomputers in the Soviet Union, another use could have been found for them. The rapid growth of computer technology offered perpetrators of Communist disinformation opportunities totally unknown in the past. If an American whiz-kid of high school age can break computer codes and manipulate sophisticated business and university computers, professionally trained KGB operatives and computer specialists could do the same. Extracting valuable intelligence from a computer or feeding a computer network with disinformation created a new challenge. Successful penetration of a computer center would temporarily disorient and eventually paralyze the nation's military defense. It could lead a group of scientists to the wrong conclusion on an important project, and it could interrupt trade between companies or between countries.

## CONCLUSION

In summing up, it would not appear too fatuous, considering the rate at which things are moving in both East and West, to suggest that some day the Soviets might enter the personal computer marketplace. One computer analyst wrote in a popular American magazine that by their very participation, the Soviets would "legitimize the computer market . . . and the new buzzword to arise from the freer exchange of information technologies between East and West would be (after our putative software) *detenteware.*"[26]

Whether or not the Soviets reformed their economic system, nothing should have prevented them from continuing to build their own computers. If they did badly at it, they would look to the West for guidance and, failing that, they would acquire whatever they needed by illicit means. It was generally acknowledged that at the moment Western computers were faster and more powerful and had larger memories than those in the USSR. Even small computers like Apple's TM Lisa had state-of-the-art programming. Many of the microchips found in Soviet fighters were exact replicas of Western chips. A single 8-bit chip found in an electronic game had more power and complexity than the 9-bit chips found in many missile guidance systems. The problem was compounded by the fact that microchips and computers had been licensed for foreign production, which further reduced American or COCOM control over their distribution. In the world computer market, stopping the determined Soviets from obtaining hardware and sophisticated programs was all but impossible because of patent violations, cloning, distribution, and foreign licensing.

Gains in computer use and computer technology undoubtedly constituted progress. Every nation aspired to progress not only to survive but to enhance its standard of living. This progress was achieved at a great expense and resulted from a curious blending of a nation's intellect, dedication, and artistic and business skills. The Soviets, like the Americans, were obsessed with this form of progress, whether the particular form was conducive to human fulfilment or not. Americans may have been on the road to a re-examination of the role of technology as a universal panacea, now that they were aware that even the computer-assisted inquiry and problem-solving that they called artificial intelligence was socially induced and greatly influenced by social constraints and politics.

But the Soviet policymakers, who had once resisted this science with a passion, stood in awe of the miraculous advances of the computer age. They were quickly realizing that humans had to bend themselves; old ideologies had to be adapted. Any society that did not adapt to the era of computers was bound to be left behind. Either Orwell's prophetic *1984* was on its way to becoming an inexorable and frightening reality in the USSR, or the system was going to break from the stranglehold in which it had been held for so long. In my view, it was the computer that turned into a catalyst, the harbinger of a new social era; Orwell's prophecy was not entirely fulfilled. The computer did not sustain the

Orwellian system already in place; on the contrary, it slowly started gnawing at its weak foundations.

## NOTES

1. Microelectronics offers the best example of how commercial-origin technology can improve military performance. Integrated circuits have made it possible for entire new weapons systems to come into being. Its successful application to "Star Wars" was a very controversial issue. But electronic warfare was widely used by the allies against Saddam Hussein during the second Gulf War.

2. See, for example, M.G. Iaroshevski, "Kibernetika--Nauka Mrakobe-sov" in *Literaturnaia Gazeta*, 5 April 1952.

3. See Friedrich Engels, *Dialectics of Nature* (New York: International Publishers, 1940).

4. *Voprosy Filosofii*, no. 4, 1955.

5. Yurii Kolbanovski, *Filosofskie Voprosy Kibernetiki* (Moscow: Nauka, 1960), p. 55.

6. Lee Kerschner, "Cybernetics: Key to the Future?" in *Problems of Communism*, Nov./Dec. 1965, p. 65.

7. See Linda Melvern, Nick Anning and David Hebditch, *Techno-Bandits: How the Soviets are Stealing America's High-Tech Future* (Boston: Houghton Mifflin, 1984), pp. 42-43.

8. Gouzenko was a Soviet cipher clerk working in the Soviet Embassy in Ottawa. He defected to the West and revealed all the secrets he was privy to. Some of his revelations led to the arrest of the Julius and Ethel Rosenberg in the U.S., as the famous "atom bomb spies."

9. Greville Wynne, *The Man from Odessa* (London: Robert Hale, 1981), p. 418, quoted in Melvern, Anning, and Hebditch, *Techno-Bandits*, p. 50.

10. See M. M. Kir'yan, ed., *Voyennotekhnicheskiy Progress i Vooruz-hennyie Sily SSSR* (Military-Technological Progress and the Armed Forces of the USSR) (Moscow: Voyenizdat, 1982). Command, control, and communications is basic military cybernetics, usually designated in military parlance as C3. It is a systems approach to combat operations. Computers are used for troop control (issuing orders), staff assessments and performing calculations with regard to the position of the enemy to prepare for sudden, radical changes in the combat situation. The command and control of large-scale combat operations involves a very complex cybernetic system that is simulated by microcomputers. Two articles on this subject are John Erickson, "Soviet Cybermen: Men and

Machines in the System," *Signal*, Vol. 3 (8): 1983, pp. 48-53; and Judith K. Grange, "Cybernetics and Automation in Soviet Troop Control" in *Signal*, Vol. 3 (8): 1983, pp. 54-57. See also Valentina Volkova et al., *Teoriya Sistem i metody sistemnovo analiza v upravlenii i svyazi* (Moscow: Akademia Nauka, 1983).

11. Anton Grigorov, *Eksperty v sisteme upravleniia obshchest'vennym proizvodstvom* (Moscow: Mysl', 1977).

12. David A. Wellman, *A Chip in the Curtain--Computer Technology in the Soviet Union* (Washington, D.C.: National Defence University Press, 1989), p. 103.

13. Ibid., p. 106.

14. Ibid., p. 114.

15. Wilson P. Dizard and S. Blake Swensrud, *Gorbachev's Information Revolution--Controlling Glasnost in a New Electronic Era* (Boulder, Colorado: Westview, 1987), p. 26.

16. William K. McHenry, "Computer Networks and the Soviet-Style Information Society," in *The Future Information Revolution in the USSR*, ed. Richard F. Starr (New York: Crane Russak and Company, 1988), pp. 88-89.

17. Ibid., p. 89.

18. Ibid.

19. Ibid., p. 91.

20. Ibid., p. 95.

21. Dizard and Swensrud, *Gorbachev's Information Revolution*, p. 22.

22. McHenry, "Computer Networks," p. 85.

23. Ibid., p. 86.

24. Dizard and Swensrud, *Gorbachev's Information Revolution*, pp. 38-55.

25. Leo Bores, "AGAT," *Byte*, November 1984, p. 135.

26. Alexander Besher, *Infoworld*, 12 November 1984.

# *Chapter 4*

# Strategic Minerals and Energy

A strategic material is one for which the quantity required for essential civilian and military uses exceeds the reasonably secure domestic and foreign supplies, and for which acceptable substitutes are not available within a reasonable period of time.
                                                    --U.S. Office of Technology Assessment

Industrial performance and military prowess are indissolubly linked. This maxim has held true for all ages and for nearly all military confrontations. The United States of America is not only the most advanced industrial country in the West but an economic giant because of its ability to influence the world's economies. It is not surprising that natural resources, or access to them, play a vital role in a nation's industrial production. This is the first and most important premise of the "realist" theory of state behavior (promulgated by H. Morgenthau et al.), in which "statesmen think and act in terms of interest defined as power."[1]

What made the U.S. such a great nation was, above all, its steel production, which is in direct proportion to a country's ability to wage war. No better example of this variable is needed than the one furnished by the American Civil War, when the industrial pre-eminence of the North was underscored. In the period before World War I, steel production was the chief index of the strength of nations, and when Germany began to overtake Britain and France as a steel producer, it was a tangible sign of the growth of its economic and military power.

When the Bolsheviks came to power in Russia, they had the highest regard for America's industrial potential. Lenin, Stalin, Trotsky--all of them clung to the conviction that production statistics are a yardstick of a given country's power, and they repeatedly extolled American industrial techniques. By the end of World War II, the U.S. could roll over 90 million tons of steel ingots a year--more than Britain, prewar Germany, Japan, France, and the USSR combined. With its economy in ruins, the USSR was able to produce only 10 million tons of steel. If the Soviet economy did not hurry and catch up, it could not for long tout its newly won status of a superpower.

With the American steel industry in decline, it did not take that long for the USSR to become the second largest industrial power in the world. It overtook the United States in steel output during the early 1980s. Without steel, coal, and iron ore--which are components of the same thing--there can be no large-scale production, no transportation, no rail system, and no infrastructure of any kind. These are the sinews of economic growth and industrial might. While today we live in an information age of rapid communications and of the microchip computer, we cannot function without the basic ingredients of the vital resources and materials, of energy in particular. Without them, the whole array of new technologies would never have been developed and improved.

## THE PROBLEM

The above statements are certainly all platitudes. The problem, however, is that in light of American foreign and defense policies, many analysts and policymakers have in the past decade argued that the Soviet Union was trying to deny Western industrial societies access to raw materials, minerals in particular, which they generally characterized as critical and strategic.[2] This "resource-war thesis" was with us throughout the Reagan and Bush administrations. It was not taken seriously in Western Europe, Canada, or NATO; its proponents were mainly from the Republic of South Africa and from strong American foreign-policy lobbyists like the Committee on the Present Danger. It was a theme in Ronald Reagan's 1980 campaign speeches and no fewer than four American "think tanks" studied this issue and propagated this view.[3] The minerals in question were typically thought to be oil from the Persian Gulf and steel alloys whose production was concentrated in southern Africa. These were chiefly cobalt, chromium, manganese, vanadium, and the platinum-group metals (uses to be discussed later), but precious metals and conductors cannot be excluded from this list.

This concern in the United States culminated in the passage of several bills under the Reagan administration: the National Materials and Minerals Policy, Research and Development Act of 1980, and the National Critical Materials Act of 1984. At the time, the American defense authorities were worrying about Soviet mineral policies. The defense sector already had a stockpile of critical materials, but this stockpile was not intended to protect U.S. industry from supply disruptions caused by economic or foreign policy disturbances. American policymakers were also beginning to worry about civilian consumers of strategic materials in the event of possible peacetime supply disruptions.[4]

Actually, there is a historic basis for this fear. More than four times since World War II, American (and consequently Western) supplies were jeopardized. The first episode came in 1949, when the USSR stopped exports of manganese and chromium to the United States following the Soviet blockade of Berlin in 1948. Another episode occurred when the U.S. decided in 1966 to participate in a United Nations embargo on chromium from Rhodesia (now Zimbabwe). In 1969, nickel workers in Canada went on strike, and in 1978, in the rebellion-torn Shaba province of Zaire (formerly Katanga), the world cobalt supply seemed to be disrupted and a wave of panic buying raised the price of cobalt almost seven-fold in a fortnight.

The 1973 Arab oil embargo exacerbated the fears of most American resource specialists when they realized how sharply the price of imported oil can rise and how crucial this can become to a Western economy. That disruption was caused by the OPEC cartel. It resulted in a loss of 500,000 jobs and reduced the U.S. GNP by $10 billion dollars. With the upheaval in the Republic of South Africa (RSA), there was increased concern over excessive Western dependence and the threat of supply disruptions seemed to loom large again.

It must be pointed out that little mining of some of these materials takes place in the United States today, and the known U.S. deposits are poor in quality. It is the RSA that provides the West with platinum-group metals, including more than half the chromium (an essential component of stainless steel) and about one-third of the manganese needed for steel making. Cobalt is produced mainly in Zaire and Zambia (the region referred to as "Southern" or "High Africa"),[5] and its supply is shipped to the Western market on South African (RSA) railways and from South African ports.[6] The Soviet Union was the other large world producer of chromium and manganese.[7]

Indiscriminate statements made by Soviet leaders did not lessen

American fears of a real or perceived resource war. One such intemperate remark was made by Nikita Khrushchev in 1960 when he said that the USSR ought to influence the mineral-rich Third World nations in order to hold the West hostage to Moscow.[8] In 1973, Leonid Brezhnev allegedly declared: "Our aim is to gain control of the two great treasure houses on which the West depends: the energy treasure house of the Persian Gulf and the mineral treasure house of central and southern Africa."[9] According to Soviet analysts, there was a strong conviction in the Soviet leadership that the "racist regime of the white minority will go when the system of apartheid goes" and when that government was replaced by a black-majority government, "the activities of foreign corporations will be drastically curtailed, changing the raw materials policy of the country."[10] It was further argued by Soviet "think tanks" that "under such circumstances, one cannot exclude a definite convergence of the RSA's raw materials policy with that of the developing states,"[11] primarily focused on chrome, manganese, platinum, and gold. Other Soviet analysts discerned that just as decrease of oil deliveries was capable of critically affecting industrial production in the U.S., Japan, and Western Europe, so too could a sharp reduction in export of South African gold cause serious impact on "capitalist" currency circulation, which is part of the whole financial mechanism of the West.[12]

Although most of the foregoing assumptions were made by the Soviets in their analyses of Western problems or serve simply as declaratory statements, can it also be said that they reflected official Soviet policies? What was Soviet behavior in the world with respect to minerals, political or economic? For it became a truism to argue that monetary chaos would be triggered by a gold shortage, and that the USSR would ultimately profit by it, as I quoted the Soviet source above.

One thoughtful Western writer summarized the reasons that advocates of the resource-war thesis in the West would be inclined to think along these lines. He maintains that there were many in the United States who embarked on an unqualified scare-mongering campaign to create the impression that the Soviets were trying to deny resources to the West because they knew it would deal a crippling blow to Western economic and military strength.[13] There was also the possibility that the Soviets might have coveted certain materials because their own economy needed them. Lacking adequate foreign exchange to purchase, Moscow was intent on seizing the resources.[14] One of the most outspoken advocates of this theme was Bohdan Szuprowicz,[15] who emphasized Moscow's close relationship with the anti-Western governments of the materials-rich nations bordering Zaire and the RSA. He cited the example of Angola, which was a member of the CMEA (Comecon) economic coalition and which bartered its mineral resources for Soviet goods, machinery, and military equipment.

## THE REALITY

It was certainly true that the USSR and other East European countries bartered for material resources from Third World countries in exchange for Soviet goods, thus avoiding the need for the hard currency that both the USSR and the Third World were usually required to pay for transactions with the Western nations. It was also conceivable that the Soviets would try to influence the materials policies of many Third World nations. Such nations had formerly known colonial domination and exploitation, and they were an easy prey to Soviet blandishments. Indeed, the cornerstone of Soviet policies throughout the underdeveloped world was support for either Marxist or nationalist liberation movements.

From the Soviet perspective this was of course a political issue, not an economic one. To be sure, the following examples of Soviet activities were always cited in relation to southern Africa.

1. Presence of Cuban troops, as well as East German and Soviet advisers in Angola.
2. Military interventions in Angola, Ethiopia, Mozambique, and Zaire, and installation of a Marxist-oriented government in Zimbabwe.
3. Reported covert or subversive Soviet operations within Namibia, South Africa, the Shaba province in Zaire, and so on.

But there was no evidence to suggest that any of these pro-Soviet countries had refused to export to or trade with the Western nations, especially since they themselves lacked the foreign exchange that was necessary to compete in world markets for all the imports they required and which the USSR was unable (though not necessarily unwilling) to deliver. In late 1984, this writer was led to believe (erroneously, I admit) that the USSR was pursuing an aggressive minerals policy in this region as part of a grand design to bring the West to heel. My argument centered on the Soviet military threat to the region from its base in the Seychelles, off the southeast African coast,[16] which could easily be seen as a direct military threat to South Africa.

More than anything else, Soviet policies may be said to have been economic and based on national self-interest rather than on any ideological considerations. That was the easiest way to explain how and why the Soviet authorities took such an interest in the metals trade, in pricing and in volumes of mineral production, and why they were not averse to influencing international commodity markets to their advantage. The best-known example of this manipulation came just before the rebel invasion of the mineral-producing province of Shaba in Zaire, which completely cut off cobalt production from Shaba's mines. Anticipating the political unrest, which the USSR may or may not have fomented, the Soviets instantly bought up a two-year supply of cobalt on the London Metals Exchange. There followed a sudden seven-fold increase in the value of cobalt on the world market, an almost prohibitive price that significantly destabilized an already unsettling minerals market. This was one of the reasons that prompted French military intervention in Zaire in 1978.

It was around this time, too, that the Soviet Union aggressively began purchasing many more ferrous and non-ferrous minerals abroad. Soviet export of some prominent materials suddenly ceased, and there was a fear in most foreign chancelleries of a perceptible Soviet transition to "selective resource dependency," which would further destabilize commodity prices in the West. Worse than this, in the early 1980s some American observers questioned the ability of the USSR to maintain its mineral self-sufficiency. These analysts argued that the only strategic material the Soviets had been heavily dependent upon until then was natural rubber. Led by Daniel Fine of MIT, these scholars pointed to such factors as changing trade patterns, rapid increases in domestic consumption, ore grade declines, economic difficulties, a slowdown in the development of Siberian deposits due to technological deficiencies and to problems in transportation to industrial centers; even the possibility of an accelerated military stockpiling was evoked.[17]

Alarmist voices were also heard in the press. By 1981 the case became an emotionally charged media event, not just an academic issue.[18] The most startling revelation, furnished by foreign trade statistics, was that, while the Soviets had been net exporters of chromium, the platinum-group metals, and manganese (all of which are strategic materials), they were now importing high-grade chrome ore from Iran, buying up cobalt as well as copper, zinc, aluminum, and molybdenum--materials in which the USSR had always been self-sufficient.

Further, since the invasion of Afghanistan, the Soviets had been tapping that country's copper, gas, and uranium, thus adding reserves to the USSR's already large share.[19] Words used in the American media to describe Soviet behavior were tellingly partisan: "mysterious," "ominous," "sinister," and "shifty." Because of this there were many U.S. government inquiries into the matter.[20]

Despite the concern in government circles in Washington, it appeared that nothing much would come of the anxieties expressed. Opinions remained divided. The U.S. Congress tried to circumvent the issue; minerals experts in the Central Intelligence Agency and the National Security Council admitted they had no evidence of a master plan of subversion on the part of the USSR. Even the U.S. State Department was skeptical about this affair.[21] Apparently only the Reagan administration was fostering the view in order to promote efforts to build up America's national defense and to cater to American mining interests.[22] The American mining industry would in fact welcome the opportunity of exploring for strategic minerals on federal lands,[23] possibly in Canada, too[24] (if ever U.S. resources were depleted). It would certainly not be averse to legislation for a more favorable tax treatment for the mining companies. Most businesses in mining and in the field of international minerals marketing were notorious for their advocacy of the resource-war theme. For all the reasons mentioned above, it would make good business sense to support such a scenario. It served as a rallying point for protectionism in the United States, where fears of diminishing world resources were taken seriously by the American corporate establishment.

Yet anyone knowledgeable about the export/import activities and the actions of the Soviet government with respect to mineral policies ought to know that they were based wholly on self-interest and motivated by a purely economic and business rationale. The Soviets were indeed fostering such a business rationale. They advertised as any capitalists did in the *Wall Street Journal*; they sold their patents and inventions for profit to foreigners; they were worried about work efficiency and the computerization of industry and production and even of craftsmanship. It would be misleading for us to take Soviets' belligerent words and empty rhetoric seriously. This point cannot be overstated. Let us examine the evidence.

First, as mentioned above, there was the abiding need in the USSR for the foreign exchange necessary for the purchase of equipment from the West in order to develop their own resources further, particularly in the far-flung regions of Eastern Siberia and the Far East. Second, whenever world-market prices tended to rise, (as they did in 1980) it would not be surprising that the Soviets made massive purchases, as a hedge against further inflation. This was plausible if the Soviets found that their own costs were rising substantially and as they began to shift to newer production areas in the East where the tempo was more rigorous and where the climatic conditions were far more severe. The Soviets would do everything in their power to compete on the international mineral market to benefit from the trade advantages to their economy.

## THE SOVIET UNION WAS A FORMIDABLE COMPETITOR--WHY?

Very little reliable data concerning Soviet production, consumption, and mineral trade are available. Neither cost nor output statistics of any non-ferrous metal have been published since World War II in absolute quantities (though some index numbers have been issued),[25] and the foreign trade returns on any non-ferrous metals were suppressed in 1977. Output and trade statistics in regard to gold were suppressed forty years ago. Data on individual deposits, mines, and refineries were still to be found, notably in the journal of the Ministry of Non-Ferrous Metallurgy of the USSR (*Tsvetnye Metally*, published in both English and French), but within rigid censorship constraints designed to conceal all output and much unit-cost data. In fact, the transmission to any unauthorized person of information on the production of non-ferrous metals was a criminal offense under Soviet law.[26]

Proliferation of information would have adversely affected the power structure of the elite and of the leadership. Information, as the maxim goes, is power. In the USSR information was always highly compartmentalized. The Soviet system is was essentially esoteric and closed, although with strong liberalizing forces at work under *perestroika*. However, it was one in which accurate statistics on minerals extraction were still secret and ideologically suspect. The economic advantage that the Soviet Union enjoyed from this was that it could produce more cheaply than suppliers in other countries.

Such important information as is needed on production and trade statistics in the USSR was obtained from the U.S. Bureau of Mines in Washington, the *Metallgesellschaft AG* in Frankfurt and the Institute of Geological Studies in London. They alone were able to corroborate data from the sale and purchases of Soviet minerals over the years. It will be observed, however, that world mineral prices had much less of an impact on Soviet mineral production than on a market economy. For instance, low 1982 prices reduced Canadian nickel production to almost 50 percent of its 1981 output.[27] This affected more than the nickel industry, however, Canadian production of platinum-group metals, a by-product of nickel, fell 51 percent. By contrast, even though Soviet platinum metals were also a nickel by-product, output in 1982 increased by more than 150,000 troy ounces, accompanying a 4 percent rise in nickel production. This seemed to indicate that both the primary metal and its important by-products (in this case, a foreign currency earner), would be produced despite the world market conditions for the primary commodity.

What did the USSR actually do? By increasing nickel production from its Arctic regions (Norilsk and the Kola Peninsula) and by heavily investing in Cuban production of nickel,[28] Soviet competition created a situation in which Canadian companies like INCO and Falconbridge ceased to set the world price for nickel. Whereas in 1950 Canada produced 95 percent of the world's nickel, by 1986 it was barely producing 10 percent. As a result of the price war, these Canadian producers lost a sizable portion of the international market share (primarily in Western Europe), largely to Soviet dumping practices.[29] What was so startling here was not so much that the USSR was able to undercut Western producer prices, but that for the first time in the international economic order, Soviet marketing tactics had allowed them to influence the world market price. Up until a few years ago, the Soviet Union was a price-taker, not a price-maker, in the market. This was especially true of precious metals like gold and platinum because the USSR would sell not as a regular export item, as do South Africa and Canada, but as its balance of payment required.[30] There was nothing in the actions of the Soviet Union that was even remotely connected with a resource war. Neither was there any evidence to suggest that the Soviet Union was inclined to act malevolently against Canadian companies like INCO out of regard for the way that the company had exploited its Sudbury employees (or, one might add, the way INCO rejected its union demands or even treated foreign workers in Guatemala not so long ago).

We must realize that it was the CMEA, not the West, that was the primary trading partner of the USSR. Approximately half of all Soviet trade, and most of its mineral exports, went to these countries, subsidized at low prices to better integrate the East European economies with that of the USSR. Soviet exports furnished three-quarters of CMEA oil and chromite, two-thirds of its iron and manganese ores, and half of its aluminium, lead, and zinc.[31] Precedents also existed for preclusive purchases of certain strategic minerals and their subsequent resale to the

West at inflated prices. Often, too, the minerals were resold to the CMEA at reduced rates as a goodwill gesture.[32]

The USSR tried to integrate into the Western trade network and into the world economy as a whole. It intimated on several occasions that it would have liked to have joined GATT the way Hungary had, first as an observer and then eventually as a full member. This implied that if it were allowed to join it would agree to the main GATT regulations, except, of course, the disclosure of state subsidies and production costs. The idea was turned down in 1986 by the majority of GATT's member states. The USSR tried its luck again in the summer of 1987 after state subsidies were reduced drastically. The USSR certainly had an interest that its own sales minimize downward pressure on price, subject to the objective that the required revenue was earned by a combination of volume and price in the plan year. When the gold price peaked in the 1970s, the USSR authorities frequently refrained from selling within any one year when the price rise slackened. During the sharp downswing of the early 1980s, they also held off the market to cushion the fall. Thus, in contrast to their policies for nickel, in early 1982 they put it about that they had made no sales at all for a stated period in a clear attempt to hold the price steadier.

Such business acumen certainly went against the grain of an American and South African resource-war thesis. Furthermore, there was some likelihood that the USSR might have agreed to a formal participation in a producers' cartel to help stabilize the prices of certain minerals. This author was told in Moscow, however, that cartelization would be a possibility provided the Soviet government was able to conclude such agreements with the producers' governments themselves, not with Western mining companies that the USSR in effect refused to recognize on the grounds that corporations had no treaty-making capacity.[33] In any case, there were other problems associated with cartels that suggested that it was not the USSR alone that might have been opposed, as I shall discuss later.[34] This did not mean that the USSR never did business with private companies when it served Soviet purposes. There is ample evidence on record to account for the "tacit" cooperation between the Soviet government and South African (RSA) companies in the production and pricing of platinum.[35] Of course, with joint ventures, the Soviet government was directly dealing with Western businesses. The same held true for Soviet and South African collusion in the production and pricing of diamonds.[36]

Admittedly, there was more than a touch of cynicism in the way the

USSR conducted its international commercial activities. But we must remember that gold, diamonds, apatite, and platinum--to name some of the major metals--were minerals of exceptional value. The mining of platinum, until recently, never attracted the same attention as that of gold. The Soviets were always eager to keep world prices as high as possible. About three-quarters of Soviet production of these metals was thought to go into reserve for foreign currency purchase, and the other quarter was for industrial use, for jewelry, for medical uses, and for sale (or outright gifts) to other members of the Soviet bloc. The whole industry was always subsidized at a generous rate until the Gorbachev reforms sought to institute greater incentives on the enterprise level, with greater decentralization of the managerial apparatus. Until 1970, for example, the Soviet mining industry sold gold to the Soviet State Bank at two roubles per gram (roughly $70 per ounce) while the State Bank sold it at one rouble per gram. Then came the dramatic rise in the price of gold in the wake of world inflation; with a world price well over $400 per ounce, not only the Soviet State Bank, but Soviet industry itself, should have been making a substantial profit.[37]

But the Soviet government had yet to admit publicly that its State Bank sold bullion, since the official Soviet balance of payments had never been disclosed.[38] As was the case with most precious and strategic metals, actual deliveries were still given an aura of secrecy and ambivalence by the Soviet practice of buying as well as selling and also by shifting trade in bullion away from Zurich to London.[39] Net bullion transactions with CMEA countries were further complicated by gold production in Mongolia and Romania (in the same way that Cuba now was a major producer of nickel, subsidized by Soviet funds) and by substantial dealing by the Hungarian National Bank.[40]

Gold was in any case considered a "noble" metal in the USSR. Its link to the entire economy and to technological innovation was absolutely essential. Gold does not rust like iron, does not get covered with a bluish-green oxide like copper, and does not darken like silver. It is a heavy metal, malleable and ductile, and melts at a temperature of 1,064 degrees centigrade, which makes it one of the best superconductors. It is therefore used in electronics, space technology, and communications, together with other alloys like copper and silver. When hammered into an extremely thin, almost transparent pellicle, it looks like a wire, even thinner than a human hair (1 gram of this wire stretches two kilometers). Only metals of the platinum group are heavier than gold. As early as 1921, Lenin expressed the Communist attitude to gold in his article,

"The Importance of Gold Now and After the Complete Victory of Socialism." His article was written during the NEP period, when it was important to re-establish normal commodity and monetary relations in a country ravaged by many years of war and to establish trading relations with the capitalist West. Somewhat naively, Lenin wrote:

When we are victorious on a world scale I think we shall use gold for the purpose of building public lavatories in the streets of some of the largest cities in the world. This would be the most 'just' and most educational way of utilising gold for the benefit of those generations which have not forgotten how, for the sake of gold, ten million men were killed and thirty million maimed in the war of 1914-18. . . . Meanwhile, we must save the gold in the RSFSR, sell it at the highest price, buy goods with it at the lowest price.

If he had lived longer, Lenin might have witnessed Stalin's penal gold colonies at Kolyma, Noril'sk, and on the Kola Peninsula, where the barbarous conditions beggared the horror of even bourgeois capitalism's quest for gold.

Considering that Soviet practices were motivated by economic self-interest, the threat to the West was an economic one and was of no political significance. To read into this some "political" ulterior motive or to misconstrue economics with politics would be self-defeating and a travesty of the available evidence. Such economic rivalry was characteristic of every interstate relationship and did not carry the same importance as a political relationship and a strategic rivalry.

## PRESENT OPTIONS, FUTURE PROSPECTS

Notwithstanding the social turmoil in South Africa, the USSR's exports outside the Eastern bloc grew to such an extent in the 1970s and 1980s that they eroded not only the RSA's traditional Western markets but Canada's as well. Barter arrangements, price discounting (dumping), and long-term contracts with clients in the U.S., West Germany, France, and Japan more than doubled since 1977. In that year alone, Soviet exports of asbestos to Japan replaced some 100,000 tons of Quebec asbestos, which gave the USSR more than 50 percent of the Japanese market. The only consolation was that the quality of Soviet asbestos shipped to Japan and Western Europe remained inferior to the Canadian product. In nickel, asbestos, or potash, Canada, hitherto a major exporter, can no longer be considered a price leader, nor will it be in the future. For this reason alone there appeared to be increased interest among major Canadian mining firms in the possibility of participating with Russia in a cartel.[41]

A good number of mining analysts firmly believed that, since Canada, East Germany, and the USSR controlled about 89 percent of world potash exports, these countries should have formed an effective potash cartel. Others even believed that the Soviets might have been persuaded to support Canpotex prices. (Canpotex is the marketing arm of Canadian potash companies for all sales outside North America.)[42]

The idea of cartels, however, was not a feasible proposition. As with De Beer's South African gold (see Note 35), there was always the possibility that the USSR might one day undercut the Canadian price. Moreover, as argued above, because the USSR was secretive about production, consumption, and stockpile data, it could not formally or legally belong to a cartel.[43] A cartel, after all, required disclosure of such statistics. Besides, the United States, more than anyone else, was opposed to such cartels and was prepared to react against it through American antitrust legislation; this could be invoked against American corporations and their subsidiaries. We must remember that most mining firms today are still owned or controlled by American banks and corporations.[44] Cartels are therefore illegal. Britain, too, has a sizable share of equity capital in foreign companies through corporations like Consolidated Gold Fields. Moreover, cartels and commodity agreements in any event will only hasten the ongoing process of substitution of critical materials, and that will undermine any artificial price increase.

Asbestos is one mineral in which Canadian producers will never need a cartel. There indeed was a kind of tacit cooperation between them and the Soviets on prices in order to prevent drastic fluctuations. During the 1970s and 1980s, Soviet production of asbestos grew at a higher rate than the world output. This trend continued as new mining capacities were brought into production in the USSR. Asbestos was not recycled, and stockpiling was negligible; consequently, annual world consumption of asbestos tended to be approximately the same as annual world production. Moreover, Canadian asbestos is considered less dangerous to human health and to the environment than the Russian or South African varieties.[45] Therefore, when the Soviets lowered their price relative to the price of Canadian asbestos, the share of Soviet exports on the importing markets had a tendency to increase.

Because the Soviet Union was also the most formidable consumer of its own asbestos and because the demand in the USSR and in Soviet bloc countries continued to grow faster than in the Western countries (the OECD had in fact tried to put a ban on asbestos products), most of the Soviet asbestos was needed to cover intra-COMECON needs. By decreasing their demand for asbestos through limitation of its use and through a continuing search for new substitutes, Western countries became less dependent on Soviet asbestos than in the past.[46]

The Europeans were least of all concerned about alleged Soviet disruptions to world minerals supply. To compensate for any shortages, France extended its commercial relations with its former colonies to ensure a constant supply, primarily from Africa. France in effect received ample uranium from Niger and Gabon (prices even decreased enormously, hurting Niger's economic growth), manganese from Gabon, iron ore from Mauritania, phosphate from Senegal and Morocco, and cobalt from Morocco. One particular study established beyond any doubt that the Federal Republic of Germany, which was absolutely dependent on almost all mineral imports for its economy, had set up an array of mechanisms, including equity investments in Third World explorations, to ensure a constant mineral supply.[47]

To be sure, most West European countries were improving relations with the Soviet Union in resource policies, and one area of cooperation was that of joint ventures in exploration and refining of minerals. German companies that pursued this avenue were August Thyssen, Degussa, Preussag, and Urangesellschaft. Joint ventures, for instance, were very successful for the People's Republic of China and the Canadian mining concern Galactic. Taking their cue from this, Soviet officials expressed an interest in pooling their resources with Canadian and Scandinavian companies as well.[48]

But the greatest effort of all to obtain technology and expertise in producing, refining, processing, and recycling Siberian and Far Eastern mineral resources was focused on Japan. Soviet analysts themselves observed the mutually complimentary character of the two economies; in gross terms, Japan imported about 90 percent of its non-fuel mineral requirements, compared with 75 percent for Western Europe and 25 percent for the United States. The Soviets regarded Japanese technology as the world's best, especially in the area of minerals extraction. The combination of Japan's geographical location (its proximity to Siberia and the Soviet Far East) and the enormous supply of Japanese investment capital that was seeking productive use outside Japan made it a natural partner in mineral mining.[49] Moscow negotiated numerous deals to acquire a wide range of Japanese technologies.[50]

One of the prime movers in the improvement of Japanese-Soviet relations was I. I. Kovalenko, the deputy head of the International Department of the Soviet Communist Party's Central Committee and the chief party specialist on Japan.[51] Gorbachev also visited Japan to cement relations. After the Soviet Army invaded Afghanistan, Japanese participation in the U.S.-led economic sanctions against the Soviet Union explicitly excluded a prohibition on joint resource development projects. The Japanese were known to be the least observant of COCOM rules on export controls and U.S. regulations banning strategically sensitive technology transfers to the Soviet Union.

Last but not least was a prospect that is more futuristic than immediate. There was a worldwide interest in developing "advanced materials" that could reduce Western reliance on strategic materials. The process was extremely costly and still in the planning stages but, unlike metal substitutes, advanced materials will soon be used as direct replacements for alloys. These materials are ceramics, composites, polymers, plastics, and others. George A. Jewett wrote, "Materials technology is almost certainly the most significant science of our age. . . . [P]olymers have achieved their greatest market penetration in replacing metals."[52] As G. Peeling and W. Chambers cogently argued, "Certain scientific advances and technological developments create a demand for new materials. . . . This kind of material requirement is evident in aerospace, rocketry, information-communication networks, and the use of lasers."[53] Between 1970 and 1991, the U.S. telecommunications industry consumed an average of 300,000 tons of copper per year; between 1991 and 2000, consumption is expected to drop by one-half because glass fiber optics are now replacing copper as an interconnection in photonic communications systems.[54]

The information-carrying capacities of fiber optics wires are revolutionizing communications. A pair of copper wires is needed for a single telephone call, but a pair of hair-thin optical fibers can carry nearly 2,000 calls simultaneously. Their cost is negligible because the basic material out of which they are made is silicon, one of the cheapest substances available. Their first use seems to have occurred at the end of the 1950s in a non-surgical probe inside the human body known today as endoscopy. Then the idea developed that optical wires could be used as substitutes for copper wires in electronic equipment such as computers and high-speed telephone switching systems. In 1983, AT&T completed the first long-distance fiber optics "circuit" between Boston and Washington. In 1988, the first trans-Atlantic fiber optics cable was laid with a 40,000 circuit capacity, which doubled the capacity of the seven North Atlantic cables already in place that had a 19,500 circuit capacity. Many are predicting that prospecting for cast-off copper wires will in the future be like the gold rush of a bygone era.

Other "technological" means to reduce or supplant the need for strategic materials are:

1. Recycling and conservation. The Office of Technology Assessment (OTA) estimates that by the mid-1990s between 400,000 and 500,000 troy ounces of platinum-group metals could be recovered from scrapped cars each year, which is equal to 16 percent of U.S. consumption.
2. Technological improvements in manufacturing processes.
3. Substitution of alloys and advanced metals. Fully developed substitutes exist for cobalt and platinum.
4. Supply diversification.
5. Development of a substitution data bank, or a materials information stockpile to which all firms might have access for information on the feasibility of substitutes and advanced materials.

Needless to say, the Soviet Union embarked on the same program of substitution to ensure improvement and future supply.

The above options certainly reduced Western imports of strategic materials and gave the lie to the specter of supply disruptions by the Soviet Union. The American Office of Technology Assessment made several studies on technologies to reduce U.S. import vulnerability and described the concept of minerals vulnerability (hence, the resource war) as a "misconception." Materials science was not the only alternative in the quest for strategic minerals: deep ocean nodules represented other sources of manganese and ferro-manganese ores, and any notion of supply shortages throughout the 1990s should be dismissed. In addition, work was well under way in both the USSR and the West to exploit offshore deposits of tin, zinc, gold, copper, and other metals. The time is not far off that we shall be able to extract rare metals on an industrial scale directly from sea water.

## ENERGY

Energy was a major concern for the Soviet Union since the early days of the revolution. Lenin himself felt that the electrification of the Soviet Union was an essential technique in building the technical and material base of Communism. Technical progress such as electrification, mechanization, and the automatization of production were linked to the growth of energy consumption.[55] The USSR produced one-fifth of the world's output of energy and fuel. It was the only industrialized country that completely satisfied its fuel and energy requirements.[56] Approximately one-third of the USSR's capital investments were allocated for the development of its fuel and energy complex.[57]

The USSR realized that it would need more and more energy as industry developed, as the population grew, as the motorization of the economy broadened, and as its chemical industry developed. In the future, the main consumer of solid fuel will be some industrial sectors and large thermal power stations. Ninety percent of the Soviet Union's energy resources were in the east (94 percent of the USSR's coal reserves, 73 percent of its natural gas, and 81 percent of its hydropower reserves).[58] A vast network of pipelines was needed to cut down the cost of transportation. The miles of pipelines already in place would circle the equator five times.[59] Base towns and outposts had to be built to supply these pipelines with maintenance workers. Hydroelectric power stations would be surrounded by industrial complexes to better utilize the energy output. The Soviets realized that they had to accelerate the construction of dams so that the time needed to build a dam could be reduced from ten to twelve years to seven or eight. Dams allowed more farmland to be utilized by preventing annual floods. Nuclear plants also had to be constructed with industrial complexes located nearby. They should have been built in sparsely populated areas with a shortage of usable farm land, and a shortage of water resources in order to best utilize the space available. Work had already begun to create "fast" reactors that allowed a more complete utility of uranium resources.[60]

Since the Chernobyl nuclear accident in 1986, the USSR has held an interest in energy conservation as a new resource of power. The United States' energy use between 1973 and 1984 dropped by 24 percent due to energy saving from improved energy efficiency (thus saving 100 quadrillion BTUs of energy).[61] With a fall in the earning potential of oil and increasing energy demands, the USSR sought new means to satisfy its energy needs. Thus, in December 1983, the United States and the USSR entered into a collaboration in energy conservation. Eugenii Velikhov, a vice president of the Academy of Sciences, designated the Institute for High Temperatures as coordinator of the Soviet contribution to this study. A number of symposia and workshops were held between the two countries in which many ideas were exchanged. The Soviets saw future energy production as highly energy-intensive and believed that other areas had to become less so if the economy was to remain self-sufficient in energy.[62]

There was an energy interconnection between the USSR and Eastern Europe, especially through the CMEA. Eastern Europe depended on the USSR for 80 percent of its energy imports and over 90 percent of its oil.[63] In the past, the Soviets used oil as a means of political and economic control. A development in cooperation between the socialist countries was signified by a Comprehensive Program adopted in 1971 for the further extension and improvement of cooperation and the development of socialist economic integration through the CMEA.[64]

The USSR was self-sufficient in its energy requirements. However, the Soviets did realize that with an expanding population and industrial base, they would need more energy. To this end, they developed more effective uses of energy to counteract a decline in oil production and coal miners' strikes. The future of these developments seems to be bright.

## CONCLUDING REMARKS

From my findings so far and the limited data available on Soviet mineral production, a general summary is in order. Were the Soviet Union not so resource-rich, it would have been impossible for that nation to maintain a superpower status and at the same time remain almost economically self-sufficient. Without self-sufficiency in the major minerals, ideological imperatives would have been undermined long ago; the revolution itself would have amounted to little more than what orthodox Marxists like to call "a storm in a teacup." There was gigantic investment, which was both costly and wasteful, in maintaining that mineral self-sufficiency, and the whole Soviet mineral industry was anything but a declining force. At a time when the international minerals sector (with the exception of gold and platinum mining) remained severely depressed, Soviet production, unimpeded by profit constraints, maintained its expansion. When profit eventually did become important, to the extent that it was necessary to reflect the true value of goods in the USSR (and the services of commodities in particular), it would be many years before the USSR experienced the same problems as the West, due to the developing nature of the entire Soviet economy, which was highly dependent at this stage on cheap minerals.

Given their resource abundance, the Soviets tended to be very wasteful; thus they had very low input productivities. It was primarily from these mineral resources that the Soviets were able to generate the hard currency imports. These imports in turn had been used to raise productivity in Soviet industry and to increase productivity in Soviet mining and drilling. Given the fact that most of the Soviet equipment appeared to be twenty years out of date, imports of Western, and increasingly Japanese, equipment did much to increase the rate of recovery and production for the future, when energy and raw materials will become less abundant, even in the Soviet Union.

The notion of a resource war should not have been taken too seriously in view of Soviet dependence on foreign trade with the technologically advanced countries. The Soviets had significant debts to the West. The USSR simply attempted to undercut Western mineral producer prices in order to carve out a greater share of the Western market. And the West itself, because of substitutes, cooperation deals with the USSR, deals with the Third World, ocean mining, synthetic chemistry, and advances in materials science, never became as vulnerable to foreign supply disruptions as we were led to believe. If the resource-war concept held true, the Soviets on the one hand and the Americans and the French on the other would be more involved in Chad, where a rich uranium deposit was discovered in the Aozou Strip.

Today France is not maintaining a 1,300-troop garrison in Chad because of the uranium--which has yet to be confirmed--but rather because of Libya's expansionist designs in the whole area. And even if Libya were seeking out uranium-rich deposits, the Soviet Union was certainly not supporting Libya for the sake of the uranium.

## NOTES

1. Hans J. Morgenthau and Kenneth W. Thompson, *Politics Among Nations: The Struggle for Power and Peace*, 6th ed., (New York: Alfred A. Knopf, 1985), p. 10.

2. Although distinctions can be made, the words "critical" and "strategic" are used interchangeably and mean the same for this writer.

3. One institution was the Resources Institute run by Bohdan O. Suprowicz in New Jersey; others were the RAND Corporation in Santa Monica and the Institute for Defense Analyses in Washington. A more recent "think tank" was established by the Washington-based National Strategy Information Center called CENS (the Council on Economics and National Security), sponsored by both business and government and focusing on overseas raw materials.

4. The U.S. Office of Technology Assessment has recently completed a study. See W. Fletcher and K. Oldenburg, "Strategic Minerals: How Technology Can Reduce U.S. Import Vulnerability," *Issues in Science*

*and Technology*, Vol. 2 (4): Summer 1986, pp. 74-95.

5. It is sometimes called "Central" and "Southern" Africa and comprises Angola, Botswana, Gabon, Mozambique, Namibia, Zaire, Zambia, Zimbabwe, and the Republic of South Africa.

6. There is no cobalt mining in the United States today. Cobalt alloys are used in jet engines to withstand high temperatures and in the hard facing of mining and drilling tools. Cobalt is a by-product of copper and nickel ores.

7. Canada, the West's second-largest supplier of critical minerals, produces no chromium and no vanadium.

8. American Die Casting Institute, *Position Paper on Minerals and Metals* (ADCI, May 1981), p. 8.

9. William K. Severin, "Soviet Nonfuel Minerals: Resource War or Business as Usual?" *Materials and Society*, Vol. 7 (1): 1983, pp. 27-34.

10. A. A. Arbatov and A. F. Shakai, *Obostreniye Syr'evoi Problemy i Mezhdunarodniye Otnosheniya* (*The Intensification of Raw Materials Problems and International Relations*) (Moscow: Mezdunarodniye Otnosheniya, 1981), p. 75. This study, articulating the "New Resources Order," is important because one of the co-authors is a brother of Georgy Arbatov. The latter is a leading Soviet specialist on the United States and a member of the party's Central Committee who reportedly has access to the highest Soviet political circles, including the Politburo.

11. Ibid.

12. Ibid.

13. David Haglund, "The West's Dependence on Imported Strategic Minerals: Implications for Canada" Working Paper (Vancouver: University of British Columbia, June 1983), p. 11.

14. Ibid.

15. Bohdan Szuprowicz, *How to Avoid Strategic Minerals Shortages* (New York: John Wiley and Sons, 1981), pp. 69-89.

16. My article was published in the *Whig Standard*, Kingston, November 14, 1984.

17. Daniel I. Fine, "Mineral Resource Dependency Crisis: Soviet Union and United States," in James A. Miller, Daniel I. Fine, and R. Daniel McMichael, eds., *The Resource War in 3-D: Dependency, Diplomacy, Defense* (Pittsburgh: World Affairs Council of Pittsburgh, 1980).

18. D. Fine, "Moscow's Ominous Shift Towards Buying Minerals," in *Business Week*, September 8, 1980, p. 54; Herbert Meyer, "Russia's Sudden Reach for Raw Materials," *Fortune*, July 28, 1980, pp. 43-4.

19. After the 1979 invasion, Soviet specialists continued to map finds of bauxite, uranium, lead, zinc, and so on. See J. Spooner et al., *Mining Annual Review 1983* (London: Mining Journal Limited, 1984).

20. See the Non-Fuel Mineral Policy Review, Oversight Hearings, U.S. Congress, House Subcommittee on Mines and Mining, Committee on Interior and Insular Affairs, 1979, 1980, 1981, 1982, 1983, 1985.

21. For an excellent discussion of official U.S. pronouncements, see L. Harold Bullis and James E. Mielke, *Strategic and Critical Materials* (Boulder, Colo.: Westview Press), pp. 155-56.

22. Ibid., p. 155.

23. Ibid., p. 21.

24. American mining companies have expressed an interest in funding exploration and refining ventures in Canada as both an investment and as part of the ill-fated free trade arrangements between the two countries.

25. See, for example, a recent one by Vasili V. Strishkov, *The Soviet Copper Industry of the USSR: Problems, Issues, and Outlook* (Washington, D.C.: Department of the Interior, Bureau of Mines, 1984).

26. *Vedomosti Verkhovnogo Sovieta (News from the Supreme Soviet)*, p. 36.

27. *Mineral Commodity Summaries* (Washington, D.C.: Department of the Interior, Bureau of Mines, 1983), pp. 107, 117.

28. "Nickel--Downhill Battle," *The Economist*, November 22, 1980, p. 98. Cuba wanted to increase its nickel production by 400 percent by 1990.

29. In November 1982, the price of nickel on the London Metal Exchange was $1.90 (U.S.) per pound, compared with the producers posted price of $3.20 (U.S.). John Caragata, *Northern Miner*, November 4, 1982, p. 7.

30. Michael Kaser, "The Soviet Impact on World Trade in Gold and Platinum," in M. M. Kostecki, ed., *The Soviet Impact on Commodity Markets* (Toronto: Macmillan, 1984), p. 167.

31. N. A. Tikhonov, *Sovietskaia Ekonomika: Dostizhenia, Problemy, Perspektivy* (Moscow: Novosti Press, 1984), p. 37.

32. Several informants in the mining industry of the USSR and at the Foreign Trade Ministry have admitted this to the author.

33. The author was told in Moscow that cartelization would only be a possibility if the Soviet government concluded agreements with other governments and not with mining companies, which the USSR did not officially recognize.

34. For an interesting discussion of opposition to cartels and commodity agreements, see Patrick James Caragata, *National Resources and International Bargaining Power* (Kingston: Queen's University, Centre for Resource Studies, 1984), pp. 98-102.

35. Ibid., p. 102.

36. Ibid. See also J. E. Tilton, *The Future of Non-Fuel Minerals* (Washington, D.C.: Brookings Institution, 1977), p. 85. For an argument that the USSR quietly agreed to form a cartel with De Beers, see E. J. Epstein, "Have You Ever Tried to Sell a Diamond?" in *The Atlantic Monthly*, February 1982. It now appears that the USSR no longer uses De Beers' Central Selling Organization to sell diamonds, but has broken off formal cartel contact by selling through a London merchant house and undercuts the CSO price by up to 15 percent. "How DeBeers Dominates the Diamonds," *The Economist*, 23 February 1980, pp. 101-2; "Diamonds--Flawed Monopoly," *The Economist*, 17 January 1981, p. 65.

37. Consolidated Gold Fields, U.S. Bureau of Mines, and the Institute of Geological Studies in London corroborate these figures.

38. Regular estimates are made, however, by many U.S. government agencies such as the CIA and by various think tanks and are published through the Joint Economic Committee of the U.S. Congress and the Congressional Reference Service.

39. "New Push for Gold Standard," *Financial Times*, November 20, 1981, p. 11; "Russia Under Gorbachev," *The Economist*, November 16, 1985, p. 22.

40. That bank held $2,433 million in gold and securities on December 31, 1981 (National Bank of Hungary, *Information Memorandum*: $400 million Term Loan, April 1981, p. 30). In 1981-82 it valued gold at $226 per ounce. See Kostecki, "The Soviet Impact on World Trade in Gold and Platinum," p. 157.

41. Representatives of INCO asked me to broach this subject with the Soviet mining officials before my trip to the USSR in the summer of 1986.

42. Caragata, *National Resources*, p. 106.

43. The USSR was a member of the international potash cartel. It joined in 1938, but this ceased on the eve of World War II.

44. INCO is itself only 54 percent Canadian-owned. There is now an increasingly greater bid by Japanese banks in Canadian and American mining ventures.

45. G. O. Vagt, *Asbestos*, MR. 155 (Ottawa: Energy, Mines, and Resources, 1976), p. 24.

46. See *Statistical Yearbook, Member Countries of the Council of Mutual Economic Assistance* (Moscow: Statistika, 1986, 1987, 1988, 1989); see also U.S. Bureau of Mines, *Asbestos, Minerals Yearbook* (Washington, D.C.: Bureau of Mines, 1985); and Kostecki, "The Soviet Impact on International Trade in Asbestos," pp. 173-93.

47. Andrew Fenton Cooper and Ashok Kapur, "La Vulnérabilite stratégique des Minéraux: Le Cas de la République fédérale allemande face à l'Afrique du Sud et a l'Union Soviétique," in *Etudes Internationales*, Vol. 15 (1): March 1984, pp. 121-56.

48. From my interview with officials at the Soviet Ministry of Foreign Trade, summer 1985.

49. For a Soviet view of Japan's production and technological capabilities, see V. A. Vlasov, *Yaponskaya Promyshlennost: Nauchno-Teknicheskiy Progress i Yego Posledstviya (Japanese Industry: Scientific-Technical Progress and its Consequences)* (Moscow: Nauka, 1979).

50. *Yaponiya Yezhegodnik* (Moscow: 1985), p. 19.

51. Because of the importance of his position, Kovalenko very likely has been involved in the formulation of Soviet policy toward Japan. He also participates in joint meetings on Soviet disarmament proposals. See Pavel Brusov, "Rabota Kovalenka," *Pravda*, February 2, 1984.

52. M. J. Wojciechowski, ed., *Structural Changes in the World Mineral Industry: Implications for Canada*, Proceedings No. 18 (Ottawa: Centre for Resource Studies, 1986), p. 21.

53. Ibid., p. 27.

54. For the best analysis on the new materials science, see *Scientific American*, Vol. 255 (4): October 1986, entire issue.

55. Igor Koslov, *Socialism and Energy Resources* (Moscow: Progress Publishers, 1981), p. 5.

56. Ibid., p. 10.

57. Ibid., p. 11.

58. Ibid., p. 14.

59. Ibid., p. 17.

60. Ibid., p. 24.

61. Diana B. Bieliavskas, "U.S. Soviet Discussions on Energy Conservation," *American Association for the Advancement of Slavic Studies Newsletter*, Vol. 27 (5): November 1987, p. 1.

62. Ibid., p. 3.

63. "Return to the Gold Standard," *The Economist*, April 20, 1985, p. 77.

64. Koslov, *Socialism*, p. 7.

*Chapter 5*

# Space Technology: Was It Really a Success Story?

The early Soviet space program was perhaps the country's most impressive technological achievement. American journalist Robert Kaiser wrote: "The Soviet reputation for scientific and technological prowess comes almost entirely from the success of its rockets and satellites in the late 1950s and early 1960s."[1] Unfortunately, the Soviet program followed no set pattern and the failures soon began to outweigh the successes. On the basis of these early accomplishments, however, the West conceded to the Soviets a self-made image of a scientific and technological superpower. The Americans then set themselves the goal of having to outwit and outperform the Soviets for ideological reasons. A space race began, fueled by American paranoia, perpetuating the bogus threat of the Soviet lead when there really was none. The truth of the matter is that in the critical areas of science and space technology, the Soviets were woefully behind. They may have been competitive in a few areas, for a short period of time. But if one is behind in one technology, then two or three, it will impair one despite some initial breakthrough. Space technology has had many interconnections. What essentially amazed everyone was the USSR's impressive ability to get into space before the Americans. That is what will forever stand out as the premier Soviet technological feat.

Interest in space technology and its uses and applications is a Russian tradition dating long before the October Revolution. An early nineteenth century scientist, Alexander Zasiadko, proposed using rockets for artillery weapons. One of the earliest aeronautical theoreticians, K. I.

Konstantantinov, used mathematics to prove that rockets could eventually be used as a means of travel. Even Nikolai Kibalchich, the revolutionary accused of assassinating Tzar Alexander II, designed a platform to be powered by rockets.[2]

Among the three founding fathers of modern rocketry and astronautics was the Russian Konstantin Tsiolkovskii (the others were the American Robert Goddard and a German, Hermann Oberth). Tsiolkovskii became the first theoretician to propose interplanetary flight. His voluminous works contain ideas involving the laws of motion on bodies in cosmic space, the velocities required for earth orbit and escape, the use of multistage rockets for space travel, of liquid hydrogen and oxygen as rocket fuels, and of liquid fuels to cool rocket engines, the need for heat shields in a re-entry from space, and the creation of permanent space stations in orbit with self-contained regenerative environments.[3] Because of his theories, which were eventually almost universally used and accomplished, the Soviet Academy of Sciences established the Tsiolkovskii Gold Medal for outstanding work in the field of space travel in 1954. But Tsiolkovskii was certainly not the only Soviet scientist working on such ideas. The stellar list included Ivan Meshcherskii and Fridrikh Tsander, a man who pioneered work in spacecraft and rocket design.

When the Soviet government took a keen interest in space travel, a number of institutes were set up to study rocket and spacecraft design. The best and the brightest scientific and technical minds were gathered to work on various projects. As early as 1918, barely a year after the revolution, the All-Union Society for the Study of Interplanetary Communications was established. A year later it was followed by the Zhukovskii Academy of Astronautics. Then 1924, the Central Bureau for the Study of the Problems of Rockets (TsBIRP) was created.

Of the most illustrious personalities in early space technology, three names stand for excellence: Mikhail Tikhonravov (known as the chief theoretician), Valentin Petrovich Glushko (the chief designer of engines) and Sergei Pavlovich Korolev (the chief designer of spacecraft). Under the Stalin and Khrushchev governments, these men were known only by their titles of Chief. Tikhonravov was the first to understand the applications of rockets on space travel. He became the vice chairman of the Commission on the Exploration and Use of Space and served on the State Commission for Space Exploration. Glushko, under the pseudonym G. V. Petrovich, suggested a plan for the development of space research, including earth orbit, moon exploration, and the exploration of the planets in 1959. During the 1960s, he developed a rocket motor that was far ahead of anything the Americans had developed at the time. He went on to become director of the Leningrad branch of the Gas Dynamics Laboratory.

It was Korolev, however, who became the best known of the three and the leading scientist in the Soviet space program. He built almost everything the Soviets sent into orbit in the 1960s. A native Ukrainian, he had spent fifteen years in the Gulag before Stalin realized how useful he could be. While being kept anonymous he was given the military commission of general-engineer and worked with the V-2 team from Germany after World War II. By 1947, however, he concluded that the V-2 technology was not the way the Soviet missile program should go. Rehabilitated after Stalin's death, Khrushchev had him promoted. Hired subsequently to work on ways to deliver intercontinental missiles, he worked on the R-7 rocket to act as a missile booster, but this proved to be more useful for launching objects into space. After several failed attempts, he launched the world's first artificial satellite.

Khrushchev approved of Korolev's plan to launch a satellite into space for a number of reasons. First, it would show Khrushchev's rivals that he was totally in charge. It would also allow him the leeway for a reorganization of armed forces. Third, it would demonstrate that the Soviets had a long-range missile system sophisticated enough to discourage an American attack.[4] He gave Korolev six weeks to prepare the rocket and satellite.

With most of the preliminary work completed, on October 4, 1957, the Soviet Union became the first country to put into orbit around the earth an artificial satellite, Sputnik I. As William Schauer wrote: "Perhaps no space achievement has had the impact of Sputnik I, and it is from October 4, 1957, that the age of space and the space race can be dated."[5] World reactions to this development ranged from shock to alarm. It must be remembered that the Cold War was then at its height. The McCarthy era had ushered in a deep-seated fear of both Communism and of the Soviet Union. In just five years time the Americans and Soviets would come to the brink of a nuclear war, closer than they ever would. Sputnik represented what the Soviets could do to the Americans. If the Russians could get into space, they could attack from the ground, sea, air, and outer space. The Soviet Union saw it as a great victory, a blow to American "capitalist" prestige. Embittered and jealous American commentators and scientists told anyone who would listen that Sputnik was the result of captured German technology. While it was true that the

Soviets had captured a few German scientists, the Americans had captured many more and had benefited more directly from their ideas. Whatever Soviet breakthrough there might have been in this area, the one sure thing was that the U.S. had to keep up if its own space program was to succeed. Soviet Premier Nikita Khrushchev would occasionally bluster about space vehicles being used to fire off Inter-Continental Ballistic Missiles (ICBMs). Space, as a popular television show later emphasized, was the "final frontier," and Americans understandably wished to claim it no less than the Russians.

The ensuing space race rivaled the English/French/Spanish competition for colonies in centuries past. Russian and American space programs developed out of their need to create delivery systems for nuclear warheads. But this rocket technology was important for more than just the weapons. The justification was always explained as national security and defense. To the Soviets, the Americans were inherently aggressive. In response, President Dwight Eisenhower insisted that satellites would only be used for civilian purposes.[6]

The Soviets set themselves many long-range space goals on the basis of five-year and seven-year plans. The Soviet leaders ultimately hoped to explore and colonize the solar system, perhaps spreading Soviet-style Communism throughout the cosmos. Their efforts seemed more concerned with bioastronautics while the Americans seemed to be interested only in whatever technology was needed to get into space. Both countries did agree, however, that they wanted to use space as a forum for eventual cooperation.

Khrushchev was extremely pleased with the launch of Sputnik. He quickly promised support to Korolev, even if their association was not always a pleasant one. Khrushchev refused to share the credit with anyone, and he kept Korolev in the background, making him dependent on government funding.

The USSR is on record for having achieved a number of other "firsts" in the space age. As early as 1957, the first animal, a dog, was put in space on board Sputnik II. Then in 1959 came the first moon shot. Soviet science was advanced enough to launch the first photographic reconnaissance and anti-satellite system, geodetic, meteorological, electronic reconnaissance, navigation, early warning, ocean surveillance, and communications satellites, all between April 1962 and December 1970. In April 1961, the first man, Yuri Gagarin, was sent into space on Vostok I. This was followed two years later by the first woman, Valentina Tereshkova, aboard Vostok 6. The Soviets were first to conduct a spacewalk from Voskhod-2. And in 1970, Venera 7 successfully landed on Venus. The following year the first manned space lab, Salyut I, was launched.

The setbacks were just as prominent, although less publicized. The catalogue of failures is too numerous to cover in great detail. Simply put, many of the early Sputniks produced virtually no usable scientific data. They were more valuable for propaganda purposes. Luna 2 and Spaceship 1 were destroyed on the launch pads. Between 1958 and 1960, five moon shots failed and a number of rockets blew up. On October 24, 1962, a Mars shot backfired and the debris fell back to earth. American experts picking it up came to the false conclusion that it was a Soviet nuclear attack, which nearly touched off World War III.[7]

In 1960, a Mars probe was set to be launched. At that time Khrushchev was using the space program to punctuate his major speeches with insults about the lackluster space technology of the West. His top missile general, Field Marshall Mitrofan Nedelin, was at the missile site and under pressure to make sure that the missile was sent up in time for one of Khrushchev's major speeches in the West. But pandemonium burst out when the rocket failed to launch. Despite designer Korolev's objections, Nedelin ordered the scientists to find out why the missile had misfired without first draining the fuel, one of the most basic rocket safety precautions. The missile exploded, killing everyone there, including Nedelin who sat nearby. Korolev miraculously escaped because he, along with a few other scientists, were seated safely in an underground bunker. Nedelin was given a state funeral amid the usual pomp, and it was perfunctorily reported that he had died in a plane crash. For the unfortunate scientists and soldiers who also died, very little was said. All were quietly buried with almost no acknowledgment.

Soviet cosmonauts were treated to the same degree of adulation as their American counterparts, sometimes even more. But if one closely examines the official pictures of the first class of twenty cosmonauts, several of the men have unmistakably been cut out in the retouched photos. Author James Oberg investigated the reasons that the men had been unceremoniously cropped out of the picture and eliminated from their rightful place in space history. One of the men missing was Grigori Nelyubov, an arrogant young man who, along with two other candidates, Ivan Anikeyev and Valentin Filatyev, got into a drunken altercation with a few army officers. When asked to apologize, he refused. He and his two friends, both of whom had apologized, were drummed out of the cosmonaut program.[8] Anatoli Kartashov and Dmitri Zaikin were grounded for medical reasons, and Mars Rafikov (the only non-Slav) for political reasons. Valentin Varlamov was injured in a diving mishap and thus also disqualified.

Perhaps the most tragic story of all was that of young Valentin Bondarenko, who was in an oxygen-rich pressure chamber when he inadvertently dropped a cotton ball dipped in alcohol onto a burner. It ignited everything in the chamber. The fire burned as the scientists struggled to pry open the chamber. So badly was Bondarenko burned that doctors could only insert intravenous pain suppressants through the soles of his feet, which had been protected somewhat by his boots. He died just a short time later.[9] His image and name were suppressed for years. Perhaps if the U.S. had been made aware of the dangers of fire in an oxygen-rich environment, NASA might have prevented the deaths of Astronauts Virgil Grissom, Edward White II, and Roger Chaffee on board Apollo 204 in a tragic launchpad fire.

A number of cosmonauts have died in space and in launching and recovery accidents. In 1967, Vladimir Komarov on Soyuz 1 was killed when his parachute fouled on his return from space. The first and arguably greatest cosmonaut, Yuri Gagarin, was killed in a flight accident in 1968. In 1966, Korolev died from complications from surgery. The first men from the Salyut space station returned to earth dead in 1971, having lost their air on the trip home. Although this was a record the Soviets surely did not want, these were the first humans to die in space.

Equipment failures were also extremely prevalent. In April 1968, an off-course test moon ship fell in China. A large number of moon and Mars probes failed, and innumerable rockets simply exploded on the launch pad or in flight. In 1975, a manned launch abort crashed in the Ural mountains, and the men had to fight off freezing temperatures and starving wolves while waiting for their rescuers. In 1979, two cosmonauts were nearly stranded in space. On September 26, 1983, a Soyuz booster exploded on the launchpad, the two cosmonauts having ejected just seconds before.[10] If NASA had known about this, it might have somehow managed to save the crew of the Challenger.

Khrushchev treated the space program as a propaganda tool. He had little regard for its scientific uses and cared only about how much it would humiliate the Americans. For instance, the decision to launch a female cosmonaut was purely propaganda to prove that women were equal in a Communist society. The woman chosen had to be an ordinary, everyday person; of the four trained, Valentina Tereshkova, a textile worker, was the prime candidate, almost the epitome of an all-Soviet woman. Khrushchev had her marry the only bachelor cosmonaut, Andrian Nikolayev, in a public relations circus of which only Hollywood romances are made. When Khrushchev later fell from power, their marriage broke up.

Khrushchev's successor, Leonid Brezhnev, seemed less interested in space. Soon after the Americans landed on the moon, the Soviets announced that they never wanted to send a man to the moon in the first place. But this was pure bravado. The Soviets had in fact sent four Zond probes to the Moon and announced that one of them was supposed to be a manned probe. But with the death of their chief designer, Korolev, it is likely that this would have been a very important contributing factor preventing them from reaching the moon. Their attitude was that if they were not able to beat the Americans, there was no sense in going at all. Instead, they sent unmanned probes and vehicles to collect whatever samples they needed. Newly acquired information today shows that after the U.S. Apollo lunar program ended, "the USSR was considering sending cosmonauts to the Moon as late as 1978-1990 for stays of up to 14 days."[11] A spacecraft was even developed for the mission, including larger compartments, an attached lunar module in which one cosmonaut would land on the moon and return to the orbiting vehicle, which would then be jettisoned when the mission was over.[12] However, the N-1 boosters that were to be used were all destroyed in launch explosions, one a few days before the American Apollo 11 that landed on the moon and the last before America's last lunar mission, Apollo 17. Plans were made to go again sometime between 1978 and 1980, but were later canceled.

Humbled, the Soviets turned to working with space stations and labs. Salyats 3 and 4 were able to spy on the Americans and conduct scientific research, such as growing vegetables and astronomical research. The mid-1970s were times of some relaxation in the Cold War between the superpowers, and space ceased to be a bone of contention and grew to become the object of cooperation and mutual understanding. In 1975, the detente linkup of an American Apollo and Soviet Soyuz spacecraft occurred. The Soviets were the first to hit on the idea of taking along guest cosmonauts into space with them. Most of these men were invited from Eastern Europe, some from Mongolia, Vietnam, India, France, and Cuba. It proved to be more than just a goodwill gesture. The Eastern European cosmonauts were shown off as proof that Western Europe was far behind Eastern Europe in the space race. As public relations. It turned out to be little more than a farce. Everyone knew that Third World economies could only produce astronauts as a luxury. It resembled another superb performance at the Olympic Games and reflected nothing of the truly low standard of living of these peoples.

Considering the various military, political, and economic benefits of the different Soviet space programs, general control and the future direction of the Soviet space effort rested with the Politburo. The decisions for military space systems research, design, development, testing, and production at the national level were carried out by the Soviet Defense Council. Both of these organizations came under the jurisdiction of the new General Secretary of the Communist Party, Mikhail Gorbachev. Actual program management was overseen by the Military Industrial Commission (*Voenno-Promyshlennaia Kommissiya*), which reported to the Council of Ministers. Furthermore, all five components of the armed forces took part in the development of the space program. The Strategic Rocket Forces provided the launch and tracking support, and the Soviet space agency, *Glavkosmos*, oversaw the various programs.[13] Most of the cosmonauts were in fact members of the Red Air Force, and the Air Force was the only body that trained them. Stellar Town, or *Zvezdniy Gorodok*, was the home of the cosmonaut detachment; Star City, *Zvezdagrad*, was the home of the technicians. Both were known for their well-stocked shops and bigger apartments, which showed up the importance of cosmonauts as Soviet heroes and the space program as a monumental achievement of socialism. It was the same pattern of lifestyle and the flaunting of a technotopia that we witnessed in connection with Russia's Silicon Valley at Zelenograd or the model science city at Akademgorodok.

The Soviets emphasized scientific discovery and the exploration of space in the service of humanity as the exclusive goal of its space program.[14] However, the space doctrine found its way into the overall military doctrine. Moscow's military planners believed in a combined arms style of warfare in which all forces were integrated into military operations. A U.S. Defense publication stated, "Space assets play a major role in this equation in the areas of antisatellite warfare; intelligence collection; command, control and communications; meteorological support; navigational support; and targeting."[15] It was no secret that all Soviet military support systems were linked to ground, naval, and air forces through earth terminals, permitting Soviet forces to receive orders and information by satellite from command headquarters thousands of miles away. Civilian satellites always had military projects piggybacked on them. By late 1984 an auxiliary ship named after the first commander of the Strategic Rocket Forces, Marshal Nedelin, was put into use as a space and missile support ship capable of a variety of missions, including support to worldwide strategic forces.[16]

## SATELLITE TECHNOLOGY

One of the most useful applications of space technology was the construction and deployment of satellites. Ever since the launching of Sputnik I, the Soviet Union had a key interest in the use of satellites (Sputnik actually means satellite in Russian). The Soviet satellite program was soon used for everything from prospecting and communications to navigation and weather forecasting, to the production of materials and medicines to the transmission of solar energy to earth. Satellites by definition had both military and civilian applications. At the time of the USSR's dissolution, nearly two-thirds of all Soviet satellites were military in nature. The three main space complexes from which the satellites were launched were at Plesetsk, Kapustin Yar, and Tyuratam.

However, the problem with Soviet satellites was that they could not last as long as the U.S. satellites. Until the mid-1980s, the Soviets used nearly the same kind of rockets as the ones that put Sputnik into orbit. Their Energia booster--similar, although larger, than the Saturn V booster of the U.S.--was able to lift over 100 tons, thus making it capable of launching space stations. Unfortunately, the Energia was not without its problems. Although it works and has been successfully launched, as one analyst contends, "The booster's structure is 7.5 tons overweight, reducing actual payload capability by the same amount."[17]

### Photo-Reconnaissance Satellites

The USSR launched its first photo-reconnaissance satellite (Cosmos 4) in April 1962. Between 1975 and 1982, up to thirty-five were launched annually. These satellites constituted the largest single element of the entire Soviet space program. Separate satellites were needed for high-resolution, medium- and low-resolution photographs and were used for monitoring activities in remote parts of the world.[18] During the 1980s, their average lifespan was only fifteen days. The reason for this was that the Soviets needed to recover their film, which became the common practice, given the poor resolution of their transmitted pictures. The satellites were used for strategic, earth resources and tactical missions. During the period of 1980-85, Soviet photo-reconnaissance satellites accumulated almost as many mission days as those logged in the previous eighteen years.[19] There were five basic types of photo-reconnaissance satellites: (1) medium resolution (for broad area surveys); (2) earth resources; (3) miscellaneous third generation (characterized by slow decay rates, limited maneuvering capability, and lifetimes of two weeks); (4) fourth generation (which returned film capsules to earth, had high resolution photography and fifty-four to fifty-nine-day missions); and (5) advanced photo-reconnaissance (nature unknown, data must be electronic; one flight lasted 207 days).[20] There were some problems with these satellites such as their uselessness once their films were used up, the time needed to analyze the photographs, bad weather problems, and the need for substantial electric power.

## Meteorological Satellites

In 1963, the Soviet Union launched its first meteorological satellite, Cosmos 14. It was the first Soviet civilian application satellite project. The two programs, Meteor 1 and Meteor 2, up to the mid-1970s, were designed to provide: (1) information on the distribution of cloudiness, ice and snow cover; (2) temperature fields, cloudtop heights, and water surface temperatures; (3) radiation levels; and (4) television images of cloud, ice, and snow covers.[21] The Meteor 3 program was characterized by its higher altitude. These satellites also had military applications in that they provided information about weather over target areas.

## Communications Satellites

The first Soviet communications satellite (Cosmos 41) was launched in August 1964, and this class came to constitute the second largest element of the satellite program, designated by the Molniya (literally, lightening) series. Molniya 1 began in 1965, Molniya 2 in 1971, and Molniya 3 in 1974. Between 1980 and 1985, an average of seventeen such satellites were launched per year. The Molniya satellites were used for simultaneous transmission of military telephone, television, facsimile, and telegraph messages. A three-tiered network was used consisting of low-altitude, highly elliptical, and geosynchronous (above the equator) satellites. Communications satellites were also used to increase the country's control over the widely dispersed armed forces and to provide a link for crisis management.[22]

### Ocean Surveillance and Navigation Satellites

The Soviet Union launched its first ocean surveillance and navigation satellites in December 1967 (Cosmos 198) and December 1970 (Cosmos 385). Within its ocean surveillance system, the RORSAT (Radar Ocean Reconnaissance Satellite) system was used for a broad area of detection, while EORSAT (Electronic Intelligence Ocean Reconnaissance Satellite) was used for pinpoint accuracy. The radar systems on board vessels were able to detect the most obscure naval movements in the world's oceans. They were even capable of identifying submerged submarines by monitoring water disturbances; hitherto this was all but impossible in view of the impenetrability of sonar waves. It was widely believed in the West that low-depth submarines were virtually undetectable and therefore invincible. It was thought that submarine-launched nuclear missiles were the ultimate in war-fighting. The Soviets preceded their naval build-up with these surveillance satellites.

But there were a number of problems. In late 1978, Cosmos 954, an ocean surveillance satellite, disintegrated over Canada and spread radioactive waste over a wide area. A similar incident took place in 1983, when Cosmos 1402 disintegrated in the atmosphere.[23] These satellites were programmed to orbit at a height of 150 miles and then separate so that the nuclear reactor, which contained over ninety pounds of the extremely radioactive U-235 isotope, would ascend to the height of 500 miles and go dead.[24] In both cases, this option failed. The Soviets were not willing to offer the Canadians any help in their joint U.S.-Canadian operation "Morning Light" cleanup.

Navigation satellites could be used to allow armies, navies, and air forces to plot their positions. They could also be used to update guidance systems on submarines. The Soviets operated these satellites through their Global Navigation Satellite System (GLONASS), which provided latitude, longitude, and altitude positional data. In 1982, with the launching of Cosmos 1383, the Soviet Union entered into an agreement with the United States, Canada, France, Norway, Britain, Bulgaria, Finland, and India to establish the COSPAS-SARSAT satellite search and rescue services. Through it, distress signals are received by satellites and transmitted to the proper authorities; it has an accuracy of up to 2 kilometers. There are currently five orbiting U.S. and Russian satellites with ten data reception stations on the ground.[25]

*Geodetic and Earth Resources Satellites*

The first geodetic satellite (Cosmos 203) was launched in February 1968. Geodetic satellites are used to determine the size and shape of the earth and plot points on its surface while providing information on the earth's magnetic and gravitational fields. This is not only essential for mapping and remote sensing, but also allows for accurate targeting of weapons.

Earth resources satellites are used to give information on the state of the world's crops, temperatures, minerals, oceans, and rivers. They can identify various plant species, diseases in forests and crops, earthquake fault systems, terrain rich in oil and mineral deposits, water pollution trends, ocean currents, iceberg tracks, and ice thickness measurements.[26] According to official Soviet estimates, the use of satellites for oil and gas prospecting, charting routes for railways, and predicting spring floods benefited their economy in the order of 500 and 600 million roubles per year ($790 million to $950 million).[27] On July 25, 1988, the Soviet Union launched the largest satellite studying earth resources (Cosmos 1870).

## MILITARY SATELLITES

### Early-Warning and Nuclear Explosion-Detection Satellites

In the late 1960s, the Soviet Union began working on an early-warning satellite system. However, that system was plagued with equipment problems. Early-warning satellites use infrared sensors that are able to discern the radiation emitted from nuclear weapons as they take off. They are able to give a half hour's warning and provide the location of the launch site. Nuclear explosion-detection satellites were used to check for violations of the Partial Test Ban Treaty, which banned nuclear explosions in the atmosphere and outer space. But some of these military satellites remained passive. They were not lethal devices, yet they could enhance the lethality of other weapons.

### Electronic Reconnaissance Satellites

Electronic reconnaissance satellites (ELINT) provided the armed forces with intercepted enemy signals. They collected data on the transmissions and emissions of electronic signals from armies (including radar, radio, data relay, and so on), and provided the location of these signals.[28] Ocean surveillance satellites fall within this category.

## Fractional Orbital Bombardment System

The Soviet Union began development of a Fractional Orbital Bombardment System (FOBS) in 1966. FOBS was an interceptor-style satellite designed to place a weapon into temporary low orbit for a surprise attack. After its first revolution of the earth, it slows down and drops onto its target. The Soviets began the program with the Scrag SS-9. There were a number of advantages to the FOBS system. It reduced the American warning time and penetrated U.S. defenses from the south, the least defended areas. The FOBS project was abandoned in 1980.

## Anti-Satellite Weapons

The USSR's first anti-satellite (ASAT) system (Cosmos 185) was launched in October 1967. ASAT was viewed as a way to combat the future threat of orbiting nuclear weapons. There were four main systems that could be considered ASAT: (1) co-orbital ASAT; (2) ground-based airborne and space-based lasers; (3) the ABM (anti-ballistic missile) network around Moscow; and (4) electronic warfare.[29]

Perhaps the best-known component of ASAT was the co-orbital satellite. One observer defined it thus: "The USSR anti-satellite system works by placing a small satellite with an explosive warhead in orbit next to the target satellite and then detonating a conventional explosive shrapnel system aboard the anti-satellite, which then destroys the target."[30] These were tested only at limited altitudes and angles of inclination. The ground-based lasers were capable of attacking satellites in various orbits. At Saryshagan, near the Sino-Soviet border, the Soviets began constructing a hybrid weapon combining laser and particle beam features in November 1979. The ABM system around Moscow consisted of nuclear-armed Galosh interceptors that could become ASATs through a direct ascent attack on low-orbiting satellites.[31] Electronic warfare (or, as the Soviets called it, Radio-Electronic Combat (REC)) could be used to jam transmissions and to seize control of enemy satellites.[32]

The key to these weapons was laser and particle beam research. Lasers (or Light Amplification by the Stimulated Emission of Radiation) had continued as an obsessive study of the Soviets as early as 1971. Nicholai Basov was Russia's shining light in this field. He experimented with three basic kinds of lasers: gas-dynamic, in which the rapid expansion of carbon dioxide gas provides the initial energy input; chemical, which uses chemical reactions to produce energy; and electrical discharge, which uses the collision of electrons with lasing material through an electric discharge.[33] Another type of beam weapon is the charged particle beam, which emits a stream of subatomic particles consisting of electrons, protons, and heavier ions accelerated to high velocities in an electromagnetic field.[34] The Americans had been following Soviet developments very closely, well before President Reagan unveiled his "Star Wars" project. The weapons were futuristic. Radio frequency weapons, such as a microwave generator, for instance, could be used to overload and damage critical electronic components used in satellites and ballistic missile warheads; they could also be used to jam frequencies.[35] Kinetic energy weapons, which use high-speed collision of a small mass with the target as a kill mechanism, may also be used. X-ray lasers can be utilized through the use of radiation from a nuclear explosion as the pumping source.[36]

Soviet ASAT targets included American photo-reconnaissance, communications, and meteorological satellites as well as armed space weapons. ASATs could be used for tactical, intimidatory, preemptive, preventative, and retaliatory measures. It has been argued that an ASAT system is a very humane method of conducting war since it involves the death of machines rather than people. In 1980 alone, the Soviet Union spent thousands of millions of dollars on beam weapons research. Moscow apparently considered this research to be extremely important to its future weapons systems, especially in the light of the much-heralded Strategic Defense Initiative in the Pentagon's strategic defense plans.[37]

## SPACE STATIONS, SHUTTLES AND PLANES

The Soviet Union created the first space station in 1971. This ship, Salyut 1, was a prototype for a manned space station that could be used for many different purposes. The different stations spent varying percentages of their orbital lifetimes occupied: Salyut 1 (1971) spent 13 percent of its time occupied, Salyut 2 (1972) 0 percent, Salyut 3 (1974-75) 7 percent, Salyut 4 (1974-77) 12 percent, Salyut 5 (1976-77) 16 percent, Salyut 6 (1977-82) 38 percent and Salyut 8 (1982-   ) 56 percent.[38] In effect, the Soviet Union logged over fourteen man-years in space against five man-years for the United States.

The space station Mir (in Russian, peace) was launched on February 20, 1986. It was the largest and most sophisticated space program designed to become the first permanently manned space station and orbiting lab. Unfortunately, the Mir was seriously overweight; only about

20 percent of the crew time on Mir could be devoted to mission objectives, with 80 percent devoted to maintenance and system operations.[39] The Soviets then developed Cosmos 929 which consisted of a number of modules that could be attached to a space station. The Progress Cargo spaceship allowed supplies to be brought to the station. The Soviets ultimately wanted to develop a permanently manned space station, the K. E. Tsiolkovskii, by the year 2000. All of these stations had military applications, such as performing research and development, reconnaissance, and operating weapons and sensors.

The Soviets were also well advanced in developing viable space shuttle and space plane programs. These programs were meant to utilize reusable spacecraft like the American space shuttle. On November 15, 1988, their prototype unmanned shuttle, Buran (meaning snowstorm) was launched and recovered successfully. They hoped to launch a manned shuttle by 1990, although this never materialized. Although the Soviet military wanted to create ten orbiters, software development and problems with thermal protective tiles hampered development. Between 1979 and 1987, more than 32,000 changes were made to the design documentation for Buran.[40] In 1983, the Soviets began tests on a reusable space plane with the flights of Cosmos 1445 and 1517. Possible missions included reconnaissance, crew transport, satellite repair and maintenance, anti-satellite operations, and service as a manned space station defender.[41] The newly independent Russian Republic is talking about scrapping these programs altogether.

## MANNED SPACE FLIGHTS AND OUTER SPACE PROBES

Thus, from Yuri Gagarin's first flight to the first multi-man spaceship, to the first spacewalk (1965) and the first space station (1971), the Soviet Union sought to pioneer efforts to live and work in space.[42] Most of the time in space was spent in space stations, averaging about six months' occupancy per year.

The USSR officially took part in a test project with the U.S. On July 17, 1975, Soyuz 19, containing Colonel Aleksei Leonov and Valery Kubasov, made a rendezvous with Apollo 18, carrying Brigadier General Thomas Stafford, Donald Kent Slayton, and Vance Devoe Brand. This historic undertaking proved that the two countries could work together in space and set a precedent for future cooperation.

In the realm of outer space probes, the Soviet Union confined its main projects to the moon, Venus, and Mars. In fact, the USSR pioneered moon probes by landing the first probe on the moon, creating the first lunar satellite, and performing the first circumlunar fly-by and return to earth. The Soviets' outer-space probes began with the Zond series: Zond 1 (launched in 1962) explored Venus; Zond 2 (1964) explored Mars; Zond 3 (1965) the moon; and Zond 4 (1968) the far reaches of earth space. The early 1980s saw a space program dedicated to the investigation of Venus. The Venera 9-16 program probed the planet Venus and sent radar maps of the surface back to earth. The Vega 1 and 2 program explored Halley's Comet in its last fly-by.

By the late 1980s, the Soviet Union's space program seemed to have shifted to Mars exploration. Russian scientists launched a series of increasingly sophisticated probes that they hoped would climax in a joint U.S.-Soviet manned mission to Mars by the year 2010. To this end, they were pinning their hopes on the Phobos project. For 1994, they planned to launch a Mars mission that was to consist of an orbiting craft for remote sensing surveys and a lander equipped with a drill for terrestrial surveys. The U.S., the European Space Agency, and twelve European nations were ready to take part in the Phobos project, with the U.S. helping the Soviets with their Deep Space Tracking Network.[43] The Phobos project was not restricted to studying Mars, however. It was also intended to study the composition of interplanetary plasma, the physical properties of solar wind particles, and Mars' magnetosphere and its interaction with the solar wind.[44] It would undertake solar research by photographing the side of the sun that is invisible from earth, study the structure and dynamics of the solar corona and chromosphere, identify solar flares, and study solar oscillations.[45]

While on Mars, Phobos was intended to determine the chemical composition, profile, and seasonal variations of its atmosphere; study its magnetosphere; obtain surface video images and images using infrared rays; and study the chemical composition of the surface.[46] On Mars' satellite Phobos, it would determine the elementary composition of the surface layer with laser and ionic beams; do a radio sounding of its inner structure; study the terrain and surface structure; obtain video images of the surface; obtain surface images in infrared rays and study the chemical composition of the surface; and investigate the surface with a lander probe.[47] This would have provided the Soviet Union with the most detailed study of Mars. The project was touted as a Soviet first.

Roald Sagdeyev, director of the Institute of Space Research (IKI), stated that the Soviet Union had a four-point program as its objective: radio astronomy, X-ray and gamma ray astronomy, studies of solar plasma and the Earth's magnetosphere, and the exploration of Mars. To study space, the Mir space station was equipped with telescopes that could automatically observe and investigate neutron stars and black holes with X-rays.[48]

## THE PEACEFUL APPLICATIONS OF SPACE TECHNOLOGY

There were a number of areas in which space technology could be put to peaceful application. For instance, existing technology could be put to a more civilian use such as communications, weather, navigation and traffic control, geodesy, data collection, and earth resources management. Orbital operations could be used for the manufacturing and testing of various products, medicines and so on and provide health and recreation through the development of vacation resorts in earth orbit. In the area of transportation, space could be used for point-to-point travel on earth, earth orbit flights, earth-lunar flights, and interplanetary flights. Finally, in the area of extraterrestrial resources, space technology could be used to discover rocket fuels, develop specific environmental technologies, discover certain materials (like diamonds), exploit asteroid mining, and terraform different planets and asteroids.[49]

## PROPOSALS AND TREATIES

A number of proposals and treaties were signed by the Soviet Union and the United States. The Limited Test Ban Treaty of 1963, for example, banned nuclear explosions in space and in the atmosphere. The Outer Space Treaty of 1967 stated that the superpowers could not place into orbit objects that carried nuclear or any other type of weapon of mass destruction. The spirit of cooperation was in the air, as it were. However, these treaties did not deal adequately with the delicate problem of the militarization of outer space. In 1958, the USSR had indeed tabled a proposal to the United Nations for a ban on the military uses of outer space. It was rejected. Two decades later, the Soviet government proposed an arms-control agreement to the U.S. that would have established a weapons-free zone and involved some demilitarization of outer space. The Reykjavik summit between Gorbachev and Reagan ended in a deadlock on space-based weapons. The USSR had suggested a limitation on space-based missile defense to lab research for the next ten years, but the U.S. refused to consider it. It thus seemed that the USSR did its part to dissuade the deployment of space-based weapons. The USSR, it seemed, was committed to the peaceful uses of outer space. The Americans were not always so sure of this. The ball was in the American court.

## EXCHANGES

The Soviet Union took part in a number of scientific space exchanges with other countries. The largest area of exchange was through the Intercosmos International Program, created in 1967. Through it, the member states shared in space technology. Members included Bulgaria, Hungary, Vietnam, the German Democratic Republic, Cuba, Mongolia, Poland, Romania, and Czechoslovakia. Between 1978 and 1987, cooperative exchanges sent astronauts from the following countries into space: Czechoslovakia, Poland, GDR, Bulgaria, Hungary, Vietnam, Mongolia, Cuba, Romania, and even France, India, and Syria. The Soviet Union offered to train Chinese astronauts as well. The USSR also signed an agreement with Iran to send an Iranian cosmonaut into space and an agreement with Britain for a joint, privately financed space mission that would have included one English astronaut with two cosmonauts.

In addition to Intercosmos, Intersputnik, in which the Eastern bloc or socialist countries made up the great majority of members, Russia widely advertised its cooperation in space communications. Intersputnik had helped various nations launch satellites. The cash-strapped USSR began offering to launch satellites for the West for tens of millions of dollars. The Russians also leased satellite capacity or complete satellite systems as well as offering boosters and satellite photographs for sale.

In April 1987, representatives of government, industry, and academia from Brazil, Canada, China, Europe, India, Japan, Sri Lanka, the USSR, and the United States met at the Massachusetts Institute of Technology to found the International Space University. Through it, courses would be offered in engineering, physical sciences, life sciences, business and management, policy and law, resources and manufacturing, architecture, and satellite applications.[50] The ISU held two-month summer sessions at different world universities until a permanent campus was established in 1993. These courses were held in France in 1989 and in Canada in 1990.

Ever since the Soyuz-Apollo Test Project, it seemed that the U.S. and USSR had a mutual interest in space cooperation. They could have done much to advance space science and fill in information gaps. There were a number of problems with this arrangement, including the question of money and of not wanting to become dependent upon each other and, at worst, political rivalry and hostility.[51] However, there are nine areas in which cooperation would be helpful: (1) exchange of data; (2)

activities such as space meteorology; (3) activities in which information uncovered by one can be profitably applied by the other; (4) activities with little or no military significance; (5) very expensive projects; (6) tracking and the observance of space vehicles; (7) communications; (8) activities involving the safety of astronauts; and (9) activities that reflect joint concerns for the regulation of space activities.[52]

During Gorbachev's 1987 visit to Washington, U.S. Representative Robert Roe, chairman of the House Science, Space, and Technology Committee, and Roald Sagdeyev, director of the IKI, met and decided that the two countries had a common interest in a joint manned mission to Mars. The USSR first brought up the possibility in 1986, but NASA turned down the idea.

## THE FUTURE

With the discussions over the American Strategic Defense Initiative and Ballistic Missile Defense, it seemed that space technology was moving in a different direction, away from peace. The USSR saw SDI as an extension of the geopolitical competition between the U.S. and the USSR. Soviet policymakers viewed SDI as the potential harbinger of a new era of unstable strategic relations with the United States.

The Soviets, as we have already seen, began developing a Ballistic Missile Defense of their own in the 1960s. However, they reappraised this policy and began negotiating an Anti-Ballistic Missile (ABM) Treaty that restricted their BMD activities. They wished to avoid an all-out race in the BMD program because they were afraid that they would fall behind. By the late 1970s and early 1980s, they undertook a significant modernization of the Moscow BMD system, which included maintaining an extensive research effort to reveal the feasibility of applying high-energy lasers and particle beams to BMD.[53] Soviet scientists believed that if they could deploy both ASAT and BMD in space, this might have assured the survival of their society and their allies' societies against an attack by most bomber/cruise missile and ballistic missile threats. However, it was domestic, nationalist, and political forces, not military ones, that ultimately caused the collapse of the Soviet Union.

The specter of this type of space technology loomed over the world. It was hoped that this type of military space technology would be replaced by peaceful, scientific endeavors. The potential spinoffs of SDI research were expected to lead to discoveries in the areas of transportation, energy production, communications, and medicine for both the

United States and the USSR. Overall, advances were in the areas of computer science and applied physics. The development of more sophisticated hardware and software had tremendous civilian applications in areas such as weather forecasting and the creation of mathematical models of the atmosphere and oceans.[54] The SDI research also served to resurrect old programs. The development of lasers has clearly led to civilian applications; medicine is just one example. There is much paradox in this story. One result of SDI research was how American SDI agencies were planning to buy a Soviet Topaz 2 space nuclear power system so they could eventually develop a similar system. As the Soviet Union was disintegrating, the Moscow science institute was willing to sell, or license, this technology to bolster its own decreasing budget.[55] Here is an obvious case of reverse technology, but this time, it is one in which the Americans are the guilty party.

With the very real possibility of a joint US-Russia Mars mission in the not-too-distant future and other announced cooperative deals, it is hoped that international cooperation in this type of space exploration will lead to cooperation in other areas. The vast reaches of outer space may hold the key to U.S.-Russian understanding and scientific exchange.

A more fitting comment on this cooperation lies in a recent tale of penury and hope. A bizarre event took place in mid-December 1993 in London, when Sotheby's Auction House auctioned many irreplaceable Soviet space relics, including two space capsules, space suits, moon rocks, and so forth. Many of these items were the personal effects of the cosmonauts, whose families were so poor that they had to sell these keepsakes to survive. It is truly sad when part of a country's history must be sold off to put food on a family's table. Bizarre too is the fact that the two capsules were purchased by an anonymous American who promised to return them to Russia one day--an ironic development in comparison to the days of Khrushchev.

Since the fall of the Soviet Union, Russia has continued its space program. The Russian economy today lies in ruins. Much of the vaunted space program has had to be cut back, while the space budget and projects like the space shuttle face cancellation. Reductions in spending are likely to continue in the foreseeable future. The public has been upset over the space programs' siphoning of resources from consumer production, although some foreign companies and guest cosmonauts have helped to pay for the Mir station. The Glavkosmos space agency has been compelled to deal with foreign joint ventures in order to earn badly needed hard currency.

The space budget has been cut by 8.7 percent; manned flight activity has fallen by 25 percent.[56] Still, Russia did manage to launch seventy-five missions in 1990, compared with America's twenty-seven. Most involved military operations or satellites with dual military-civilian purposes.[57] As one report indicated, "The failures occur more frequently than in the U.S. and European programs, a trend that is likely to continue given the state of overall Soviet technology and the space management structure."[58] Such failures have included booster malfunctions, explosions, and various equipment failures and production delays.

To add to losses due to financing is the struggle for control of the space program itself between the military and a civilian agency created by President Boris Yeltsin. The military believes that the civilian agency has too much control, especially over the purse strings, and interferes with military operations.[59] There is also the continuing administrative struggle over who should retain control of the Baikonur/Tyuratam launch site in Kazakhstan. It would take a lot of work at Russia's Plesetsk Cosmodrome for it to be able to launch manned missions.

Yet despite its problems, the Russian Space Agency plans to continue to develop satellite-based communications as part of the government efforts to help to upgrade Russia's infrastructure; surveillance and remote sensing; improvement of launch and ground logistics; and the development of a shuttle.[60] The Russians plan all this despite severe cutbacks. The Mir-2 space station is set to be launched in 1997. The Russian government is also expected to work with the Americans on a U.S. space station. NASA has been working with the Energia booster, and Washington appears to be interested in acquiring the Soyuz crew transport as a cost-effective way to develop its own such crew transport.[61]

Several joint Russian-U.S. missions and Russian-French missions are planned, as is a flight to Mars in 1994 with help from France and Germany. Russia and Canada are also working on an international satellite communications system. It seems that joint Western ventures are the way to continue Russian space technology research, while the Russian military continues to launch surveillance spacecraft and revive its ocean surveillance program. During the first quarter of 1993, the Russians launched twelve military spacecraft, including three military navigation, two military communications, two imaging reconnaissance, two missile warning, two electronic intelligence and one ocean surveillance satellite.[62]

The Soviet Union had a very sophisticated space technology program.

In a sense, the Russians were advanced beyond the Americans in the early years. Russian failures cannot be taken at face value--after all, Americans have failed in their space endeavors on a number of occasions and generally never undertook the sheer volume of the Soviet program. A telling quote to end this chapter sums up Soviet space technology and Soviet science in general: "No previous government in history was so openly and energetically in favor of science, but neither had any modern government been so ideologically opposed to the free exchange of ideas, a presumed prerequisite of scientific progress."[63]

## *NOTES*

1.  Robert G. Kaiser, *Russia: The People and the Power* (New York: Pocket Books, 1976), p. 320.
2.  William I. Schauer, *The Politics of Space: A Comparison of the Soviet and American Space Programs* (New York: Holmes and Meier Publishers, 1976), pp. 2-3.
3.  Ibid., p. 3.
4.  James Oberg, *Red Star in Orbit* (New York: Random, 1981), p. 29.
5.  Schauer, *Politics of Space*, p. 14.
6.  Ibid., p. 87.
7.  James E. Oberg, *Uncovering Soviet Disasters: Exploring the Limits of Glasnost* (New York: Random House, 1988), p. 152.
8.  Ibid., p. 158.
9.  Ibid.
10. Ibid., p. 192.
11. Craig Covault, "Russians Reveal Secrets of Mir, Buran, Lunar Landing Craft," *Aviation Week and Space Technology*, Vol. 136 (6): February 10, 1992, p. 38.
12. Ibid., p. 39.
13. U.S. Department of Defense, *Soviet Military Power*, (Washington, D.C.: U.S. Department of Defense, 1983), p. 66.
14. Schauer, *Politics of Space*, p. 84.
15. U.S. Department of Defense, *Soviet Military Power* (Washington, D.C.: U.S. Department of Defense, 1985), pp. 54-55.
16. Ibid., p. 59.
17. Covault, "Russians Reveal," p. 38.
18. Paul B. Stares, *Space and National Security* (Washington, D.C.: Brookings Institution, 1987), p. 52.
19. Nicholas L. Johnson, *Soviet Space Programs 1980-1985* (Science

and Technology Series, Vol. 66) (San Diego: American Astronautical Society, 1987), p. 38.

20. Ibid., pp. 40-42.

21. Ibid., p. 85.

22. Paul Stares, "U.S. and Soviet Military Space Programs: A Comparative Assessment," *Daedalus*, Vol. 114: 1985, p. 129.

23. Bhupendra Jasani and Christopher Lee, *Countdown to Space War* (London: Taylor and Francis, 1984), p. 44.

24. Oberg, *Uncovering Soviet Disasters*, 1988, p. 199.

25. Arnold Selivanov, "Rescue from Outer Space," In Vitali Goldansky, ed., *Soviet Science and Technology--87* (Moscow: Novosti Press Agency Publishing House, 1988), p. 165.

26. Sir Bernard Lovell, *The Origins and International Economics of Space Exploration* (Edinburgh: University of Edinburgh Press, 1973), p. 75.

27. "The Great Siberia in the Sky," *The Economist*, October 3, 1987, p. 94.

28. Stephen M. Meyer, "Soviet Military Programmes and the New High Ground," *Survival*, Vol. 25 (5): September/October 1983, p. 207.

29. Johnson, *Soviet Space Programs*, p. 138.

30. Hans Mark, "Introduction." In Uri Ra'anan and Robert L. Pfaltzgraff Jr., eds., *International Security Dimensions of Space* (Hamden, Conn.: Archon Books, 1984), p. 12.

31. Lt. Col. Ray P. Linville, "Emerging Soviet Space Systems: Prospects for Military Application," *Armed Forces Journal International*, January 1987, p. 32.

32. David G. Chizum, *Soviet Radioelectronic Combat* (Boulder, Colo.: Westview, 1985).

33. Jasani and Lee, *Countdown*, p. 80.

34. Curtis Peebles, *Battle for Space* (New York: Beaufort Books, 1983), p. 16.

35. Stares, *Space and National Security*, p. 76.

36. Jasani and Lee, *Countdown*, p. 81.

37. The Strategic Defense Initiative, or "Star Wars" as it was colloquially known, was announced by President Ronald Reagan in 1983 as a space-based ballistic missile defense in which surveillance satellites, space-based lasers, and battle stations would destroy nuclear weapons before they could harm anyone.

38. Johnson, *Soviet Space Programs*, p. 171.

39. Covault, "Russians Reveal," p. 38.

40. Ibid.

41. *Soviet Military Power*, 1985, p. 57.

42. Johnson, *Soviet Space Programs*, p. 148.

43. Leon Jaroff, "Onward to Mars," *Time*, July 18, 1988, p. 66.

44. Roald Sagdeyev, *Deep Space and Terrestrial Problems* (Moscow: Novosti Press Agency Publishing House, 1987), p. 9.

45. Ibid., p. 11.

46. Ibid., p. 13.

47. Ibid., p. 15.

48. Ibid., p. 8.

49. Charles S. Sheldon II, *Peaceful Applications in Outer Space-- Prospects for Man and Society*. Lincoln P. Bloomfield, ed. (New York: Praeger, 1968), pp. 37-74.

50. Bill Knapp, "Space University Coming to Canada," *The Globe and Mail*, August 12, 1989, p. D4.

51. Schauer, *Politics of Space*, p. 217.

52. Ibid., pp. 218-19.

53. Bruce Parrott, *The Soviet Union and Ballistic Missile Defense* (Boulder, Colo.: Westview Press, 1987), p. 36.

54. Malcolm W. Browne, "The Star Wars Spinoff," *The New York Times Magazine*, August 24, 1986, p. 66.

55. Breck W. Henderson, "U.S. Buying Soviet Topaz 2 to Boost Space Nuclear Power Program," *Aviation Week and Space Technology*, Vol. 134 (2): January 14, 1991, p. 54.

56. Anonymous, "Aggressive Soviet Space Program Threatened by Budget, Policy Changes," *Aviation Week and Space Technology*, Vol. 134 (11): March 18, 1991, p. 153.

57. Ibid., p. 154.

58. Ibid.

59. Craig Covault, "Russians Locked in Struggle for Space Program Control," *Aviation Week and Space Technology*, Vol. 138 (5): February 1, 1993, p. 57.

60. Jeffrey M. Lenorovitz and Boris Rybak, "Feeble Russian Economy Hinders Space Efforts," *Aviation Week and Space Technology*, Vol. 138 (11): March 15, 1993, p. 91.

61. Jeffrey M. Lenorovitz, "Russia to Expand Role in Manned Space Flight," *Aviation Week and Space Technology*, Vol. 139 (5): August 2, 1993, p. 62.

62. Craig Covault, "Russian Military Space Maintains Aggressive Pace," *Aviation Week and Space Technology*, Vol. 138 (18): May 3,

1993, p. 61.

    63. Walter McCougall, . . . *The Heavens and the Earth: A Political History of the Space Race* (New York: Basic Books, 1985), p. 23.

*Chapter 6*

# The Economic Fallout

As with anything else, technology exacts a price from its users. In East and West, whatever the benefits, technology always has its costs. After the Russian Revolution brought the Communists to power, Lenin realized that Russia's mostly agrarian, land-based economy had to be industrialized in order to make the Communist state viable. Under the tsars, cities were indeed beginning to build factories, but the countryside was still run like feudal fiefdoms, despite the abolition of serfdom in the 1860s. Russia's government in pre-revolutionary times was alternately a cruel Asiatic despotism or a benevolent one. Lenin, like Tsar Peter the Great before him, decided to do what was necessary to bring his people to Western European and American industrial standards. Russia and most of the rest of the Soviet Union was thus dragged kicking and screaming through industrialization, a process that had taken over a hundred years in the West itself. In just a few years the leadership thought Soviet history would establish, as Harley Balzer once wrote, "a technological quick-fix that will enable the USSR to leap past the messier stages of capitalist development into an age of material abundance."[1]

Large programs were planned that at first seemed possible but later turned into great disappointments, such as the plans to divert northern running rivers to Central Asia. People were turned into faceless automatons as they struggled to keep up with and surpass Western progress for the grand cause of the Soviet Motherland. There was an ideological imperative behind it all, the inherent superiority of Marxism as a scientific doctrine that generated "a faith in the USSR's capacity to carry out technological transformation."[2] Yet no single system can be a perfect one. The government's emphasis on keeping up with and surpassing the West in weapons technology alone drained much-needed resources from the civilian economy. Lenin's drive to develop an industrial infrastructure led Soviet industry to sacrifice consumer goods to producer goods. To be sure, the production standards for consumers and the military were virtually the same; the only difference was the way in which they were adhered to. The people did not seem to be a priority, or even an adequate concern. They were entitled to the basic necessities, including a place to live, adequate food, and clothing. They were also to have adequate entertainment, such as ballets or sports events to keep them occupied and give them some leisure, but little else. To acquire these necessities, the citizens usually expected to stand in line for hours to buy shoddy merchandise. The goods available were produced in factories or grown on collective farms that took little or no interest at all in the air, the water, or the soil pollution. The trade-off was unequal and unfair.

The Soviet economy was always influenced by changing political circumstances and technological progress. The Soviet Union, with all the constituent republics, had about 40 million more people than the United States, while its gross national product was never more than one-half that of the U.S. Its ordinary people, however, had virtually nothing.

Much of this population's misery could easily be blamed on the obsessive Soviet need to outdistance the Americans militarily. Soviet military spending was far too high. The hidden or illegal economy (sometimes called secondary economy) was far too deep. The regular economy needed to produce high-quality manufactured goods for export in order to survive. It was often quipped that the Soviets were "first in space, first in tanks, far behind in computers and last in ladies' lingerie."[3] Were the economic reforms started by President Mikhail Gorbachev and his advisers like Abel Aganbegyan, Alexander Yakovlev, and Tania Zaslovskaia the real answer to this dilemma? I intend to deal with this issue in the following pages now that Mikhail Gorbachev is no longer the leader of the country, the Communist party is no longer in power, and the Soviet Union as we knew it has died a timely death. Only a nationalist Russia remains in place. Let us look first at how the socialist system was supposed to work and then at the grim circumstances of its demise.

## THE IDEAL ECONOMIC SYSTEM

Socialism is one of the few systems of government that is entirely justified in economic terms. Socialism seeks the transformation of the capitalist economic system, and consequently the sociopolitical system, by emphasizing the power of a collective and of social control over individualism. It was at first popularized by the followers of the English philosopher Robert Owen (1771-1858) and the French revolutionary François Babeuf (1760-97) and his colleague François Fourier (1772-1837). German intellectuals also became involved in the movement in the 1830s and 1840s, including the philosopher Ludwig Feuerbach (1804-72), who in addition to Hegelian thought, had a direct and profound influence on the young Karl Marx.

Karl Marx (1818-83) and Friedrich Engels (1820-95) wrote extensively on the exploitation of the workers in industrial England and on the abject life of factory workers in other countries. They saw the Dickensian conditions of long hours, meager pay, squalid living conditions, and the generally poor health of the industrial working classes, immortalized by the character of Bob Cratchet in Charles Dickens' *A Christmas Carol*. They also dissected the causes of this social affliction and attempted to predict what society would be like in the future when the capitalists were eventually expropriated. They extolled the virtues of a classless society in such works as *Das Kapital* and *The Communist Manifesto*.

Marx believed that men were, by nature, communalistic and that capitalism had forced people apart from each other. Individualism was the downfall of the ordinary person. Members of the working class were in so much misery that their class consciousness was growing and they would eventually put an end to capitalism and overthrow their oppressors.

Furthermore, Marx believed that socialism would rise like a phoenix from the ashes of the capitalist system, but only as a bridge to true Communism. The people would return to their inherently communal nature. All land and property would belong to the people, by which he meant the political state. Everything would be centralized, including health care and education. Socialism was thus to be the bridge between the individualistic capitalist state and the true communal Communist state in which men and women would enjoy full equality and no class structure.

Marx stressed that the socialist revolution would have to take place in a capitalist country where the forces of industrialism had already alienated the working class to the point that they were to begin to desire the promise of socialism and communism. The last place he would have expected the first socialist revolution to take place was Russia, which was still largely agrarian with a very small industrial working class and a nearly feudal farming system. He argued further that, while agricultural workers were alienated in their slave-like conditions, they were not nearly as alienated as industrial workers under capitalism. But at other times, he wrote that Russia could become socialist without achieving capitalism. Yet Russia was destined to be the place where the great socialist experiment first began.

Russia at that time was governed by the feckless Tsar Nicholas II, who had no concept of the hardships of his people: starvation in the cities and feudalism on the farms, where peasants were literally still enslaved as little better than serfs. World War I ended with tragic losses and nearly half the army of over 15 million killed, wounded, or taken prisoner. Social unrest was becoming harder to stamp out. The atmosphere was ripe for revolution.

One of the leaders of the revolutionary forces of socialism was Vladimir Ilyich Ulyanov, alias Lenin (1870-1924), a gifted orator, organizer, and writer who wanted to adapt Marxism to Russia. In doing this, he revised Marxism to include a paramilitary structure and discipline in a Marxist Party, and an alliance between the proletariat and the peasants. Since Russia was the weakest link in the capitalist chain, he held that Russia ought to be the first to fall to socialism so that the others would quickly follow.[4] He believed that the capitalists would have to finish exploiting their colonies before they too would fall to Communism.

He applied the socialist concepts in which the economy was managed by the state to the Soviet state. All production was centrally planned. The factory enterprise was the basic unit of production. All output was to be raised. Moreover, the aim of socialist production was to satisfy as fully as possible the constantly growing requirements of each individual and the entire society through unceasing, rapid development of socialist production on the basis of technical progress.[5]

The key to economic management was central planning in which all aspects of production were given specific goals within a certain period of time, usually a five-year plan. Theoretically, each enterprise's plan was to be made by the workers, then sent upward for approval. In actuality, the central planning organization sent plans down to the enterprises. Tried experimentally in the early 1920s, the process was formally adopted in 1928. Of course, the problem with this system was that consumer demand could not be predicted. However, in a socialist state this was irrelevant. Lenin wanted to rapidly industrialize his country and felt that the plans would be the best way to carry out this task. He especially stressed electrification and put most emphasis on heavy industry that would make the Soviet Union competitive.

One area of social development that concerned Lenin was the problem of self-determination among the non-Russian minorities. He held the view that nationalities that had not attained nationhood before the Revolution developed into nations under the socialists (e.g., Tajikistan) by eradicating the notion of a backward nation. Furthermore, it was Lenin's belief that the socialist philosophy would cause all cultures to draw together and become one. In the early decades of Soviet rule, relatively high levels of investment in the more backward regions of the USSR were rooted in the Marxist belief that industrialization, urbanization, and economic equality would reduce ethnic consciousness by forging a deeper awareness of common class interests.[6] Nevertheless, nothing made more impact than the policies of forcibly introducing Russian as the national language and the Sovietization of all national cultures. If the minorities wanted to be modern and progressive and industrialized, all they had to do was to speak Russian.

Lenin's death at the relatively young age of 54 in 1924 brought one of the world's greatest despots to power: Joseph Vissarionovich Dzhugashvili who took the name Stalin (meaning steel in Russian) (1879-1953). American journalist Anna Louise Strong, a Maoist, somewhat excused Stalin's behavior when she wrote:

This was one of history's great dynamic eras, perhaps its greatest [1930s and 1940s]. . . . It gave birth to millions of heroes and to some devils. Lesser men can look back on it now and list its crimes. But those who lived through the struggle, and even many who died of it, endured the evil as part of the cost of what was built.[7]

Strong's attitude may be taking things a bit too far. Under Stalin's leadership, millions died from starvation, and untold thousands, including hundreds of scientists, were shot or exiled to Gulag labor camps in Siberia on the slightest whim or pretext of dissension. Terror was the political byword of the Stalin era.

When Stalin came to power, he took over the dictatorship of the proletariat (a term used by Marx to describe workers' control of the government); the state became synonymous with Stalin. He created a cult of personality in which he was set up as a demigod. Stalin's will was carried out. He believed that the Soviet Union needed a modern industry in order to maintain its independence and strength, and it needed that industry in a hurry. In 1931, his prophetic words were: "We are 50 or a hundred years behind the leading countries. We must make up this distance in ten years. Either we do it, or we shall perish."[8]

This was accomplished mainly through the use of terror. Stalin centralized planning and had all resources allocated by the state. New sectors of industry were created and industrialization began at a dizzying rate. However, Stalin was not satisfied and set limits and goals that were totally unrealizable. Production rose slowly in a world economy going through an economic depression. To import one needed raw materials; Stalin ordered food exported to pay for equipment, causing hunger in his own land. Prices were fixed, and the standard of living began to decline. Most of his goals were not met and that infuriated Stalin. He forcibly collectivized the farms, displacing thousands of peasants, and introducing sterner discipline by denying housing and social insurance to unproductive workers. Absenteeism and tardiness were treated as crimes. To increase high production, he created "Stakhanovism" (named after an especially productive coal miner named Stakhanov), in which high production was rewarded with bonuses and perks. Naturally, this encouraged the worker to hurry production along with little regard for quality. Stalin's interference in different sectors in which he had little knowledge, resulted in severe problems for enterprises trying to fulfil impossible goals. He suffered from gigantomania--wanting to create large enterprises. His obsession with heavy industry led to an expensive arms race. Anyone who criticized Stalin's way of thinking was repressed. The great Scottish sovietologist Alec Nove once wrote, "It is hard to compute the damage done by this deliberate Stalinist campaign to secure total obedience of intellectuals to the Party line, and to cut Russia off from all Western influence--and so also from Western science and technology."[9] Not only did he expect workers to perform miracles in setting new production quotas; he also denied them access to the very technology that could help them do so.

But did all this suffering, the waste and death, truly advance the cause of Soviet industrialization? Was it justifiable? Eminent Soviet historian Roy Medvedev thinks not: "And if the extreme exertions and sacrifices which the people made for the sake of industrialization are compared with the results, the conclusion cannot be avoided: the results would have been far greater without Stalin."[10]

Still, it must be remembered that the Soviets had many obstacles to overcome. After the Revolution, they were reeling from the losses of World War I and the Revolution itself which cost millions of lives and untold millions of rubles in loss and damage to the country's infrastructure, agriculture, and industrial potential. The population itself was not trained for industry; most were agricultural workers, sharecroppers, and peasants. For years after the Revolution, the entire country suffered from a Western economic blockade. Then, World War II swept away the lives of countless more and caused a disruption in plans. The Cold War also resulted in the diversion of untold millions of rubles to the production of arms.[11] Thus, it is a miracle that the Soviet economic system did not totally break down instead of--at least marginally--succeeding.

After Stalin's death, Nikita Khrushchev (1894-1971) came to power. He stressed agriculture and made impractical plans that unbalanced the economy. He tried to expand the economy too quickly. In 1961, he promised that the Soviet Union would overtake the United States in output by 1980 and would win the war of capitalism and Communism through peaceful competition.[12] He promised more consumer goods and housing and vowed to listen to workers' grievances. He stated several times that heavy industry had finished its mad rush to develop and that light and heavy industry would develop at the same rate. To give him his due, there was some real improvement under his leadership. However, his exaggerations and generally poor leadership qualities combined with international political problems (the 1963 Missile Crisis) ended in his overthrow in 1964.

Khrushchev's successor was Leonid Brezhnev (1906-84). Like Stalin, Brezhnev also believed in heavy industry and its importance. He put a priority on agriculture and stressed the importance of arms production. Although he stated that he was for the growth of consumer goods and services, little was accomplished. He did reorganize industry to create large economic units by combining enterprises into associations that gave them more freedom to make decisions. While there may have been some sincere desire to accomplish some substantial changes in the Soviet economy, by the last five years of his rule (1977-82), Brezhnev had created a personality cult of his own. Corruption was rampant, extending into the Politburo and even to Brezhnev's own family. These last few years saw a decline in industry and agriculture, and food shortages. There was a more balanced economy, but necessary reforms were either not attempted or were canceled.

Brezhnev was briefly succeeded by Yuri Andropov (1914-84), former head of the KGB. Andropov set out to increase production, improve management, improve the quality of goods and work, introduce better planning, improve coordination, and increase the number and variety of consumer goods. Unfortunately, Andropov only ruled a few months before he succumbed to a debilitating kidney disorder. His successor, Konstantin Chernenko, a conservative follower of Brezhnev, wanted to continue Andropov's reforms and decentralize decision-making. Unfortunately, Chernenko, seen by many as being merely a fill-in for Andropov's chosen successor, Mikhail Gorbachev, was dead within a year and was succeeded by Gorbachev.

## WHAT DID THE SOVIET CONSTITUTION CALL FOR?

Before we discuss the Gorbachev reforms, we should take a closer look at the Soviet Constitution of 1977, the last time that this basic law spelled out what the Soviet economy and Soviet society were supposed to be. Articles 10-18 addressed the economic system. They stated that the foundation of the economic system was the socialist ownership of the means of production and that state property was the principal form of social property, including that of collective farms. Earned income, clothing, personal accouterment, homes, and savings were the only form of personal property. The source of growth was labor free from exploitation. The goal of production was the fullest satisfaction of people's growing material, cultural, and intellectual requirements. People were allowed the individual labor of handicrafts, farming, and provision of services for the public. All land, water, and other resources had to be preserved.

Articles 19-27 fell under the title of Social Development and Culture and stated that the social basis was the alliance of workers, peasants, and intelligentsia (traditionally, party members, teachers, scientists, scholars, doctors, military, police, artists, writers, actors, and business managers). All Soviet citizens were free to apply their creative energies and develop their personalities. The state promised to improve working conditions and raise incomes through increases in productivity. The state further promised to extend and improve health care, social services, education, trade, and public utilities, and to develop science and technology.

Articles 39-69 dealt with the basic rights and freedoms of the Soviet citizen. They were called full social, economic, political, and personal rights and freedoms, including the right to work; rest and leisure; health protection; maintenance in old age, in sickness, and in the disability or loss of the breadwinner; housing; education; cultural benefits; freedom of scientific, technical, and artistic work; the right to take part in management and administration of the state and public affairs; freedom to submit proposals to state bodies and public organizations; freedom of speech, press, and assembly; association in public organizations to promote political activities; freedom of religion; protection of the family; child care; inviolability of the person and home; and privacy. These Articles stated that all officials must respect the individual and proclaimed the right to lodge a complaint against officials and public bodies. All persons were to observe the Constitution and its laws; they had to work conscientiously in their occupation and preserve and protect socialist property; and they were obliged to safeguard the interests of the Soviet state. Military service was decreed an honorable duty. Citizens were to respect the rights and national dignity of others and be concerned with the upbringing of children. They were also obligated to protect nature and historical monuments and sites. Finally, citizens had to promote friendship with other lands.[13]

This was the ideal. The reality was quite different. The Soviet Union had the second-largest workforce in history, which was imposed on a backward land at an impressive rate of growth. Jobs were created, homes were built, and the people were fed. Railways were built as well as electric power plants. However, industry was uncompetitive. Workers were half as productive as American workers; they were only one-tenth as productive in the agricultural field and had poorly made industrial goods. Soviet industrial technology was second-rate or worse.[14]

There were reasons for this. Although the Communist Party declared that bureaucracy was a capitalist invention, the Soviet Union had the largest bureaucracy in the world, due mainly to the idea of democratic centralism (in which leaders were elected by their subordinates, and power was supposed to come from the bottom up). They had literally smothered the economy, unwilling to introduce anything innovative that could have thrown off a plan. Planning ensured "inefficiency, waste and irrational behaviour, and discourage[d] technological innovation."[15] Fulfilling the plan's objectives was all that counted, and product quality and consumer demand had nothing to do with the plan. As a result, the public was skeptical of the quality of Soviet-made goods and desperate for Western-made items. With workers struggling to exceed the plans in order to earn a bonus, there was little desire or time to deal with possible delays caused by introducing new technology. Robert Kaiser encapsulated the dilemma thus:

A new product means new raw materials, thus new sources of supply and the uncertainty that inevitably accompanies the search for them. It means new, unpredictable customers. A new process may also require new raw materials, and it will mean reorganizing the factory's labour force, perhaps adding new-- and hard to find--skilled workers. If the Planning Commission thinks the new process is more efficient than the old, it will raise the factory's targets.[16]

Each ministry acted independently, and there was little cooperation. Yet if there was any shortfall in a commodity, this would have had an effect on other sectors (i.e., a shortage of a particular mineral could cause one plant to fail to fulfill its plan for one part of a component needed to produce a larger product, and so on). Corruption was rampant. Many high party officials were taking bribes or taking advantage of their positions to gain favor. Since production was supposed to be for the people, workers felt they could take things home to use or sell somewhere else. Many officials moonlighted by having other jobs; for example, government drivers used their cars as taxis. *Blat*--the exchange of favors for bribes or gifts--was very prevalent. All prices were fixed and staples were subsidized so as not to reflect their true value. Thus bread was very cheap, but a new coat could cost a month's salary. Because it was so hard to get anything of good quality, a large black market existed, which was more expensive but had better quality products than did peasant markets and cooperatives. There were constant labor and supply shortages as each enterprise tried to become self-sufficient. To cover up their mistakes and failures, or to earn bonuses, most enterprises misreported statistics. As discussed in the chapter on computers, there would have been no point in feeding false information into a computer network, or using computers to build models and forecast future productivity or gauge unproductive forces.

Often a system such as this discourages initiative, inventions, and even Western products; it would have meant too many delays in production. Indeed, any new technology was considered suspect. While the government tried to impose technological progress from above, it was an uphill struggle with the Russian popular mind-set. It was a foregone conclusion that the only truly innovative area of the economy was going to be the military, in which state-of-the-art technology was immediately applied. Perhaps this was because the civilian economy was considered a seller's market while the military was a buyer's.[17]

All this points up the contradictions in the Soviet command economy: "The basic criticism to be leveled against this system is that it has come into contradiction with the requirements of a modern industrial economy and of a society with rising living standards and even more sharply rising expectations."[18]

The state did not succeed in following its social guidelines. The state became as oppressive as the capitalists were considered. It became a police state in which peace and true freedom were virtually not to be found. A person could have been arrested for the slightest offense. Incomes and the standard of living dropped. Although necessities were subsidized, staples such as meat and fish were not always to be found. Some people even suffered from nutritional deficiencies, and there was some starvation. Homes were small and crowded and--although it did not officially exist on the books--homelessness was widespread. The health care system was not efficiently run, and bribes were needed to get the most basic supplies. Pensions and child care were not always adequate. Although women were said to be equal, their salaries were kept down and few were in high political or executive positions. Nationalities were discriminated against, officially and unofficially, and such minorities as the Germans, Poles, and Jews were considered non-native. Each person was guaranteed the right to work but was not always effectively employed. In despair, many Soviets turned to alcohol. It became a very serious social problem, especially since the budget was partly dependent on alcohol sales.[19] It was into this atmosphere that Mikhail Gorbachev (1931- ) came to power. He was determined to change attitudes and the entire economy.

To understand the vast change in thinking in the late stages of the Soviet Union and how it differed from prevailing attitudes, one must understand the idea of Gorbachev's *perestroika* itself. Gorbachev defined it as follows:

Perestroika is the all-round intensification of the Soviet economy, the revival and development of the principles of democratic centralism in running the national economy, the universal introduction of economic methods, the renunciation of management by injunction and by administrative methods, and the overall encouragement of innovation and socialist enterprise.[20]

Gorbachev knew the problems of the Soviet economy and thought that political and economic changes could be handled quickly enough to prevent the collapse of the Soviet economy. Unfortunately, this was not to be. Other economic revivals and changes had been tried in the past under Lenin's New Economic Policy of the 1920s with only limited success. The most recent and comprehensive reform movement took place in 1965, and it too failed. It seemed that such reforms could not work in a Communist system.

The economic structure of the USSR deteriorated steadily beginning in the mid to late 1960s, and was in desperate need of change. As the Western world surged ahead economically, the Soviets were struggling to, at least marginally, keep up. They did, but only partially.

Gorbachev found that the ordinary Soviet citizen was forced to live a life of harshness and need. The government was repressive and citizens had very little to do besides work and worry about when they could afford a new pair of shoes, a home of their own, or even fresh meat. All of this took place while billions of rubles were pumped into developing newer, deadlier, and, above all, either American-equivalent or superior weapons of mass destruction. Nuclear bombs and missiles, more effective tanks, military and spy satellites--all of these seemed to be much more important than producing good clothing, or shipping good food from the south to the north. Although they were known for their proficiency in the construction of advanced nuclear submarines and space stations, the people of the Soviet Union were forced to stand in line for hours to receive shoddy merchandise and meager food supplies. Because of the low quality of their civilian products, few could be exported to the West for much-needed hard currency.

The Soviet Union was the world's largest producer of such commodities as oil, gas, steel, iron and non-ferrous ores, mineral fertilizers, cement, metal-cutting machine tools, tractors, refrigerators, and so on. It was also the leader in several areas of science such as space research and technology, laser technology, and thermonuclear fusion.[21] However, there were problems, such as technical inefficiency, lack of equipment, falling growth rates, falling labor productivity, centralized and politicized administration, the production of low-quality goods, official economy, and imbalances in the system (especially in the supply-demand sector).[22] The system was hierarchical and rigid. Although the Soviet Union was known for its abundance of raw materials, it still lacked modern manufacturing technology and managerial expertise.

Although it is obvious that changes had to take place, there were a number of obstacles that had to be overcome. For instance, changes were met with resistance from some top-level political leaders, the bureaucracy, and the people themselves. Gorbachev had to deal with unsupportive bureaucrats, resentful managers, antagonized workers, and outraged consumers.[23] As well, inflationary pressures and the absence of any form of market for capital and equity also formed economic obstacles.[24] The Soviet Union was also forced to support some of its dependencies like Cuba and North Vietnam and suffered substantial losses in expenditures and personnel during the war with Afghanistan. As Richard Ericson has written:

Economic attitudes and understanding are still to a great extent mired in the paternalistic socialist ideology that guaranteed economic security and the social direction of all economic activity. While that is changing, there is a legacy of social attitudes that resists marketizing reforms, and fails to value economic experimentation, entrepreneurship, and risk taking.[25]

The basic aim of Gorbachev's reforms was a renewal of growth with less investment and with an accent on modernization and discipline. He, like other leaders, felt that science and technology could help provide answers to economic difficulties.[26] A central theme was the scientific technical revolution, including automation and information technology.[27] He also wanted to increase the price of raw materials, which would cut pollution and inefficiency; transfer raw materials and land to local Soviets, which would limit central planners; and make factories self-financing, which would discourage the old mentality of "fulfill the plan and damn the consequences."[28] During the period of the mid-1980s until 1990, the process involved a number of economic policy changes and some partial reforms in order to start the acceleration (*uskorenie*) of the economy. After 1990, the reforms were to move quickly into place and rapidly change the economy.

The first major reform was the Law on Individual Labor Activity, signed in May 1987, which allowed for small production facilities and redefined the role of the worker. After a number of disappointing attempts at reform within industry, the Law on State Enterprises (Associations) and Basic Provisions for Fundamental Perestroika of Economic Management were adopted in June 1987 by the Supreme Soviet and the Central Committee, respectively, but they failed to meet their objectives. The *Economist* placed the blame on the ambiguity of the law, which envisaged central control and managerial independence working together.[29]

Also set for restructuring were investment policies. In particular, the government wanted to hasten technical progress. Abel Aganbegyan, Gorbachev's chief economic adviser, stated, "Technological reconstruction and acceleration of re-equipment in all branches of economy are the most important components of the economic strategy."[30] Technological re-equipment of industry was to be a priority, along with an increase in the quality of all products produced. Financing was also slated for restructuring. Such fields as applied science were to be self-financing. Research financing would be available from central ministry funds and bank loans. Priority projects would receive state budget allocations. Accordingly, large enterprises would either rely on research institutes or operate their own research labs, while some might have had to close entirely. Thus changes would be effective "only when enterprises choose to adopt new technology because of its economic profitability and suitability to specific needs, not because some artificial mechanism makes profitability dependent on introducing new technology."[31]

As Guri Marchuk states, the technological modernization of the economy would be impossible without the restructuring of the management system. Thus, only large enterprises would be administered by the central authorities, while the rest were left to either local or republican associations. Peter Havlik has written, "Ministries will in future become scientific, technical, planning and economic headquarters of individual industries."[32] Each republic or local body would plan enterprise output. The production of consumer goods would be promoted through industry, cooperative, and individual work efforts. The pricing system would be reformed to take into account social costs, utility, and quality characteristics as well as demand.[33]

One obstacle to the implementation of a market economy was the existence of a dual economy based on the civilian and military facets of society. Traditionally, the civilian sector was insufficiently developed technologically and cash poor, while the military sector was very advanced and opulent. Research and development for each sector was also separate. In the past, over 60 percent of public research and development financing went to the military sector. Scientists working in this area had the advantage of better equipment, higher salaries, and better financing.

The most significant reason for the reforms in the economy was to change the productive power of society from producer-oriented to consumer-oriented in order to satisfy the demands of consumers through increased efficiency and quality. Thus, a market economy became important.

The results of some of the changes within the Soviet economy caused consternation. Proposed legislation that would have tripled bread prices was put off for months as a result of waves of protest, panic-buying, and hoarding. These proposed changes did not meet with favor among Soviet citizens. Placards of protestors at the 1990 May Day parade in Moscow carried such slogans as: "No Unemployment," "No Private Enterprise," and "No Price Reform." The Soviet people feared these changes. Unfortunately, the economic changes that the Soviet Union went through needed public support to show that their citizens would be ready to make sacrifices and work harder to improve the economy. Apparently, that was not the case.

## THE NEEDS OF SOVIET CITIZENS

Valentin Pavlov, the minister of finance for the USSR, stated: "Our efforts must be exclusively oriented toward the person, toward the individual human being. We must have a new slogan: Up with the standard of living. Let us make money. Let us give people financial incentives."[34] However, what were the priority needs of the average Soviet citizen?

Perhaps the most important concern for the Soviet consumer was the prevalence of food and consumer goods. These commodities could be acquired through state and cooperative stores and eating establishments. However, food and consumer goods were traditionally accorded a low priority within Soviet industry. Thus, food was often rationed and consumer goods (even essentials) could not always be purchased. As discussed above, food was often of low quality and variety and, because of an inefficient distribution system, it often rotted before it reached the stores. Citizens were forced to stand in line for hours. This represented a loss in labor productivity because a person may have had to take time off from work just to acquire the staples of life.

The currency within the Soviet Union was meant for internal use only. Its value was often reduced because it was used to buy goods that did not exist, and the purchasing power depended upon the status of the purchaser. Frequently, connections within shops, government, and so on were more important than money. Thus within this type of economic environment, people were forced to carry a lot of cash around in case they come upon a sudden supply of goods in a store. Since distribution was so poor, goods could have come in at one store and be totally absent at another. Thus, hoarding became necessary in order to maintain a steady supply of most crucial items. Goods were not the only thing that was hoarded. Before the Revolution, it was estimated that over 400 billion roubles were being saved by Soviet citizens since they had nothing to spend their money on. All of this became an expected part of life. Gorbachev promised to help alleviate the problems in housing and to improve health care which, although free, was inefficient and suffered from shortages in drugs and other essential supplies.

A problem with *perestroika* and the subsequent modernization of industry was the possible loss of millions of jobs. There was no official unemployment or inflation within the Soviet system. However, although employed, the Soviet citizen was not always effectively employed. Labor productivity was often low, and the system suffered from overstaffing and general inefficiency.

## REFORMS

The Gorbachev government moved slowly toward a market economy to allow the Soviet people time to adjust to the necessary changes. One of the first steps was the allowance of cooperatives. Gorbachev stated, "We need highly efficient and technically well-equipped cooperatives, which are capable of providing commodities and services of the highest quality and competing with domestic and foreign enterprises."[35] Cooperatives served a dual purpose of providing goods and services for the population while improving the standard of living for their members. Although they undoubtedly offered better products at competitive prices (although their prices were sometimes high above state prices), their existence created hostility in some Soviet quarters. Paradoxically, the black market flourished for years and was tolerated if not wholeheartedly supported by most Soviet citizens. Although black market prices were often unreasonably high, up to 85 percent of all Soviet citizens had, at one time or another, used it.

Part of the blame for this type of thinking could be found within the state itself. Since the Revolution of 1917, the government taught the Soviet people to be dependent upon the state and to think collectively. It therefore came as no surprise to the state that the people had very little empathy with capitalist ideals that emphasized individualism rather than collectivism.

As the Soviet Union sought to enter the international market, it also sought to borrow money from the West to upgrade its own production facilities. Since it had little to sell for hard currency, it tried to increase the quality of its manufactured goods. In the past, the USSR had to rely on the sale of energy, gold, and weapons. However, as production declined and extraction became more expensive, both oil and gold seemed less stable. Also, the USSR's best clients for weapons, such as Iraq and Syria, were hit by the declining price of oil.[36]

Although the Soviet Union's industrial production constituted one-fifth of the world's total industrial production, this area of the economy needed massive reform. For the most part, the ministries administered the enterprises and set quotas for production, which had to be met. These state orders represented about 75 percent of total industrial output, making it almost impossible to set up other kinds of trade. As a result of having to meet these orders, most factory equipment could not be replaced and upgraded because the industries could not afford to slow down production. Factory equipment was, on average, twenty-five years old and of poor quality. Maintenance and repair were inadequate. Because of state orders, there was poor specialization in products, low product variety, and waste. The bureaucracy at work in these industries was resistant to innovation.

What was needed was a supply of high technology plants and equipment. The manufacturing and engineering industries had to be upgraded in order to help industrialize the rest. Machine building was also important. A market had to be created between companies. In early 1986, eleven institutes of the Academy of Sciences and eight institutes from various industrial ministries were given control of several industrial enterprises and called Interbranch Scientific Technical Complexes (MNTK).

In the past, quality control was undertaken by the enterprises themselves. In 1987, teams of quality control inspectors from the State Standards Committee were placed in a number of enterprises. The prototype for this new quality control was the technical inspection department and its military representative, which were prevalent at military facilities.

One aspect of these enterprises that seemed to work was the practice of an enterprise providing its workers with housing, in-plant goods and services (e.g., refrigerators, clothing, meat), and raising food and manufacturing consumer goods at the factory itself. These ideas made these industries seem like the self-supporting feudal estates of old Russia.[37] By providing their workers with such things, and perhaps by issuing shares to them as well, these industries fostered a sense of self-interest in their workers to make sure their industry succeeded and was profitable.

## CONVERSION--BEATING SWORDS INTO PLOUGHSHARES?

A major undertaking of the Soviet government was the process of converting sections of the military complex into consumer goods-producing enterprises. In recent years, as the Cold War warmed considerably and the fear of nuclear war dwindled, the Soviet Union came to realize that it could no longer devote as much of its economy to the defense industry. While they might have been matching and, in some cases, even surpassing the Americans in military hardware, the Soviets were falling woefully behind in consumer goods production. To generate popular support for other economic changes, this seemed a perfect way to garner widespread goodwill for other changes. The military industry had always been more productive and technically advanced. Another advantage to using these industries to produce consumer goods was that they could be readily converted to produce military goods again if the need arose.

In 1989, the goal was to produce civilian goods valued at 27 billion roubles at munitions factories.[38] Former Prime Minister Ryzhkov stated that 40 percent of the defense industry's output was civilian. However, the goal was to raise it to 50 percent by 1991 and 60 percent by 1995.[39] Three hundred and forty-five defense industry enterprises and over 200 major research institutes and designing offices working for defense were targeted to produce consumer goods,[40] involving a 37 percent rise in the production of washing machines, a 300 percent rise in VCRs and 200 percent in agricultural machinery.[41] All of this would involve a retooling of military munitions factories without a drop in production. Dual-use technologies like microelectronics, computers, and aviation equipment were to be turned over increasingly to the civilian sector.

This type of activity provided ready-made jobs for personnel released from the military sector, although retraining would be necessary. One major problem was that some military equipment could not be used for civilian production and had to be destroyed or converted. However, the military saw this as a threat to its technological superiority. The advantages to the entire economy would have been immeasurable if this could have been accomplished. Not only would the domestic consumer economy have benefited from this conversion but, if goods could have been sold at competitive prices on the world market, consumer goods could have been purchased from the West with the hard currency from such sales.[42] Joint ventures with Western firms could have also aided conversion and brought in required hard currency.

## TECHNOLOGY IN THE SOVIET ECONOMY

"Before his retirement Academy [of Sciences] president A. P. Aleksandrov focused on energy issues, problems in computer technology, the rapid pace of genetic engineering, and the need for scientific aid to agriculture," wrote Loren Graham in 1988.[43] As this quote shows, one of the major priorities of Soviet science was to improve technology for use in industry and agriculture. The main problem in Soviet industry was that most enterprises were reluctant to innovate and had very little incentive to do so. Yet the integration of technology in industry and the modernization of industrial plants and equipment were vital to *perestroika*.

Robot technology was an important part of industrial development in the Soviet Union. Although it produced nearly three times as many robots as the United States, the robots were mostly unsophisticated and suffered from poor quality and service. Thus the USSR was forced to import from other countries. Between 1981 and 1985, more than 20,000 robots, manipulators, and robot complexes were put into operation.[44] The trade unions supported the implementation of robot technology since they increased labor productivity and improved working conditions.[45] The one area of the industrial process that had trouble with this was managers who had little desire for change.

Soviet industry was very energy- and raw materials intensive. This had to change in order to modernize. The Soviet Union had a wealth of raw materials, including vast forests, one-quarter of the world's oil, over half of the world's gas and coal, and a vast inventory of ores and minerals. The problem with this abundance was that most of it was located in Siberia, where the Soviets had to invest a lot of time and energy in developing and extracting these materials. They were able to export oil, natural gas, and electric power (through hydroelectric dams, coal, and atomic reactors), which earned hard currency for the economy. The Soviets, before the Revolution, took steps to economize their fuel and raw material consumption in order to ensure a lasting resource base.

Soviet telecommunications were notoriously bad. Only about a quarter of urban and less than 10 percent of rural dwellers had telephones. The lines were unsophisticated and subject to breakdown. All lines were direct dial, and there was no way to switch calls within an office. All of this was frustrating and prevented the easy use of modems by computer operators.

The Communications Ministry sought to upgrade services. It concentrated on digital signal processing, optical fiber communications, satellite communications, special machine building, and microelectronics.[46] It also wanted to organize networks for telephone, teletext, digital transmission of information, and facsimile and electronic postal service.[47] Many joint ventures were created in the telecommunications field.

## HIGH TECHNOLOGY

The Soviet Union needed a technological basis in order to raise economic outputs, and technological progress itself stems from science. High technology is the basis for Western industry and was essential to the Soviet Union in its bid to be competitive on the world market. Although rich in resources, the Soviets were poor in innovative technology. As Marshall Goldman pointed out, "Most analysts agree that economic leadership will belong to those countries that can lead the way in high technology."[48]

High technology is an industry that employs large numbers of scientists and engineers and in which a portion of sales go back into research. Industries such as the following are typical of high technology: computers and office equipment, electrical equipment, optical and medical instruments, aircraft, drugs and medicine, plastics and synthetic materials, professional and scientific instruments, engines and turbines, and some types of chemicals.[49] In the past, high technology benefited other areas of the Soviet economy. For example, the information gathered from various Soviet space vehicles helped in map making and oil and gas prospecting.

There were, however, problems within the Soviet science community that first had to be addressed. The bureaucracies involved with science were not always amenable to changes. Most scientists found problems in getting supplies and funding to be frustrating. As well, most scientists did not get the chance to work out innovative ideas and saw no material gain in pursuing their projects to completion. Most labs did not have the necessary infrastructure to provide supplies. To that end, many industries were trying to combine the lab and the factory.

It was imperative that the Soviets fostered their technological development, especially in an area such as computers. Only by advancing their own innovative technology could they hope to satisfy their own needs and compete on a world market.

## COMPUTERS

The computer industry in the Soviet Union was entering its first stages of growth. This industry consisted of domestic mainframes and several hundred thousand personal computers. The Soviet leadership under Gorbachev came to realize that the country had to become computer-based in order to remain at least in tandem with the computerized First World. Thus they had to bring in the computer revolution, which had already swept the world to their own doorstep. As Joel Schatz, a member of a joint venture with the Soviet Union, said: "It was Soviet policy for decades to resist this technology since it makes it hard to control information. But personal computers are a planetary phenomenon now. Whatever the downside, they must get involved or lose world influence."[50] Although computer cooperatives and joint ventures with Western firms became more and more prevalent, there were inherent problems with this new industry. Computers were primitive, as was software. There was a lack of trained personnel, and modems were virtually unknown. One of the most fundamental problems was the above-mentioned internal security. Since computers involved the exchange of information, authorities feared espionage or the exchange of privileged information.

To gain access to Western technology, reverse engineering, or the copying of Western technology, was sometimes practiced, but this did not seem to be a viable solution. Part of the problem was that, for the most part, the Soviets had to spend months trying to understand how the technology worked. This also discouraged domestic production of needed equipment.

To gain official access to Western technology, a ministry had to apply for hard currency and demonstrate that the required machine or license could not be made or obtained domestically. The application to purchase foreign licenses had to go through the State Committee for Science and Technology and GOSPLAN had to show that the production cost would be at least a third less than domestic research and development.[51] Militarily sensitive technology had to go through the Military-Industrial Commission (VPK), which acquired it for the KGB, military intelligence, State Committee for Science and Technology (GKNT), Ministry for Foreign Trade, and the State Committee for External Economic Relations.[52] Illegal acquisition funds were provided by the KGB, GKNT, VPK, and the Ministry of Defense.

One mechanism that placed restrictions upon technology transfer to the Soviet Union was the Coordinating Committee on Multilateral Export Controls (COCOM), a committee of NATO. The purpose of this organization was to restrict technology to the Soviet Union, the Warsaw Pact countries, Vietnam, Mongolia, China, and North Korea.

Joint ventures between the Soviet Union and various Western countries became prevalent. The advantage of these enterprises for the Soviets was that they brought in much-needed hard currency and technology (it was estimated that over one-third of all joint ventures were based on science-intensive technology), although Western companies really wanted only the market and used less sophisticated technology. For Western countries, these ventures represented a large market heretofore untapped.

Although joint ventures involved a risk in the money invested, they also had the potential of being very profitable. For the Soviets, they brought Western technology and expertise into the production process and produced something valuable for export (thus generating hard currency, investment capital from the West and providing a more stable source of income than risky products like the oil and weapons trade). There were, however, problems for Western companies such as information transfer. Because of COCOM regulations, it was very difficult for Western companies to transfer vital information to the Soviet Union. As well, some logistics problems arose due to the lack of paper and such things as photocopiers.

Gorbachev's changes did not work. In 1991, the following statistics proved this by showing how certain areas fell or grew:

| | | |
|---|---|---|
| GNP | | - 17.0% |
| Net material production | | - 15.0% |
| Industry | | - 7.8% |
| Agriculture | | - 7.0% |
| National income used | | - 16.0% |
| Consumption | | - 13.0% |
| Investment | | - 25.0% |
| Consumer prices | | +196.0% |
| Producer prices | | +240.0% |
| Cash issued | | +480.0% |
| Credit issued | | +210.0% |
| Budget deficit | over | +500.0%[53] |

Prices rose for the following items: beef, 350 percent; pork, 278 percent; milk, 179 percent; butter, 278 percent, eggs, 200 percent; flour, 304 percent; rye bread, 400 percent; T-shirt, 350 percent; and radio, 158 percent.[54] All of this caused hardship for the Soviet people. It was not long after that the Soviet government fell.

But independence has not helped the new republics to survive economically. They were traditionally interdependent and are now in debt and cash-poor, begging for their share of the center's gold reserves. Each republic tried to introduce separate currencies, and this caused collapse of trade among them.[55] A bank was being set up between the new states. It has become so bad that science and other institutes are selling or licensing technology in order to raise cash. The necessity of areas such as space research is being questioned. Each is trying to free itself of its past. Russification and Russian nationalism are being denied, and national cultures are stressed.

Armenia is involved in a dispute with Azerbaijan over two enclaves within each other's borders that belong to the other nationality: Nagorno-Karabakh, an Armenian land in Azerbaijan, and Nakhichevan, an Azeri enclave in Armenia. Fighting has continued on both sides for years. Only the great Russian bear prevented full-scale war. Geidar Aliev has taken over Nakhichevan and conditions have deteriorated to Bosnian levels in some areas. Iran, Turkey, and the United States are providing relief. Armenian fighters have broken through Azeri positions near Nagorno-Karabakh and briefly annexed a strip of land linking it with Armenia. However, Armenia knows that the Azeris have twice the population, and their supply lines have fallen. Refugees are fleeing from the fighting. None of this bodes well for an economy trying to reassert itself. To that end, the government implemented land and industrial privatization. Armenia is also interested in its diaspora, located mainly in Turkey.

Azerbaijan is also suffering from the war. After a number of military reverses, the Azeris toppled their government and set up Surat Hussei-nov as prime minister. Over thirty parties exist in the Parliament, and the government has refused elections because of the war. The Azeris are closely allied with Turkey (they are related by language and culture) and with Iran (which has a large population of 15 million Azeris itself, although they are not agitating to join their independent brothers). Turkey has helped by closing its border with Armenia. They have become very interested in the Soviet Muslim countries and hope to promote secularism over fundamentalism and foreign investment over economic decline.[56] Russia has been making noises about intervening in the civil war; as it is, Russians are concerned with problems on their own borders. Azerbaijan is cutting economic deals with Russia over oil production that could lead to rewards if Russia helps it with Nagorno-Karabakh.[57] Azerbaijan's oil reserves are vital to any rebuilding of their economy. Turkey and the U.S. have been involved in building new pipelines and in development deals.

Belarus is developing its own church and language. One of the first steps was renaming the Republic of Byelorussia as Belarus. However, it was reluctant to become independent and was the republic most anxious for the creation of the Commonwealth of Independent States, which is based there. Leader Stanislav Shushkevich espouses market reforms only weakly. He has found it hard going through his own bureaucratic jungle. Privatization has had a hard time coming. It is well developed industrially and quite sophisticated but it had an interdependent relationship with Russia. It was 100 percent dependent on cheap Russian energy supplies.[58] It also traded nearly exclusively with Russia. Still, Belarus has created a number of banks. A stable republic, it is still likely to remain economically troubled for some time to come.

Estonia has a stable, plural society and economy. Soon after independence, it abandoned the rouble and adopted its own currency, currently the strongest in the former Soviet Union or in neighboring Scandinavia. Bank reserves have grown, and inflation fell to 1.7 percent by mid-1993.[59]

Georgia is a multi-ethnic, paternalistic, authoritarian state that has been the site of ethnic strife since the revolution. Three areas (South Ossetia, Abkhazia, and Ajaria) want independence or self-rule. The Abkhazian revolutionaries have been especially violent, having nearly killed President Eduard Shevardnadze in mid-1993, after which he declared martial law. Abkhazia has asked Russia to make it a protectorate or part of the Russian federation.[60] Georgian politicians have accused Russia of intervening, and there is evidence for that charge. Russia offered to send troops, but Georgia sees them as an invasion force. When Shevardnadze did agree, they did not help.

Georgia privatized most of its agriculture and entered a number of joint ventures.[61] However, the economy is collapsing, and the state has no sources of cheap energy and grain.

Kazakhstan is the largest of the Central Asian countries. With its broad oil- and resource-based economy, Kazakhstan may face a bright economic future. Mostly agricultural, it has the world's largest known unexploited oil field, which could pump up to one million barrels a day. U.S. companies have already set up joint ventures in the oil industry here. Technologically backward Kazakhstan requires Western technology in order to survive. Relatively stable due to President Nursultan Nazarbaev and his Western advisors, it actively seeks foreign investment. Political rights have been expanded, prices liberalized, its privatization plans expanded, and a banking system established.[62] Natural gas and coal reserves are also attractive to Western investors, as are its metals and minerals such as gold, copper, iron ore, zinc, silver, titanium, beryllium, tungsten, and gallium. It also needs water and air pollution control equipment and help to stop the drying of the Aral Sea, all of which it hopes to get from the West.

Kyrgyzstan is tormented by ethnic tensions due to the nationalistic tendencies of the Kyrgyz. It is looking for Western partners to exploit its undeveloped hydroelectric energy and its abundant gold. It also has many rare minerals, all of which could help it recover and move into the 1990s. It adopted a comprehensive foreign investment law and provided for favorable tax relief.

Latvia is still quite economically interdependent with Russia. It has moved more hesitantly toward full market reforms. Latvia has introduced a partly new currency. Its central bank engineered a strengthening of its transitional currency by tight-money policies.[63] Still, it is working toward full reforms.

Lithuania, like Latvia, has also introduced a partly new currency. Inflation has risen, and the exchange rate has fallen. Its central bank reserves are low. *The Economist* predicted, "With the cost of energy from Russia rising, shaky export performance and a reformed communist government not known for economic orthodoxy, prudent Lithuanians may decide to change their litas for a safer and more reliable currency."[64]

Moldova is populated by Romanians who have expressed an interest in reuniting with Romania. Moldova was torn away from Romania in 1941 and, since independence, it has "established a free-trade zone, encourage[d] cultural and economic co-operation, and [formed] a committee to liaise between the two parliaments."[65] Soon after the Revolution, moves toward reunification set off a civil war. Russian-speaking natives of Trans-Dniestria in the east, the home of most of the republic's industry, wanted a separate state joined with Russia, an effort supported by Russian troops. A cease-fire has kept the civil war from going on but has also slowed any moves toward reunification. The urban elite is made up mostly of Russians and Ukrainians who want to transform Moldova.[66] Many of the Moldovians do not speak Romanian very well. Inflation is extremely high and living standards have dropped. Despite this, the government has gone a long way toward establishing a market economy, including privatization of industry and agriculture, encouragement of foreign investment, and the establishment of a banking system and a revamped tax system.

Russia has been struggling with its own moves toward a market economy and democracy. Under Boris Yeltsin, the republic started the reform process, but it has not been an easy experience. In late September and early October 1993, a move was made to impeach Yeltsin, but he called out the troops. A number of government deputies were killed. An election was scheduled for December 12, 1993. Russians were downhearted. Inflation is high and living standards have fallen. Many of the parties that ran in the election rejected the idea of economic reform and want to ease up on them. An ultra-nationalist party, the Liberal Democratic Party led by Vladimir Zhirinovsky, won the majority of votes although Yeltsin remains president. Zhirinovsky is an ultra-nationalist who demands the restoration of the empire, Alaska returned to the Soviets, and the conquering of Finland. He has spouted other fascist rhetoric. Since his election, however, he has not made as many pronouncements. What got him elected was his promise to restore Russia to its former glory and to help with the unemployment and inflation that Yeltsin's economic reforms have caused. His life story is full of holes, outright lies, and exaggerations. He is vulgar and seems to appeal to the lowest common denominator. His failure to solve economic problems immediately will no doubt cut his popularity. Some parts of Russia are also fighting secessionist movements, such as in Chechnya. Still, Russia is interfering in some of its former republics such as the Nagorno-Karabakh, Abkhazia, and North Ossetia disputes. It is a useful diversion of the public's attention from domestic troubles.[67]

Tajikistan is formed of Persian speakers who may seek to join their fellow speakers in Iran. The Tajik government is widely believed to have been helped to power by the Russians. Clan wars have broken out all over the republic. The country has the fourth-largest aluminum production plant in the world and is a major producer of metal-working machine tools.[68] The Americans have been especially interested in conducting business there.

Turkmenistan is a small republic not greatly affected by Sovietization and is still very tribalistic. It has large reserves of natural gas and oil and has instituted free enterprise zones to simplify customs and offers other perks to Western companies.[69] It has concluded several joint venture agreements and seeks to upgrade its own industries with new technology.

Ukraine has begun a process of Ukrainization. By August 1993, the currency had collapsed and hyperinflation began, causing the resignation of its deputy prime minister. Part of the problem is the infighting among the president, prime minister, and parliament.[70] The government had tried to change gradually to a market economy, but this did not work. *The Economist* observed: "Ukraine's economy is collapsing because nationalists secured their country's independence by co-opting, not overthrowing, the local communist elite."[71] The Communists blocked full-scale privatization and stole as much as they could. The only thing that the nationalist-communist coalition can truthfully claim is that they have avoided civil war between the Ukrainian and Russian minorities. The only way for Ukraine to work is for the government to lose in the next elections and for true reformers to be elected.

Uzbekistan is typical of many of the Central Asian states in that the Soviets created it. There was no nationalism here before, no working class or popular government. As Gregory Gleason has written, "The peasants tended to identify with a particular tribe, valley or oasis rather than with some large national group."[72] As a consequence, no significant nationalist problems have arisen. The cultural heart of the area is a tourist attraction. Its economy was basically a cotton monoculture forced upon it by the Soviets with results that will be discussed in the next chapter. The Uzbek government seeks to develop its own processing plants with Western aid. It also has large gold, oil, and natural gas reserves, which it hopes to continue to upgrade.

## CONCLUSION

It is obvious that the economic and social legacy of the Soviet past has not helped the people of its newly independent republics. The costs of technology for the Soviet people and economy were almost impossible to imagine in the Western consumer-oriented economy. Because of the desperate need for the Soviet government to keep up with the West militarily, the ordinary people were sacrificed. They were forced to live in crowded buildings with low-paying jobs and had to stand in line for hours for goods that were of poor quality or may not have even been distributed to the area they lived in. The ordinary person had very little. Because such a low priority was set on the consumer, goods were produced in low-technology factories while military goods were produced in high-tech factories. Before he was overthrown, Gorbachev was trying to end this trend. He was reducing the military and converting military factories into consumer-oriented factories. Joint ventures and cooperatives were helping the ordinary person gain money and good-quality merchandise. Technology was finally beginning to be used to help the population.

## NOTES

1. Harley D. Balzer, *Soviet Science on the Edge of Reform* (Boulder,

Colo.: Westview, 1989), p. 186.

2. Ibid., p. 187.

3. Robert G. Kaiser, *Russia: The People and the Power* (New York: Pocket Books, 1976), p. 317.

4. Vadim Medish, *The Soviet Union*, 3rd edn. (Englewood Cliffs, N.J.: Prentice-Hall, 1987), pp. 65-6.

5. I. Agranorsky et al. *USSR: Questions and Answers* (Moscow: Novosti Press, 1967), p. 183.

6. Joan De Bardeleben, *Soviet Politics in Transition* (Toronto: D. C. Heath, 1992), pp. 158-59.

7. Anna Louise Strong, *The Stalin Era* (New York: Soviet Russia Today, 1956), p. 9.

8. I. V. Stalin, *Sochineniya*, Vol. 13 (Moscow: Politizdat, 1951), p. 39.

9. Alec Nove, *Stalinism and After: The Road to Socialism*, 3rd edn. (Boston: Unwin Hyman, 1989), p. 105.

10. Roy A. Medvedev, *Let History Judge: The Origins and Consequences of Stalinism*. Translated by Colleen Taylor. David Joravsky and Georges Haupt, eds. (New York: Vintage Books, 1971), p. 109.

11. The information from this paragraph is taken from Harry G. Shaffer, "Soviet Economic Performance in Historical Perspective," in *The Soviet Crucible: The Soviet System in Theory and Practice*, 5th edn. (North Scituate, Mass.: Duxbury Press, 1980), p. 295.

12. Alan H. Smith, "Soviet Economic Prospects: Can the Soviet Economic System Survive?" In Martin McCauley, ed., *The Soviet Union After Brezhnev* (London: Heinemann Educational Books, 1983), p. 65.

13. "Constitution (Fundamental Law) of the Union of Soviet Socialist Republics," In Samuel Hendel, ed., *The Soviet Crucible: The Soviet System in Theory and Practice*, 5th edn. (North Scituate, Mass.: Duxbury Press, 1980), pp. 453-61.

14. Kaiser, *Russia*, p. 342.

15. Ibid., p. 346.

16. Ibid., p. 359.

17. Ibid., p. 382.

18. Alec Nove, "An Economy in Transition." In Abraham Brumberg, ed., *Chronicle of a Revolution: A Western-Soviet Inquiry into Perestroika* (New York: Pantheon Books, 1990), p. 54.

19. Ibid., p. 54.

20. Mikhail Gorbachev, *Perestroika: New Thinking for Our Country and the World* (New York: Harper and Row Publishers, 1987), p. 34.

21. *USSR Yearbook '89* (Moscow: Novosti Press Agency Publishing House, 1989), p. 17.

22. Ed A. Hewett, *Reforming the Soviet Economy: Equality versus Efficiency* (Washington, D.C.: Brookings Institution, 1988), pp. 50-52.

23. Judy Shelton, *The Coming Soviet Crash: Gorbachev's Desperate Pursuit of Credit in Western Financial Markets* (New York: Free Press, 1989), p. 78.

24. Ibid., p. 189.

25. Richard E. Ericson, "Economics." In Timothy J. Colton and Robert Legvold, eds., *After the Soviet Union: From Empire to Nations* (New York: W. W. Norton, 1992), p. 67.

26. Harley D. Balzer, *Soviet Science on the Edge of Reform* (Boulder, Colo.: Westview, 1989), p. 102.

27. Ernest Mandel, *Beyond Perestroika: The Future of Gorbachev's USSR*. Translated by Gus Fagan (New York: Verso, 1989), p. 57.

28. Dick Thompson, "The Greening of the USSR," in *Time*, January 2, 1989, p. 60.

29. "Staying On?" *The Economist*, April 28, 1990, p. 11.

30. Abel Aganbegyan, *The Challenge: Economics of Perestroika*. Translated by Pauline M. Tiffen, Michael Barratt Brown, ed. (London: Hutchinson Education, 1988), p. 99.

31. Balzer, *Soviet Science*, p. 183. Much of the discussion on financing is based on information from Balzar, pp. 180-84.

32. Peter Havlik, "Gorbachev's Reform Course Confirmed," In Hubert Gabrisch, ed. *Economic Reforms in Eastern Europe and the Soviet Union* (Boulder, Colo.: Westview, 1989), p. 92.

33. "Russian Management--Perestroika in the Factory," *The Economist*, June 9, 1990, p. 91.

34. Peter Dragadze, "Russia's Embryonic Capitalists," *Forbes*, October 16, 1989. Quoted in Minton Goldman, ed., *Global Studies: The Soviet Union and Eastern Europe*, 3rd edn. (Guilford, Conn.: Dushkin Publishing, 1990), p. 169.

35. Anders Aslund, *Gorbachev's Struggle for Economic Reform--The Soviet Reform Process, 1985-1988* (London: Pinter Publishers, 1989), p. 164.

36. Shelton, *The Coming Soviet Crash*, p. 88.

37. Richard Parker, "Inside the 'Collapsing' Soviet Economy," *Atlantic Monthly*, June 1990, p. 70.

38. Rudolf Hiltunen, "Transferring to a Peaceful Footing." In *Conversion: Goods Instead of Weapons* (Moscow: Novosti Press Agency

Publishing House, 1989), p. 11.

39. Ibid., p. 12.

40. Alexei Kireyev, "Contrasts of Conversion," *Perestroika--A Soviet Monthly Digest*, Vol. 5: May 1990, p. 3.

41. Leonid Vid, "Guns into Butter, Soviet Style," *Bulletin of the Atomic Scientists*, January/February 1990. Quoted in Suzanne P. Ogden, ed., *World Politics 1990/91* (Guilford, Conn.: Dushkin Publishing, 1990), p. 197.

42. Adam Kowalski, "Swords into Chocolate Truffles," *New Scientist*, 11 November 1989, p. 30.

43. Loren Graham, "Science Policy and Organization." In James Cracraft, ed., *The Soviet Union Today*, 2nd edn. (Chicago: University of Chicago Press, 1988), p. 229.

44. Vasili Grigoryev, *The Soviet Union: Facts, Problems, Appraisals* (Moscow: Novosti Press Agency Publishing House, 1987), p. 19.

45. Ibid., p. 20.

46. *Who's Who in the Soviet Government* (Moscow: Novosti Press Agency Publishing House, 1990), p. 126.

47. Ibid., p. 128.

48. Marshall I. Goldman, *Gorbachev's Challenge--Economic Reform in the Age of High Technology* (New York: W. W. Norton, 1987), p. 8.

49. Ibid., pp. 86-87.

50. Michael Rogers with Carroll Bogert, "Red Hackers, Arise!," *Newsweek*, March 20, 1989. Quoted in Minton Goldman, ed., *Global Studies: The Soviet Union and Eastern Europe*, 3rd edn. (Guilford, Conn.: Dushkin Publishing, 1990), p. 171.

51. Philip Hanson, "Soviet Assimilation of Western Technology," in Bruce Parrott, ed., *Trade, Technology and Soviet-American Relations* (Bloomington, Ind.: Indiana University Press, 1985), p. 66.

52. Ibid., p. 68.

53. *Ekonomika izhizn'*, Vol. 6, 1992.

54. *Pravitel'stvennyi vestnik*, Vol. 13, March 1991, p. 11.

55. "Huddled for Comfort," *Banker*, Vol. 143 (805): March 1993, p. 46.

56. "The Transcaucasus: Fiery Food, Fiery Tempers," *The Economist*, Vol. 328 (7821): July 24, 1993, p. 56.

57. "Azerbaijan: The Bear Pauses," *The Economist*, Vol. 329 (7841): December 11, 1993, p. 62.

58. "Huddled for Comfort," p. 46.

59. "Baltic States: Kroons, Lats, Litas," *The Economist*, Vol. 328

(7818): July 3, 1993, p. 50.

60. "The Transcaucasus," p. 56.

61. R. Scott Marshal, "Caucasus, Moldova--Future Depends on Reform," *Business America*, Vol. 114 (8): April 19, 1993, p. 28.

62. Rashmi Nehra, "Kazakhstan Has an Abundance of Oil and Other Resources," *Business America*, Vol. 114 (18): September 6, 1993, p. 4.

63. "Baltic States," p. 50.

64. Ibid.

65. "Huddled for Comfort," p. 47.

66. "Bessarabian Homesick Blues," *The Economist*, Vol. 329 (7835): October 30, 1993, p. 62.

67. Peter Galuszka, "Is Russia 'Trying to Recapture Lost Lands'?" *Business Week*, Vol. 114 (17): August 30, 1993, p. 57.

68. Eric T. Bruder and Kathleen A. Scanlan, "Central Asia: A New Business Frontier," *Business America*, Vol. 114 (18): September 6, 1993, p. 2.

69. Pamela Feodoroff, "Central Asia Trade Channels are Opening," *Business America*, Vol. 114 (8): April 1993, p. 28.

70. "Ukraine Over the Brink," *The Economist*, Vol. 328 (7827): September 4, 1993, p. 45.

71. Ibid.

72. Gregory Gleason, "Uzbekistan: From Statehood to Nationhood." In Ian Bremner and Ray Taras, eds., *Nation and Politics in the Soviet Successor States* (Cambridge, England: Cambridge University Press, 1993), p. 335.

*Chapter 7*

# The Ecological Fallout

The Soviet propensity for industrialization at all costs and their obsessive need to stay abreast of Western technology led to a disaster beyond their imagining. The Soviet landscape was literally poisoned and the Soviet people along with it. Their technological backwardness probably kept them from further economic catastrophe. The collapse of the Soviet Union was, at least partially, politically and economically linked to Soviet industrialization policies that had catastrophic effects on the environment. The Soviet Union had been systematically polluting its land, air, and water reserves since Stalin's first great industrialization drive. In the process, it adversely affected its greatest resource--the people. The environmental destruction was of such a magnitude that the future of unborn generations has been threatened and the children of this generation are, in some cases, doomed to early illness and death. Environmental analyst Dr. Grigory Matveyevich Barenboim, in an interview in late 1990, went so far as to say:

There is no worse ecological situation in the planet than ours in the USSR. . . . Pyotr Chadayev said 150 years ago that it was Russia's fate to serve as an example to the world of how not to live. I would say that we have become both an environmental testing ground for the whole world and an ecological threat to the entire planet.[1]

Yet, despite the sacrifices, the image of the Soviet Union as a techno-superpower proved to be a grave one. Its technological might had, in retrospect, shown itself to be a half-truth. Its technology moved ahead in leaps and bounds, but this progress was fragmented and unsteady. Lapses in research and development as well as in Soviet policymaking resulted in as many problems as there were advances. The Soviets were barely able to stay abreast of the scientific advances made in the West, with gaps in their programs, particularly in safety measures. They proved to be good at developing the poison but forgot to invent the antidote.

The damage to the environment and to the health of the people, combined with a flawed and faulty economy, helped to weaken Soviet society from within, leading to the eventual demise of the Soviet state. The unavoidable health effects related to disastrous Soviet environmental policies and the inability of the Soviet medical apparatus to address these problems raised doubts among the citizens of the USSR about the Communists' legitimacy. Among the causes of this health crisis were "inadequate diet; pervasive alcoholism; cramped living conditions; dirty, noisy and dangerous workplaces and poor sanitation."[2] Only capitalist societies were supposed to have such problems. In fact, whenever anything was published on environmental degradation, the causes were placed squarely at the feet of the capitalist exploiters and their industries. Socialism was touted as a solution to the problem.

Soviet-sponsored "ecocide" helped to unite peoples within the various republics, adding a new dimension and impetus to nationalism. The final disintegration of the Soviet Union and much of the present conflict within and between republics can be attributed to nationalism. The immediacy and universality of environmental problems were the catalyst for the rebirth of this nationalism. The damage done to the various republics by Moscow's environmental policies, or lack thereof, was seen by many grass-roots organizations as a type of Soviet (read here, Russian) domination. Many of the republics already felt as if they were colonies to be exploited in the same way that the Western capitalists were exploiting their colonies (as Lenin had written about). This was the common perception in Central Asia especially. Their machine building, food, and fuel-processing capabilities were kept at a low level by Moscow. They were to produce cotton at all costs with little other option. Yet this cotton was then taken out of the region and processed in Russia or one of the other republics. Their resources were mercilessly taken by the Soviets in return for a backward industrial base and poor living conditions. Soviets used their areas as a toxic waste dump to get rid of their own pollution. One such site was immediately outside the heavily populated city of Tashkent in Uzbekistan. Other republics complained about unwanted nuclear reactors, such as the Ignalina nuclear reactor in Lithuania, and industrially polluted waste.

Environmental awareness was originally promoted by popular fronts that pushed for the cleanup of their own individual republics. Over time, environmental demands became political demands and the fronts demanded independence. The Soviets brought much of this upon themselves. Their "self-inflicted social and ecological wounds, compounding and compounded by its economic and political failures, sapped Soviet military strength and undermined Moscow's pretense to global influence."[3]

But perhaps some of this laxness can be explained by general Soviet attitudes toward nature. In the early nineteenth century, those who thought that the future of Russia required a shift toward the West saw nature as something to be manipulated and exploited for industrialization. Slavophiles (who wanted to keep the Russian culture intact) took on more traditional Russian attitudes and emphasized humanity's unity with nature.[4] Peasants knew how to revere and subtly use nature for their own benefit. Of course, when the Communists came to power, they took the Westernizers' view and chose to exploit nature for all it was worth:

The official outlook is best expressed in the optimistic dictum that man's ability to provide for his needs grows in rough proportion to his increasing numbers and technical sophistication. In other words, the problems of resource depletion, pollution, and overpopulation will be solved by improved technology; new food sources will be found and natural raw materials will be replaced by synthetics. Little thought is given to the environmental impact of such drastic technological solutions on animal and plant ecosystems other than those directly linked to man, to say nothing of the psychological and social traumas that would ensue.[5]

The environmental problems of the former Soviet Union are manifold and the damage is too extensive to be examined in its entirety here. However, it is necessary to give some basic statistics in order to illustrate the dire situation of the former Soviet Union. As a consequence of Soviet industrial policies, 70 million people out of 190 million citizens in over 100 cities were literally poisoned, causing numerous diseases and chronic conditions to develop. The air in these areas often contained five times and more the recognized limit of pollutants. Specific harmful compounds can reach up to 200 or 300 times the allowed amounts.[6] Let us examine these statistics more closely and by category.

## WATER POLLUTION

In 1989, it was estimated that 32.7 billion cubic meters out of 44 billion were polluted in the Soviet Union.[7] The Sea of Azov, the Black Sea, and the Caspian Sea were poisoned by untreated waterborne, agricultural, and industrial waste.[8] The Volga, Dnieper, and Don rivers as well as a plethora of smaller tributaries were turned into "open sewers."[9] The lack of sewage treatment caused a great accumulation of algae that choked rivers and lakes. Most of the large cities had some sort of sewage treatment but it was inadequate. Frequently, the smaller cities and rural areas had no sewage treatment whatsoever. Often, many collective farms did not even have piped water. Oil leaked into rivers through agricultural and industrial spills. Rivers were known to burst into flame when matches or cigarettes were carelessly thrown into them. The Volga burned for hours in 1970 and the Azov is known to contain a high concentration of oil and other chemicals. The resulting oxygen deficiency of the water caused fish to die in great numbers. In other rivers, PCBs and DDTs contaminated the fish so that they could not be eaten. Many fish died trying to swim up polluted rivers to spawn. Sodium, chlorine, and sulphur salts made rivers as salty as oceans. Runoff waters from mines caused rivers to run black with coal dust. Most industries located near water released some sort of pollutant. Most lakes and rivers were not safe to swim in and beaches were closed. Since water was considered a free commodity, too much was often wasted by individuals, agricultural workers, and industries. In many ways, water could have been recycled.

Two of the most polluted waters in the Soviet Union were the Caspian and Aral seas. Both had water flowing into them; evaporation kept them from overflowing. Both were scenic holiday retreats and homes to quite large fishing fleets, the Caspian being especially known for its caviar. The Soviets began diverting water from the rivers, feeding these seas mainly for irrigation purposes, which resulted in dropping water levels of both. As a result of this and of the runoff from agricultural land, itself poisoned with tons of chemical fertilizers and pesticides, the fish died out in the Aral in 1983. The threat to the Caspian caviar beds was very real. A cannery in one Kazakh city that processed its fleet's fish had to have fish brought in from Russia because its town was miles from the water. The Aral, formerly the fourth-largest inland body of water, shrunk in volume by two-thirds, and its surface area decreased by about 44 percent.[10] Its levels have dropped so much that ships rest on sand looking like large children's toys abandoned in a sandbox, miles from any water. This was mainly because many of the rivers sustaining the sea (including the two main ones, the Syr Darya and Amu Darya) dried up because of chemical contamination including, but not exclusively, nitrites, nitrates, ammonia, and phosphates and the diversion of their courses for irrigation. Often the irrigation process was ineffective, with up to 90 percent of the water lost. Irrigation ditches were left unlined so that the water, often polluted by agricultural, industrial, or human wastes, simply seeped into the ground without ever having irrigated anything.[11] The farm workers also used collecting basins for water to be used eventually for irrigation: "When full, these basins destroyed plant life on the bottom; when empty, they allowed the soil, no longer protected by plant growth, to be carried away."[12]

A further poisoning of the land and the people resulted from the death of the Aral. Sand and salt contaminated by chemical runoff from farms was left exposed on the dried seabed. In some areas, salt now covers the earth like snow. This waste was carried by the wind, often as far as a thousand miles, where it poisoned other fields, rivers, and groundwater reserves, causing throat cancer, hepatitis, and respiratory diseases.[13] Even the climate has changed around the Aral. The sea used to moderate the incredible heat; it no longer does.

The Aral issue helped to raise Central Asian nationalism in Uzbekistan, Kazakhstan, and Turkmenistan. There were even calls to evacuate the area. James Critchlow has written:

Increased infant mortality in the Aral region, colder winters and hotter summers, clouds of salt and sand carried by wind, a result of erosion from the dried-up sea-bed; all of these were tangible phenomena that could be traced directly to the central government's plundering and mismanagement of the region's water resources. As a symbol of environmental abuse, the Aral heightened public outrage over what outsiders had done to the Central Asian homeland.[14]

When the sea began to drop, so did cotton production, which the Soviets had insisted on as their major product. The peasants were forced to give up their own lands, and because of the loss of their own garden plots, their diets worsened, resulting in malnutrition.

Because of Central Asia's water shortage, there were plans to divert two Siberian rivers running north into the Arctic Ocean, the Ob and lower Irtysh, so that they would run southward. Two plans were discussed. One would use the natural incline system but that would have resulted in vast areas of farmland and forests being flooded. That plan was generally rejected in favor of a series of pumping stations that would need immense amounts of electricity to run. Leaders Nikita Khrushchev, Leonid Brezhnev, and Konstantin Chernenko were all enthusiastic about the project. Other canal projects, like the White Sea-Baltic and Volga-Don canals, had flooded vast areas with decidedly uneven success. Unlike other similar great projects, there was public discussion of the process. The Russian intelligentsia opposed the plan, as did a grass-roots movement. It was felt that the project would lead to vast ecological destruction in the North and in Central Asia and that it would be too expensive. When Gorbachev began discussing the project, a movement called the Russian Party began to defend the Russian environment and culture by taking an aggressive chauvinistic view against Central Asians.[15] Its members also agreed that the project was unviable economically and asserted that more than water was needed to increase production.[16] In 1986, all work was ended on the project. This angered the Central Asians, who were desperate for more water and looked upon this cancelation as yet another example of Russian domination and demands for higher production while failing to help to achieve it.

To add to the problem in Uzbekistan, a gigantic chemical plant was built in Navoi in the 1970s that consumed 50 million cubic meters of water per year. Half of this was lost in production and the other half was polluted. The same volume could have been used to irrigate 6,000 hectares of cotton.[17] The irony is that most of the chemicals were sent to areas that did not have water problems.

Rivers and seas, including Lake Lagoda, the Volga, Lake Balkhash, and the Caspian, Aral, and Black seas, were further damaged because of carelessly planned irrigation projects. In the mad drive to make an ever increasing amount of land arable, the Soviets drained more lakes and other bodies of water dry and nearly dry. It was calculated by the Soviet state that using the Caspian, for example, for irrigation and letting it dry to expose valuable minerals and salts would offset any losses to fishing and transportation.[18] Ze'ev Wolfson, who wrote under the name Boris Komarov, said in disgust: "In what other economy would it be possible to squander thousands of rubles digging drainage canals and destroying lakes when it was known beforehand that no one would benefit at all from it?"[19]

Twelve percent of Soviet drinking water was polluted, but this figure is deceiving. Where there was a higher population density, there was also more pollution. The areas with the highest population density, the

Caucasus and the region west of the Ural mountains, for example, had only 16 percent of the total potable water.[20] This suggested that there was a true dearth of clean drinking water. As a result, cholera and parasitic diseases were on the rise.

Another cause of the Soviet ecocide was the proliferation of giant projects favored by its policymakers. From Stalin's first five-year plan (including the building of a canal from the Baltic to the White Sea mentioned above) to the point that the Soviets could no longer afford them, the USSR was driven to create industrial monoliths as examples of the might of the Soviet Union. Giant prestige projects were carried out without regard for efficiency or need. Often these projects resulted in unnecessary waste and failure, as in the case of the plant at Lake Baikal in Siberia.

Lake Baikal, the world's deepest freshwater lake, fell victim to industrial pollution by way of these gigantic projects. A cellulose-cord processing factory was built there in 1964 to produce heavy-duty tire cord for the military. Before the factory at Baikalsk was fully operational, the Soviet Union switched to a type of petroleum-based cord. The Lake Baikal factory continued to produce a product that was no longer needed.

Baikal was the home of over 1,200 unique aquatic life forms including the world's only freshwater seals. Because of the unique purity of its water, Baikal was considered a pristine example of nature at its finest. When a study was done to show what could result from industrial expansion here, the specialists were told to change their results to follow the Soviet government's desires more closely. The builders ignored the fact that earthquakes had occurred in the area and could occur again. Logging in the area caused much erosion of the land.

The people of the area quickly realized what was happening to their precious lake. The first protesters were called "enemies of the people," a title that usually led to imprisonment or, in extreme cases, execution. Even after the factories were built, controversy continued despite gag orders. Promises to keep things running safely were not kept. By 1986, one reserve and two national parks were created on Baikal. In 1987, the cellulose-cord factory was ordered shut down but it was not. In the end, it was making 50 percent less cord, 3,000 tons of brown wrapping paper, and 100,000 tons of nutrient yeast for pig fodder, all of which could be made elsewhere.[21] The factory was losing its efficiency as the water it required became impure and Baikal's water was tainted. Donald Kelley, Kenneth Stunkel, and Richard Wescott said: "Ironically, the much disputed Baikal pulp mill now finds it necessary to treat water it uses because the lake's natural circulation returns the mill's own wastes to the intake pipes."[22] Thus, one of the oldest ecosystems in existence was almost destroyed.[23] Scientists have said that only if all industry and the local towns were abandoned could Baikal completely recover; this is unlikely in the near future.

## AGRICULTURAL/LAND POLLUTION

To compensate for the lack of productivity on collective farms, Soviet agricultural policies called for the careless overuse of toxic agricultural chemicals. From 1965 to 1989, there was a 250 percent rise in the use of chemicals for farming.[24] Fertilizers, pesticides, and herbicides were spread lavishly on fields to the point that they did far more harm than good. One instance that illustrated the Soviet disregard for the environment and welfare of its people was the fact that tons of DDT were used on Soviet crops long after other nations had banned its use. Twenty-five million acres of cropland remain poisoned.[25] Central Asia, in particular, suffered from this policy. In order to increase cotton production, pesticides and defoliants were used heedlessly. The most significant result of this abuse was the drying up of the Aral Sea. All of this destruction occurred despite the fact that sewage recycling could easily have been used to fertilize crops. Thus, the overuse of fertilizers (along with lumbering, and heavy industry) was among the country's biggest polluters.

The health problems caused by agricultural pollution were many and interconnected. Food was poisoned by the overuse of chemicals. Produce and livestock were defiled by the toxins contaminating the soil. Much of the farming in the Soviet Union was done using primitive methods. The symbolic scythe was still very much in use. Due to this lapse in Soviet technology (which is to say, the Soviet lapse in distributing technology to the masses), these farming methods put those who toiled in the fields at even greater risk to the dangers caused by pollution. Agrarian workers worked unprotected amid these harmful chemicals and, as a result, developed skin and respiratory diseases from constant contact. Often the victims were the children who shared in the labor. It was proven that only 10 percent of the pesticides controlled the insects they were meant to attack.[26] The republics most affected were those in Central Asia, the Caucasus, and the Ukraine, although the situation affected everyone as the chemically poisoned food ended up on the shelves of stores countrywide.

Cotton was perhaps the most damaging crop to be raised in the former Soviet Union. Like every other industry, it was the subject of economic plans despite the fact that it is exceptionally hard to plan and predict crops. In sometimes vain attempts to increase production at Moscow's insistence, normal planting practices were ignored. Harvesting machinery broke up the soil; pesticides killed not only the insects but any animal life in the area. Crop rotation was also ignored. Cotton is planted on the same field year after year, resulting in the loss of nutrients in the soil and subsequently in lower crop yields. The Uzbeks, for example, used to rotate alfalfa, which enriched the soil, with cotton. The alfalfa also allowed farmers to keep livestock, which in turn provided organic fertilizer for the cotton. Boris Rumer has written, "But under constant pressure from Moscow to increase production at any price, it was impossible to let the soil rest. The classic cycle--cotton, alfalfa, manure, cotton--was broken."[27] Thus it can be said, "Wherever it is farmed, cotton consumes not just land and water, but people as well."[28]

As a result of these lower crop yields, officials had to falsify records in order to pass all demands for higher production. In 1983, this was discovered and a large number of officials in Central Asia were purged. Most were charged with bribetaking and exaggerating their reports. The prosecutor's office in Moscow sent investigators, led by Tel'man Gdlyan, to investigate. Over several years, many were questioned and arrested, although many were acquitted because the investigators were using illegal methods to extract information. Most were Uzbek and the rest were mostly Muslim, as if Russians could have no part in corruption. To be truthful, many were open to bribery (including Brezhnev's son-in-law). However, there were some who were truly trying to help. The Uzbek people were outraged. They justifiably felt victimized and that "the chief target of "corruption" was the central economic apparatus in Moscow, perceived as a monster of tyranny and exploitation encroaching ruthlessly on Uzbek well-being."[29] This was one contributing factor of the rise of Uzbek and Central Asian nationalism.

Fertile soil was used for factories, mines, other non-agricultural purposes or it was flooded by hydroelectric dams. Swampland, on the other hand, was drained, destroying berrying and hunting grounds as well as causing rivers to dry up.[30] When these areas proved to be infertile, trees were planted, most of which developed diseases. These diseases were subsequently passed on to healthy forests, causing many trees to die out.[31] Careless logging caused erosion because new trees were not planted. In this manner, arable land was further destroyed.

The cutting of grass, trees, and other foliage as well as the uncontrolled grazing of animals in Central Asia caused sand to encroach at alarming rates. The desertification began to increase until cities had to plant trees to counter this dangerous trend. Domestic and industrial dumps took up hundreds of thousands of kilometers throughout the Soviet Union. The only thing that prevented their being overrun was that paper, metal, bottles, and other goods were in such short supply that they had to be recycled. They also did not have such things as disposable diapers, which clog Western dumps.

Toxins released in accidents destroyed valuable hectares of land. Industries briefly began to inject toxins into the deep layers of the Earth with no thought or study into the consequences of such actions. The result was groundwater pollution and the poisoning of the land itself, which made it useless for agriculture.

Large tracts of land were destroyed by half-used mines. Once it became harder to find minerals, the mines were abandoned for more lucrative sites, leaving large amounts of minerals and destroying new sites. Part of the reason for this general disregard for the land was that it was considered a free commodity, like water.

## INDUSTRIAL/NOISE POLLUTION

Another cause of pollution in the former Soviet Union was laid at the feet of industry. Health problems related to industrial pollution were similar to those caused by agriculture. Industrialization was pursued at a reckless speed from the Stalin era onward, without even token consideration for safety or environmental protection measures. Its priority over consumer goods only sped up the load of effluents released into the environment. Merit was based on gross output.

Bureaucrats have long been evaluated and rewarded only in terms of gross output. Rivers were fouled and forests stripped in the rush to transform raw materials into material wealth. No premium was placed on efficiency and no environmental concerns restrained industrialization.[32]

Factory managers were under pressure to fulfill their goals at all costs. Any fines collected against the offending companies did not go toward paying the cost of cleaning the environmental mess the company had made. Instead, the money was reallocated to finance other industries and to increase industrial output (or back to the company itself). Often, several ministries would be involved in the cleanup, and they would rarely cooperate. Instead, they preferred to argue about who was to blame or how much each should contribute to the pot. Thus, "as long as enterprises have no real economic interest in ecologically clean technologies, forcing them to adopt such processes is more or less like forcing a cat to eat cucumbers by giving it a lecture on the benefits of vegetarianism."[33] As the Soviet Union disintegrated politically and economically, so did its industries. Factories and other installations were literally crumbling from misuse, lack of proper maintenance, and a total disregard for primitive working conditions.

Many industrial installations (such as iron smelters) were either moved from locations in the western part of the Soviet Union or hurriedly constructed behind the Ural mountains during World War II. Originally built for emergency conditions and to escape the advancing German army, few were modernized or re-equipped.[34] Instead, the factories were called upon to fulfill impossible plans with little time to modernize.

Soviet industrial practices polluted the air, land, and water. Untreated industrial wastes were pumped into the air and nearby bodies of water, destroying wildlife and harming residents. Recycling of raw materials was ignored. Pollution control devices, when they existed, were primitive and sometimes left unused because they impeded productivity.[35] Sanitary inspectors were known to take bribes. Associated with industrial pollution was exhaust from automobiles. While the Soviet Union had far fewer public and private vehicles than the United States, they were rarely equipped with any sort of purification device.[36]

Noise pollution was also a problem, particularly in cities. The levels in cities and factories from traffic, thin-walled apartment complexes, machinery, and a thousand other sources have been proven to cause problems with nerves, fatigue, and cardiovascular disease. Cars and trucks are poorly muffled and, since traffic patterns are extremely poor in Soviet cities, horns are used constantly. Added to this was the noise of heavy machinery in the large factories many worked in. The worker could not even find peace at home. Most lived in communal apartments where the walls were nearly paper-thin and poorly soundproofed. No one could be truly free from noise: "Effective noise-pollution control has proven difficult in the Soviet Union because of the low priority attached to such quality-of-life issues and the lax enforcement of existing standards."[37] Thus, people had this constant strain on their nerves and no one did anything about it.

## AIR POLLUTION

The air in many Soviet cities was nearly as filthy to breathe as their polluted water was to drink. Mercury, lead, chlorine, carbon monoxide, and sulphur dioxide existed in the air at many times the legally allowed limits. Millions of rubles worth of valuable raw materials were discharged annually into the atmosphere, raw materials that could have been filtered and reused.[38] Soot from smokestacks or dust often turned the snow into a dirty gray mess. A city in the Ural mountains created a workers' brigade to clean the dirt and soot off the roofs of buildings every three months; otherwise they would collapse from the sheer weight. In another city, window panes frequently had to be replaced because they became thin and brittle from all of the acid in the air.[39] The incidence of lung cancer doubled between 1970 and 1980.[40] The number of cities with unsafe levels of air pollution was staggering. Nearly every republic was represented. Examples were: Moscow, Leningrad, Minsk, Tyumen, Kharkov, Odessa, Yerevan, Baku, Tashkent, Fergana, Frunze, and Alma Ata. Over 60 million tons of pollutants were in the Soviet atmosphere.[41]

Magnitogorsk, a planned industrial city at the southern tip of the Urals, exemplified the fate of most major industrial cities in every republic of the Soviet Union. Magnitogorsk was considered one of the most polluted cities in the former USSR.[42] Pictures of the city showed an array of smokestacks spewing orange exhaust into the sky. Once considered a monument to Stalin's new breed of industrial supermen, it was a painful reminder of the human and environmental costs of reckless industrialization.

In this city of approximately 223,000 people, 34 percent of all adults and 67 percent of children under the age of fifteen developed respiratory illnesses. Such illnesses included advanced emphysema and lung cancer. Between 1980 and 1991 birth defects in Magnitorgorsk doubled;[43] however, "there were few if any other Soviet cities where industrial workers could find markedly better conditions, truly clean air and, overall, safer living conditions."[44] This air pollution affected not only the Soviet Union but also the rest of the world. The Soviets contributed more than their fair share toward acid rain and the hole in the ozone layer. Often the air was so foul that trees and wildlife would die for miles around factory cities. This and deforestation cost the Soviets in lost oxygen production. Areas bordering the USSR also had to deal with their legacy, much as Canada must deal with American-produced acid rain.

## NUCLEAR POLLUTION

Nuclear pollution was another culprit behind the devastation of the Soviet Union. Several regions were contaminated due to accidents at nuclear reactors, careless storage of nuclear waste, and atomic weapons testing. The Soviets dumped nuclear waste in the Barents Sea for thirty years. In the 1950s, they dumped nuclear waste in lakes and rivers. In fact, to this day, a person can get a lethal dose of radiation in less than one hour standing on the bank of Karachai Lake.[45] In Kazakhstan, near Semey, lies a body of water called Atomic Lake by the residents. It was created as a reservoir by the explosion of a shallow underground device in 1965. The downwind population was exposed to large amounts of vented radiation. "Over the years," Mike Edwards has written, "the Soviets used scores of nuclear devices for other 'peaceful' purposes like diamond mining and stanching oil-well fires."[46]

After 1949, aboveground nuclear testing was carried out in Kazakhstan and other Central Asian republics, as well as in the far north.[47] More often than not, those living near test sites were never informed of the testing, let alone the possible dangers from radiation. Northeastern Kazakhstan was the home of a Soviet nuclear test site that nearly caused earthquakes. Almost 500 nuclear tests were conducted there before Gorbachev, who listened to protesters, closed it in 1990. Most were underground but some were above. After explosions, unprotected and uninformed villagers would be examined by military doctors. People began to ask questions but it was not until reports of high levels of chromosome damage and stillbirths in the region and predictions of high rates of leukemia and thyroid cancer were issued that information was available.[48] The village of Dolon was drenched with the fallout from the first atomic test in the Soviet Union in 1949. Birth defects rose by over 150 percent in the area.[49] The Soviet Union was essentially turned into a nuclear waste dump.[50]

The meltdown at Chernobyl in 1986, while one of the most devastating accidents, was only the tip of the iceberg. Beginning in 1990, the Soviet Union declassified information that disclosed a list of nuclear accidents that occurred between 1964 and 1985. These accidents happened in various republics, from Armenia to the Ukraine to Kazakhstan. The amount of radiation emitted from these accidents was reportedly unknown. The most disturbing fact of these disclosures was that there was, in some cases more than one accident per station.[51] Of the thirty-seven reactors that operated in the Soviet Union, over half of them had enough safety violations to warrant closure.

In February 1958, in the town of Kyshtym in the Ural mountains, a nuclear waste dump exploded, causing the evacuation of many villages and farms. Winds carried contaminated soil over a thousand square miles and radioactive clouds for dozens of miles. The area is still considered dangerous.

It is completely unknown how many hundreds or thousands of Gulag prisoners died of radiation illnesses from mining uranium or working in nuclear plants. Safety measures were often ignored, and the dying prisoners were often dispassionately and cruelly used as lab rats for medical research. Other nuclear accidents happened during hydrogen bomb tests, at nuclear power plants, involving nuclear weapons, and during underground nuclear tests. Nuclearpowered ships and submarines were not immune to accidents. In 1966, a reactor meltdown occurred on the icebreaker Lenin. Submarines were so notorious for their nuclear instability that the joke was: How do you tell a man is from the Northern fleet (submarine fleet)? He glows in the dark.[52]

In April 1986, the Chernobyl nuclear plant, only two-thirds completed, was rocked by two explosions that blew apart the No. 4 reactor. Several tons of radioactive minerals were released into the atmosphere. The cause of the accident is not precisely known, although it is known that a test run, which had not been approved, was being carried out with all of the safety systems, including the core cooling system, shut down. The operators had been trying to finish the test quickly because it had been delayed. Normal procedures were ignored, and the emergency shutdown signals were turned off. Power built up too quickly in the core and blew the reactor apart.[53]

The Soviets did not acknowledge the accident until Swedish instruments began to pick up the increased radiation that rained down on Eastern Europe and the Soviet Union. Over 100,000 people were evacuated from their homes, some not until months later: "Outside the twenty-mile zone, authorities made rough judgement calls, evacuating some villages, such as Bober, but leaving others intact, such as Maryanivka, even though radiation exceeded norms. The housing shortage was a factor."[54] Seven years later, a National Geographic team visited a town sixty miles from Kiev called Bober. It found stark empty houses containing the remnants of people's lives--an old shoe, a jacket. Radioactive cesium 137 and strontium 90 fell on the village after Chernobyl and will continue to remain unsafe for centuries.[55] Thousands of people were involved in cleaning up and burying the core with concrete. Even now, the core remains radioactive and it is doubtful that the shield is enough. Another will have to be built. Thirty-one people were known to have died, mostly firemen who first arrived to stop the fires burning out of control. However, it is estimated that tens of thousands of people were exposed to severe radiation and could develop cancer and other diseases.

The effects of Chernobyl were widespread. Over 2.5 million acres were contaminated in the Ukraine and Byelorussia.[56] Restrictions on the consumption of certain foods were imposed on fifteen regions, affecting 75 million people.[57] Because of the speed with which contaminated grass can affect cow's milk, dairy products were banned, 50 percent being judged unfit for human consumption. Milk was made into cheese and butter to wait for the radioactivity to decline.[58] Meat supplies were similarly affected. Contaminated grain was used as food for animals except for those that would be killed within two months, because authorities believed it would take that long to cleanse them.[59]

The accident also affected Europe and Asia. In Poland, Germany, Austria, and Hungary, nearly $200 million worth of agricultural produce was destroyed.[60] In Finland, Sweden, and Norway, large herds of reindeer had to be destroyed. As a result of the scare, an EC ban was placed on fresh foods from Eastern Europe, including areas of the USSR, Poland, Czechoslovakia, Hungary, Bulgaria, Romania, and parts of Yugoslavia.

The Soviets appear to have learned little from their mistakes. After Chernobyl, there were other accidents, though not of the same proportions. For example, in 1989, at a facility in Kursk within the Russian Republic, radioactive water was allowed to spill onto the floor of the plant, overflowing into the territory surrounding the reactor. In that year, there were 118 unplanned shutdowns and 100 unscheduled "reductions of capacity."[61] This indicated that conditions at these reactors did not improve and posed a grave threat to those working in or living around the stations.

As mentioned before, poorly contained nuclear waste was dumped in the various republics of the former Soviet Union. In the Siberian city of Novosibirsk, radioactive ampules from scientific and industrial instrumentation were thrown into streets and yards. Other areas of Novosibirsk were further contaminated because of the theft of state property. Citizens stole radioactive bricks and other scrap material and built sheds and other domestic constructions.[62]

Since the dismantlement of the Soviet Union and the economic and political chaos that followed, the former USSR's nuclear arsenal has also

deteriorated. Nuclear-powered submarines leaked radiation into the
Arctic, and nothing was done to rectify this. With responsibility in
question and funds for maintenance scarce, the stockpiled warheads were
also a possible threat.

Radiation spread in the same way as chemical pollutants. Wind
carried radioactive sand from republic to republic. Radioactive produce
and meat from livestock in contaminated areas in the Ukraine, Georgia,
or Kazakhstan were sold in Russia and Belarus. For instance, after the
Chernobyl accident, 2000 head of cattle, pigs, and horses were evacuated
from a collective farm in the Ukraine. They were discovered to be
contaminated and were slaughtered. The meat was sold. Soviet health
authorities concluded that radioactivity had not yet affected the meat.[63]

Nuclear accidents affected not only the Soviet Union but also the rest
of the world. An example was the disintegration of radioactive satellites
in the earth's atmosphere. The Soviets rarely told the West when a
satellite was about to crash. In January 1978, Cosmos 954 crashed in
northern Canada, scattering dangerous radioactive material over miles of
land. The Soviets never informed the Canadian government what to look
for until everything had been recovered. They paid for damages but only
half of what Canada asked for. The satellite had passed over some of the
most populated areas in the world before it crashed and could have ir-
radiated many people. The same thing happened in 1983, but parts of
Cosmos 1402 landed in the South Atlantic and Indian oceans. The
Soviets adopted a cavalier attitude to all of this: "The orbiting reactor
graveyard, in Moscow's eyes, does not exist, and therefore, there can be
no danger from it, nor any Soviet responsibility for it."[64]

The effects of radiation contamination were widespread and incon-
clusive. Soviet authorities were both unable and unwilling to give even
approximate figures as to exactly how many people were (and continued
to be) affected by Chernobyl and other accidents. However, some say
that Chernobyl "triggered an interest in conserving energy. An anti-
nuclear--and, in turn, broadly environmental--movement gathered across
the Soviet Union."[65] It can therefore be said that Chernobyl was a
precipitator of ecological activism.

## WILDLIFE

Humans were not the only ones to suffer from environmental
disasters in the Soviet Union. There was little in the way of wildlife
conservation. Hunters killed too many animals and birds. Poachers took
more than the hunters. Military helicopters used birds of prey for target

practice and hunted wolves in the winter. Even government officials and high military officers took part in massive hunts in which hundreds of animals and birds were slaughtered. Like many carnivores--including the very rare snow leopard--wolves were suspected of killing sheep and were hunted down and destroyed in considerable numbers when, in fact, the sheep were actually being stolen or poorly managed.[66] In a manner reminiscent of the American buffalo, deer too were slaughtered for their tongues only. Game birds were killed by air pollution and made homeless by deforestation and the draining of swamp land. Agriculture took vast areas of land away from the wilderness. Although refuges and reserves were created, they were not safe for the animals and large areas of them were appropriated for roads, government members' *dachas*, and so on. Thus, another resource was rapidly disappearing, although, to be fair, the Soviets did save the beaver, sable, otter, and pine marten (traditional fur animals) and have helped to save the bison, walrus, tiger, polar bear, and wild horse.[67] In mid-February 1994, the World Wildlife Fund announced that since the fall of the Soviet Union, air and water pollution, unregulated logging, and uncontrolled poaching are threatening dozens of species. The group and the Russian government are trying to raise $17 million in order to prevent the extinction of these species.

## HUMAN COSTS

The toll this systematic destruction of the environment took was undeniable. The life expectancy of the Soviet people dropped significantly during the 1980s. Infant mortality rates rose, as did the number of birth defects. There were resurgences of infectious diseases that had been nearly eliminated, such as polio, typhoid, and diphtheria. As well, there was an increase in certain types of cancer. Leukemia, bone, and thyroid cancer were all on the rise, particularly in children. The increase was greatest in areas that were directly affected by nuclear radiation.[68]

The peoples of Central Asia and the Caucasus were perhaps the hardest hit. It was here that the infant mortality rate was the highest. In 1989, 22 percent of all Soviet births were here and 39 percent of all infant deaths.[69] Children here fell victim to parasitic infection more frequently than in other regions. Infants were literally poisoned by their mother's breast milk. There were outbreaks of cholera due to contaminated drinking water, itself caused by insufficient or nonexistent sewage treatment. In Azerbaijan it was reported that 42 percent of women between the ages of twenty and thirty-four were sterile.[70]

Other regions also fell victim to health problems as a direct result of environmental devastation. In Estonia in 1989, hair loss was reported in children, a result of radium emissions from oil and shale mining in the area.[71] A similar type of "chemical balding" was seen in over 200 children in the Ukraine that same year. Accompanying symptoms were stomach cramps and hallucinations.[72]

These were just a few of the more frightening health problems directly caused by pollution and contamination. The damaging effects of environmental degradation were compounded by deficiencies in the Soviet medical system. Conditions in Soviet hospitals were deplorable. Most were overcrowded and some did not have even the simplest amenities such as hot water. Supply shortages always plagued the Soviet Union and medical supplies were no exception. Part of the reason for this was the backdoor trade in medical supplies. Medical doctors were not respected, and in fact were among the lowest-paid professionals in the Soviet system. Thus medical personnel sought bribes to do even the simplest procedures and most cared little about the patients. Many were poorly trained and would not have passed Western medical exams. Most medical equipment was of poor quality, with high-tech equipment being found in only the most exclusive hospitals. Vaccines were not always pure or effective. Although medical care was free in the Soviet Union, only the wealthy were adequately cared for and then only because they could pay for the equipment, supplies, and bribes.

Part of the reason for the rise in infectious diseases such as polio, which had been eradicated in the Soviet Union as it had in the West, was due to the AIDS scare in the mid-1980s. Parents decided not to have their children vaccinated against these diseases as access to a single-use needle could not be assured even in a hospital.[73] Unlike in the West, hypodermic syringes could not be readily bought by the individual. There were, and still are, not enough to go around. Doctors used syringes more than once without regard for the possible transmission of HIV.

To put it simply, the people of the former Soviet Union are sick. Fifty-three percent of all Soviet schoolchildren were considered to be in poor health. The greatest indictment, however, against Soviet environmental policies was the plight of the Red Army. A report from the Red Army's General Staff in 1991 stated that 52 percent of all potential draftees were unfit either physically or mentally for duty.[74] This was ample evidence in itself of how ecocide helped in the demise of the Soviet Union.

## CAUSES

The environmental destruction in the Soviet Union was caused entirely by flaws in the Soviet socialist infrastructure and its reliance on heavy industry. There were flaws in central planning. Projects went ahead regardless of incorrect information. Studies were ignored if they did not produce the desired results or were changed to reflect the ministry's need. Plans were badly coordinated. For example, river and lakes would be diverted for more than a single project, overstraining their capacities. This was also due in part to overlapping administrative jurisdictions.

That is not to say that there were not environmental laws. In 1957, Estonia adopted the Law on the Preservation of Nature. The conservation law of the Russian Republic, adopted in 1960, stated, "Conservation is a major state task and a concern of all people." It covered land, minerals, water, forests, landscape, resort as well as green belt areas, animal life, and the atmosphere.[75] By 1963, all the republics had such laws. However, these laws were not enforced or followed: "The plethora of Soviet laws passed in the late 1950s and in the 1960s demonstrates the accepted approach to the solution of environmental disruption in the USSR seemed to be, if the first law does not work, pass another one."[76]

Soviet agencies did not properly enforce environmental laws and fines levied on offenders were insignificant. If one considered the fact that all industries were state-owned, the idea of having fines in the first place was ridiculous. The only offender to fine was the state itself, which just rerouted the money. If plant managers were fined, the plant itself paid the fine or, if not, it was usually so low that the managers' bonus for increased production exceeded it.

The Soviet Union lagged far behind other industrialized countries in developing waste disposal technology. This was once again an example of Soviet single-sightedness in the drive toward industrialization.

Natural resources in the Soviet Union were treated as free goods and were wrongly believed to be limitless. As well, institutionalized priority was given to production over any sort of conservation.[77]

A state-controlled economy also helped devastate the environment. In the case of agriculture, fertilizers and other chemicals were supplied to collective farmers in abundance. Therefore there was no frugality in their use. In a capitalist society, a farmer, by reason of expense, would not use nearly as much. Soviet land was considered "nobody's land"; therefore there was no great sense of concern for the environment or its protection.

The public did not know how serious the destruction of their environment was. In the 1970s, a ban was placed on publications on the environment for military reasons. As Keith Bush wrote in 1972:

If Soviet society is to combat effectively the environmental by-products of industrialization and modernization, its citizens and officials should have comprehensive data on ecological problems and unimpeded access to the research and experience of other industrialized societies. Until recently, however, there was a tendency to treat pollution--like unemployment, drunkenness, crime, or airplane crashes--as a necessary concomitant of capitalism and to dismiss the ecology campaign in the U.S. as a vehicle for "social demagogy" designed to blunt political opposition.[78]

This blindness to the faults of socialist production caused unbelievable suffering.

After Mikhail Gorbachev came to power, *glasnost* encouraged people to speak out, and awareness increased. At first, "both environmental deterioration and poor consumer goods supply [were] probably viewed as symptomatic of the pervasive inefficiency and skewed priorities in the economic sphere."[79] The popular media upheld the government's myth that pollution was caused by capitalism and that the solution was socialism. The Soviet scholarly media was more apt to attribute the pollution to scientific and technical progress, inadequate research and application, and poor incentives, laws, and organization.[80]

After the people became fully aware of the environmental problems and their discontent merged with the voice of nationalism, the next task at hand was to clean up the mess left by Soviet actions. Despite the desire of activists and the general population to repair the damage, an extensive cleanup of the environment did not take place. The upper-level apparatchiks

may face a potential conflict between the desire for a cleaner environment and hopes of rapidly raising the living standards and consumption levels of the people. Without pollution control, boosting production will befoul the environment even more. And money that goes into anti-pollution equipment cannot be used for industrial expansion.[81]

The economic situation for the republics of the former USSR was bleak and funds to salvage the environment were not available. An effective cleanup campaign entailed high costs that the economically strapped republics would not be able or willing to incur. One of these costs was in lost jobs and decreased production that would follow if culprit factories were shut down permanently or even temporarily for retrofitting with purification equipment. Soviet production of anti-pollution devices was limited in any case.[82] It is hard to justify environmental expenses when people had so little to begin with. Gorbachev's economic restructuring seemed to be the best time to modernize factories and clean the environment. However, the money was put toward propping up the falling economy: "Resources are being put to other uses, such as attracting Western business and building more plants and factories."[83] The environment was ignored.

Another obstacle to a proposed cleanup was in Soviet central planning, which was not completely dismantled. Central planning in the Soviet Union resulted in production monopolies. One factory might have produced up to one-third of a type of commodity. If such a plant was shut down, it would have caused a chain reaction of plant closures, lost jobs, and shortages.

An example of this type of effect happened in the city of Sverdlovsk in 1990. An installation was shut down for environmental, health, and safety reasons. This plant was one of the main producers of a certain type of analgesic used in the manufacture of non-prescription painkillers. As a result of this, several factories producing these painkillers were also closed. The result was an "aspirin famine." However, twelve days after the factory closed down, the roof fell in and crushed all of the machinery.[84] This was yet another example of the literal and figurative disintegration of Soviet industry.

Despite these obstacles, there was reason to believe that the situation would have improved. Part of the reason was the resurgence of nationalism. After Mikhail Gorbachev introduced *glasnost* into Soviet society, some of the earliest criticisms were on behalf of the preservation of the environment. The meltdown at Chernobyl served to increase these concerns and to help the original environmental activists, or Greens, gain the support of the general population.

The initial protests against the state in the early *glasnost* period were directed against Soviet environmental policies rather than for democratization. In the late 1980s, several interest groups were created, including the Social-Ecological Union, Ecological Union, Ecological Foundation, Ecological Society of the Soviet Union, and All-Union Movement of Greens. These began as pressure groups with no political connections but became involved more and more with politics. *Goskompriroda*, the state committee for the protection of the environment, was created in

1988 and handled environmental protection in each republic, but it was essentially powerless. Eventually protesters began to equate the Soviet destruction of the environment with colonial exploitation. "Nobody's land" became "our land." This was the link between the environmental movement and nationalism.

The Green movement was also beneficial to the nationalist movement because it provided an agenda that all within a republic could endorse. Ecological groups were the first to be recognized by the Soviet government while more politically oriented groups were still resisted despite *glasnost*.

When the Soviet Union finally fell apart and free elections were held, environmental groups turned into political parties because they already had the organization in place to effectively campaign and win in the 1991 elections. The emergence of ecopolitics in the Soviet Union therefore was in part responsible for the disintegration of the Communist monopoly of power.

Another culprit was the Soviet military. Suffering from massive budget cuts, it began to disintegrate after its withdrawal from Afghanistan and Eastern Europe. The army could no longer hide its deficiencies. As previously mentioned, most of the young people recruited for the military were physically or mentally unfit for duty. Many also dodged the draft. Minorities were mistreated, and some were even killed under hazing practices. Alcohol and drug abuse were rampant. Over 20 percent of all military deaths were from illness.[85] This can be attributed to the poor quality of physicians and their terrible working conditions. But the military had only itself to blame. The military-industrial complex was by far the largest polluter and the one that had kept such statistics secret.

While the havoc wreaked upon the environment by the Soviet Union cannot be denied, it is necessary to put the situation into perspective. Is the damage truly more terrible than that caused in the West? While most sources confirm this as fact, there were still many discrepancies. Figures and statistics did not always concur. When the Soviet Union opened itself up to public scrutiny, it did so with a vengeance. Party officials and a variety of "experts" were extremely anxious to tell the full story of the failures of the Soviet society. The truth was that the Soviets spent so much time hiding and distorting facts from their own people, as well as the rest of the world, that the truth may never be completely revealed. It was also possible that there were exaggerations by the republics themselves as an indictment against the Communist apparatus. The reason for this would have been to consolidate their own legitimacy.

In a capitalist society, are the people presented with the whole truth at all times? The profit motive in capitalism may also prove to hide much more than it reveals. The West cannot condemn the former Soviet Union when it continues to pollute its own resources. Atomic weapons testing was also carried out in the Nevada desert. Wind blows across the United States as well the republics of the Soviet Union.

## THE LEGACY FOR THE NEW REPUBLICS

Since the fall of the Soviet government, the separate republics have had to take stock of the environmental damage caused by the Soviet government. There is a growing green awareness as information becomes available; there are high expectations of Western wealth and environmental expertise.[86] All of the new republics are enacting environmental protection and impact assessment laws that in turn have given Western companies strict guidelines to follow for any natural resource exploitation. Let us look at the environmental legacy left to each republic.[87]

Armenia suffered from two major ecological disasters: the fallout from Chernobyl and a 1988 earthquake that devastated the area. A shortage of relief supplies exacerbated the problem. Untreated water and toxic chemicals polluting the soil are also problems.

In Azerbaijan, over half of the townships lack sewers; the result is water pollution. The soil is also polluted. The effluents in the Caspian Sea also affect Azerbaijan. The people are blessed with extensive energy resources, which will no doubt bring much to their beleaguered economy.

Belarus received a heavy dose of radiation from Chernobyl and also suffers from the overuse of pesticides.

Estonia must deal with inadequate sewage, the pollution of the Baltic Sea, and foul air created by industry.

In Georgia, the dirty water of the Black Sea has seeped into surface water, which was already polluted by untreated water. This and the overuse of pesticides have resulted in many cases of digestive diseases.

Kazakhstan suffers from the nuclear fallout from above and below-ground atomic tests and leaks from military sites used for dismantling nuclear weapons. As a result, when the independent government came to power, it outlawed nuclear testing. The waterways to the Aral Sea were diverted for irrigation purposes with devastating results. The fishery was ruined and farmlands were destroyed by salt and sand.

Kyrgyzstan also suffers from soil salinity and water pollution, with few homes having piped water. On the other hand, forest reserves increased and the state has been diversifying agriculture.

In Latvia, protests about a paper mill's pollution at Jurmala helped spark the independence movement in 1989. It has suffered from air pollution (mostly from automobiles) and water pollution.

In Lithuania, there has been an increase in childhood diseases through water pollution. The nuclear reactor at Ignalina is of the same design and poses the same dangers as Chernobyl.

Moldova has high rates of disease and infant mortality because of excessive pesticides, fertilizers, and bacterial contamination in the produce industry. There is also water pollution.

In Russia, the Ural city of Chelyabinsk may be the most radioactive place on earth because of spills and toxic waste from a plutonium plant. Deforestation and soil erosion are also problems. Life expectancy has also dropped. The rivers, air, and soil are all poisoned by industries, mines, coal electric plants, nuclear reactors, urban infrastructure, and excessive use of agricultural chemicals.

Tajikistan has inadequate sanitary facilities and suffers from soil salinity. It also has the second-highest infant mortality rate of all the former republics. Tajikistan has begun to diversify its agriculture away from cotton production.

Turkmenistan was severely affected by the cotton monoculture in much the same way as Tajikistan. The Aral and Caspian seas are also causing problems. Food supplies are inadequate, as is the delivery infrastructure. Water supplies are inadequate and, for the most part, unclean. The state has the lowest life expectancy (65.2 years) and highest infant mortality rate in all the former Soviet republics.[88]

Ukraine suffers from industrial and water pollution. An excessive use of fertilizers has caused decay in the Black Sea. The fallout from Chernobyl continues to affect the people there. Up to one-tenth of Ukrainian land is contaminated and the cancer rate continues to grow.

Uzbekistan also suffers from the cotton monoculture, particularly after a 50 percent increase in irrigation. Water quality is bad, especially in the Aral Sea. Industrial pollution was one of the underlying causes of the 1989 ethnic riots in the Ferghana Valley.

Overall, the life expectancy of the former Soviet Union was 70.0 years, lower than in Europe, Canada, or the United States. The Soviet infant morality rate was also several times the European norm, at 24 deaths per 1,000.[89] In every country but the U.S., the former Soviet

Union has the highest number of threatened species.

## CONCLUSION

Murray Feshbach and Alfred Friendly wrote: "When historians finally conduct an autopsy on the Soviet Union and Soviet Communism, they may reach the verdict of death by ecocide."[90] Regardless of whether the situation in the former Soviet Union has been exaggerated, the fact remains that damage to the environment and the resulting health effects pose a formidable challenge for the now independent republics. After all, "[t]he former Soviet policies of rapid industrialization were based on heavy industry without environmental controls, inefficient agriculture heavily dependent on toxic chemicals, and an inadequately monitored nuclear program."[91] Only time will tell if the former republics' newly regained sense of nationalism will help them to rebuild their tortured lands. It is to be hoped that active nationalism, in the form of wars, will not simply add to the ecological devastation and human suffering perpetuated by Soviet rule. As Feshbach and Friendly wrote, "Ecocide was draining the nation's wealth and strength to the tune of 43 billion rubles a year, the price, as they computed it, of working days lost to illness, of cropland made unusable, of water fit neither to drink nor to use in industrial processes."[92]

The Soviet Union's use of science and technology helped it in a number of ways but, in some cases, did more harm than good. The economy of the USSR was nearly ruined by the recklessness of Soviet central planning, the incompetence of the plans and managing techniques. There are few resources left for any recovery. The ecology has been devastated by overuse and pollution. The people themselves are paying the price of illness and death due to secrecy and the need to continually upgrade technology. The peoples of the former Soviet Union can look forward to many years of poverty, illness, and despair because of past Soviet policies. It is hoped that they can do better. They have to in order to survive. And survival is at best difficult during good times, let alone in a world just now recovering from a recession.

## NOTES

1. Murray Feshbach and Alfred Friendly, *Ecocide in the USSR: Health and Nature Under Siege* (New York: Basic Books, 1992), p. 11.
2. Ibid., p. 5.
3. Ibid., p. 11.

4. Donald R. Kelley, Kenneth R. Stunkel, and Richard R. Wescott, *The Economic Superpowers and the Environment: The United States, the Soviet Union and Japan* (San Francisco: W. H. Freeman, 1976, p. 22.

5. Ibid., p. 24.

6. Feshbach and Friendly, *Ecocide*, p. 3.

7. Ibid., p. 113.

8. Ibid., p. 3.

9. Ibid.

10. Ibid., p. 2.

11. Ibid., p. 74.

12. James Critchlow, *Nationalism in Uzbekistan: A Soviet Republic's Road to Sovereignty* (Boulder, Colo.: Westview, 1991), p. 82.

13. Feshbach and Friendly, *Ecocide*, p. 74.

14. Critchlow, *Nationalism*, pp. 84-85.

15. Boris Z. Rumer, *Soviet Central Asia: 'A Tragic Experiment'* (Boston: Unwin Hyman, 1989), p. 93.

16. Ibid., p. 94.

17. Ibid., p. 60.

18. Marshall I. Goldman, *The Spoils of Progress: Environmental Pollution in the Soviet Union* (Cambridge, Mass.: MIT Press, 1972), p. 242.

19. Boris Komarov (Ze'ev Wolfson), *The Destruction of Nature in the Soviet Union* (New York: M. E. Sharpe, 1980), p. 52.

20. Feshbach and Friendly, *Ecocide*, p. 113.

21. Ibid., p. 119.

22. Kelley, Stunkel, and Wescott, *Economic Superpowers*, p. 84.

23. Feshbach and Friendly, *Ecocide*, p. 119.

24. Ibid., p. 64.

25. Ibid., p. 2. Statistically, this means half of all fertile land is imperiled, with 13 percent marginalized; 388 million acres are saline, 279 million are eroded, and 62 million are waterlogged. Ibid., pp. 57-58.

26. Ibid., p. 66.

27. Rumer, *Soviet Central Asia*, p. 71.

28. Feshbach and Friendly, *Ecocide*, p. 79.

29. Critchlow, *Nationalism*, p. 44.

30. Komarov, *Destruction*, p. 49.

31. Ibid., p. 50.

32. Dick Thompson, "The Greening of the USSR," *Time*, January 2, 1989, p. 59.

33. Komarov, *Destruction*, p. 95.

34. Feshbach and Friendly, *Ecocide*, p. 104.

35. Stephen Kotkin, *Steeltown U.S.S.R.* (Los Angeles: University of California Press, 1991), p. 135.

36. Feshbach and Friendly, *Ecocide*, p. 96.

37. Kelley, Stunkel, and Wescott, *Economic Superpower*, p. 236.

38. Ibid., p. 67.

39. Komarov, *Destruction*, p. 20-21.

40. Ibid., p. 25.

41. "Russia's Greens--The Poisoned Giant Wakes Up," *The Economist*, November 4, 1989, p. 24.

42. However, it was not as bad as Norilsk, which had two million tons of pollution thrown into the atmosphere every year; see Feshbach and Friendly, *Ecocide*, p. 10.

43. Ibid., p. 92.

44. Ibid., p. 103.

45. Paul Hofheinz, "The New Soviet Threat: Pollution," *Fortune*, Vol. 126 (2): July 27, 1992, p. 111.

46. Mike Edwards, "A Broken Empire: Kazakhstan: Facing the Nightmare," *National Geographic*, Vol. 183 (3): March 1993, p. 35.

47. Gabriel Schoenfeld, "Rad Storm Rising," *The Atlantic*, Vol. 266 (6): December 1990, p. 44.

48. Edwards, "Broken Empire," p. 36.

49. Ibid.

50. Schoenfeld, "Rad Storm Rising," p. 44.

51. Ibid., p. 50.

52. James E. Oberg, *Uncovering Soviet Disasters: Exploring the Limits of Glasnost* (New York: Random House, 1988), p. 66.

53. Mike Edwards, "Chernobyl--One Year After," *National Geographic*, Vol. 171 (5): May 1987, pp. 641, 646-47.

54. Mike Edwards, "A Broken Empire: Ukraine: Running on Empty," *National Geographic*, Vol. 183 (3): March 1993, p. 47.

55. Ibid., pp. 45, 47.

56. Hofheinz, "New Soviet Threat," p. 111.

57. Louis MacKay and Mark Thompson, "Introduction: Chernobyl and Beyond." In Louis MacKay and Mark Thompson, eds., *Something in the Wind: Politics after Chernobyl* (London: Pluto Press, 1988), p. 6.

58. Ibid., p. 7.

59. Ibid.

60. Hofheinz, "New Soviet Threat," p. 111.

61. Schoenfeld, "Rad Storm Rising," p. 44.

186      Science, Technology, and Ecopolitics in the USSR

62. Ibid., p. 46.
63. Edwards, "Chernobyl," p. 650.
64. Oberg, *Uncovering*, p. 209.
65. Glenn Garelik, "The Chernobyl Syndrome," *New York Times Book Review*, p. 15.
66. Komarov, *Destruction*, p. 78.
67. Kelley, Stunkel, and Wescott, *Economic Superpowers*, p. 226.
68. Feshbach and Friendly, *Ecocide*, p. 147.
69. Ibid., p. 212.
70. Charles Ziegler, *Environmental Policy in the U.S.S.R.* (Boston: University of Massachusetts Press, 1987), p. xviii.
71. Ibid., p. xix.
72. Schoenfeld, "Rad Storm Rising," p. 50.
73. Feshbach and Friendly, *Ecocide*, p. 191.
74. Ibid., p. 162.
75. Goldman, *Spoils of Progress*, p. 303.
76. Ibid., p. 31.
77. Ben Eklof, *Soviet Briefing: Gorbachev and the Reform Period* (Boulder, Colo.: Westview Press, 1989), p. 139.
78. Keith Bush, "Environmental Problems in the USSR," *Problems of Communism*, Vol. 21 (4): July-August 1972, p. 26.
79. Joan De Bardeleben, *The Environment and Marxism-Leninism: The Soviet and East German Experience* (Boulder, Colo.: Westview, 1985), p. 38.
80. Ibid., p. 48.
81. Thompson, "Greening of the USSR," p. 60.
82. Feshbach and Friendly, *Ecocide*, p. 106.
83. Louise Penny, "Where Even the Air Is a Sewer" in *Globe and Mail*, July 11, 1990, p. A19.
84. Feshbach and Friendly, *Ecocide*, p. 106.
85. Ibid., p. 167.
86. Anonymous, "CIS Environmental Rules Growing Tougher," *Oil and Gas Journal*, Vol. 91 (38): September 29, 1993, p. 31.
87. The information from this section is taken from World Resources Institute, *The 1993 Information Please Environmental Almanac* (Boston: Houghton Mifflin, 1993), pp. 552-57.
88. Ibid., p. 555-56.
89. Ibid., p. 558.
90. Feshbach and Friendly, *Ecocide*, p. 1.
91. World Resources Institute, *1993 Information Please*, p. 552.

92. Feshbach and Friendly, *Ecocide*, p. 259.

# Epilogue: Utopias and Anti-Utopias in Postmodernist Times

In its headlong, fulminating dash toward industrialization that ultimately brought it to the brink of catastrophe, one comes to the conclusion that there was something inherently self-destructive in the Soviet system, something providential, immanent, almost like a classical Greek tragedy. This notion is reinforced as we are reminded of the Jewish legend of the Golem of Prague.

In the sixteenth century, the Cabbalist Rabbi Judah Löw ben Bezalel created a stupendous machine--an artificial man with superhuman powers to protect the Jews in Prague from pogroms in times of need. This humanoid could be brought to life simply by inserting into its mouth a slip of paper on which one of the secret Divine names of God was inscribed. In the closest thing the Cabbalist had to calculating machines, he used the mystical system of numerology, substituting numerical, quasi-electrical, values for Hebrew-letter inscriptions. But as we can easily guess, the Golem's powers were soon turned against his own creator, the good Rabbi. The moral of the story: imperfect human beings should not create uncontrollable forces that could easily be unleashed against them or could dominate them. The legend may have stirred the imagination of the English writer, Mary Shelley, who wrote *Frankenstein*, a novel about a monster who runs amok and the theme, at the height of the English Industrial Revolution, became not merely a Jewish but a general human concern.

Norbert Wiener, the Jewish-American mathematician and father of modern cybernetics was obsessed with this issue. In his work, *God and*

*Golem Inc.*, he was one of the first to seriously begin to question the implications of recent technological developments, including the idea of a "computerized Golem." Wiener pondered the idea of machines which can learn and reproduce themselves, and he wondered about what the proper relationship should be between sophisticated machines and their human creators. Wiener concluded that modern machines are, like Frankenstein, "modern counterparts of the Golem of the Rabbi of Prague."[1] Wiener thus reasoned that the very issue of control is a central theme. This is not in the least surprising if we imagine that God, human beings, and machines all have the ability to create in their own image.

Yet Golems and Frankensteins are the stuff of myth, tales of yore. The reality is that modern science and technology are facts, indeed ways of life, in our human existence. They have become cultural phenomena, regardless of the society they permeate, be it capitalist or socialist, religious or atheist. Science and technology are integral parts of our socialization process. Although science, and particularly technology, does bring considerable benefits, there are also limitations and dire consequences that flow from it. Some are willing to accept responsibility for these consequences; others refuse. The very idea of nuclear technology has in fact been admonished by most of its own creators, from Albert Einstein to Andrei Sakharov.

Almost everybody agrees that humans and technology are involved in a symbiotic relationship. The point to make here is that this symbiosis is not always a beneficial one. It is reasonable to make two initial conclusions: the first is that technological innovation always tend to benefit a nation, a particular group, class, or segment of society that implements it. What I am basically implying here is that technology will either be commercialized (that is, it must be owned and marketed) by capitalist society, or else it will serve a totalitarian order or the power equation of a nation for military purposes. The second point now universally accepted is that technologies, based on the motives and benefits driving them, cannot really be neutral as was commonly thought. Even the purpose of the Golem (he was Jewish) and Frankenstein preclude neutrality.

To be sure, a machine is essentially a neutral piece of hardware; but the moment it develops and begins to integrate into society it no longer remains neutral. In the Soviet context, while computers may have been regarded as neutral, at one point, as the computer developed, it became subjected increasingly to a Western cultural bias, which is why the Soviets ended up rejecting them. Having rejected capitalism and private enterprise, there would not have been much need for a market-driven management information system. Consequently, in the USSR, the question of marketing computer technology was never taken seriously. Software, too, had a distinct Anglo-Saxon bias. The applications written in such languages as COBOL, FORTRAN, BASIC, PASCAL, and others are written in English. There was no company in the Soviet Union like France's Honeywell Bull (notice the English sounding name) that was the equivalent of IBM and geared to marketing information technology using English software applications. At the machine level all computer languages are reduced to some form of representation in the binary numbering code: 0 or 1. This purely mathematical form of the systems program is not necessarily subject to any cultural bias. In fact, in early data processing, machine language was regarded as the first truly universal language. As computers were becoming more complex it became exceedingly difficult to manage the binary strings of 0s and 1s. It seems that only translation programs, or calculating machines, are still utilizing this binary code. Application programs, on the other hand, practically all become subject to cultural bias; and practically all of these software languages are in English. Even today's INTERNET--the information highway that one plies--which originated from the Penta-gon's need to control secret communications within its internal departments and its links with academic research on military technol-ogies and partly modeled on the famous French MINITEL and its *messagerie* of the 1980s--is virtually all based in English. So cultural and linguistic biases prevail, and the language barrier can impede the smooth flow of information: one either renounces that, or adapts to the English-based language culture. Soviet leaders must have discussed these problems for years, realizing that data accumulation and processing had become the preserve of the English language and of the applications software made in the USA. Wary of Western influence, the Soviets also realized, to their own misfortune, that with the rapid development of both hardware and software in the West, it became virtually impossible for them to start all over by designing their own software.

The record of the Soviet experience as I outlined in this book should be fairly straightforward: to remain a world military power, the USSR had to pursue a technological advantage--to build that proverbially better mousetrap. The sole benefit was to its military-industrial complex. There was no social accountability whatsoever. The individual alienation and the ecological fallout associated with the USSR was the direct result of heavy-industry pollution or smokestack emissions, pesticides, fertilizers,

chemical wastes, oils, nuclear power, and so on. All this went on until
Ronald Reagan's Star Wars program forced the Soviet leaders to spend
and spend until they were financially prostrate.

Clearly the Western experience has had the same problems with oil
slicks and acid rain, factory fumes and nuclear testing, but the Western
critics go far beyond that. They generally point to a growing alienation,
environmental catastrophe, even of human enslavement by machines
resulting not only from the automobile but from information technology
itself. I should again point out here that apart from the early detractors
of cybernetics, few in the USSR went on a full-fledged anti-technics
crusade. The cyber pitfalls in the West, which Russian politicians and
private enterprise are emulating today are many and varied.

For instance, Silicon Valley's microchip industry, near San Francisco,
long touted as clean and safe, is seen by some anti-technologists as
being so highly toxic that they are calling it "high-tech pollution." Lenny
Siegel and John Markoff argue that "one of the greatest ironies of microelectronics technology is that the transformation of America into an
information society relies, at its core, upon a technology from the
industrial era: chemical processing. The manufacture of chips, printed
circuit boards, magnetic media, and other high-tech products use some
of the most dangerous materials known to humanity . . . the release of
those toxins into the air, the ground, and bodies of water poses a
significant threat to public health."[2] Morris Berman in the same vein
even charges that "scientific consciousness is alienated consciousness;"
and his litany of horrors include statistics on homelessness, joblessness--
all due to modern science and technology--by illustrating how many
million schizophrenics inhabit the US, how many million "seriously
disturbed children, millions of alcoholics, millions more suffering from
depression, and millions downing benzodiazepines."[3] This he attributes
to the new mental framework of capitalism . . . "based on the scientific
mode of experiment, quantification, and technical mastery." Others have
expressed the opinion that technology drugs its user; it borders on
addiction, it dulls one's senses, like numbness; technologies are simply
not easy to switch off or leave aside.

Travel by motor car numbs one's senses to the reality of the
countryside, just like TV numbs its viewer, the computer numbs its user.
Marshall McLuhan likened technology to the Narcissus myth, the boy
who, in Greek mythology, was numbed after mistaking his own
reflection in the water for another person. He reminds us that "narcissus"
comes from the Greek word "narcosis" which means narcotic or

numbness.[4] In this respect, a fascinating book recently came out on auto-centred transport called *The Ecology of the Automobile*. Here Peter Freund and George Martin make a very interesting case against what they call the "ideology of automobility," where the symbol of auto space enhances feelings of placelessness, the mood produced is that of rootlessness and, far too often, accompanied by more mobility than we need. Again, capitalism is seen as the root of this malaise. Anti-technologists conflate capitalism with technology, in much the same way that Marxists see imperialism as an offshoot of modern capitalism. Oil companies, the auto industry, trucking, and highway construction firms, consumerism (Fordism is the term frequently used) feed the constant need for strip malls replete with the spatial derangement that comes with more highways and more parking lots and more cars.

Technology is often seen as a function of the masculine ethos and as an imperative of patriarchy (the editor of New Society Publishers, T. L. Hill, underscores all the gendered notions in the book *Questioning Technology* by subtitling it *Questioning Patriarchy*), where, in the main, it is women who are victimized on the lower social rungs of the corporate ladder and at the factory workplace. Nor does automobility and its spatial alienation free women from a gendered division of labor. The "middle-class mother" must now fulfil her role as a driver to reconnect a community "fragmented by automobility by providing links between home, school, leisure sites, shopping, and friends."[5] Further-more, the very fantasy of driving at high speeds is essentially a masculine one. So, the combination of absolute mobility, speed, technology, all encapsulated in this image of moving through space in a hermetically sealed module, transcending time, space, and the messiness of nature is, according to yet another poststructuralist writer, an alienating experience.[6] This whole concept of automobility is an enslaving and numbing experience. Freund and Martin add to this convoluted postmodernist dystopia with the following remark:

this system of technology-in-use includes supplies of metals, chemicals, fuels, roads, signals, repair sites, fuel distribution sites, traffic police, courts, insurance, scrap dealers, and various car lobbies and associations.[7]

No doubt, many of the foregoing arguments are sustainable; others are misleading. Further qualification is in order. There are truths, half-truths, and outright fallacies in these symbolic depictions. For one thing, it is advanced capitalism that spawned radical feminism and a middle-class feminist perspective to both technology and critical theory. As regards the automotive industry, energy-intensive industries do in fact fuel this unbridled automobility. Likewise, business and corporatism do encourage technological innovation and are dependent on the good-will of the government. But in the modern world it would be wishful thinking to keep government and business from being independent of each other. Why should business move from oil or nuclear energy which is making money and employing people to a cheaper solar energy and lose huge profits? As business remorselessly pursues technology, government and the large corporations must work hand in hand in order to finance and manage large-scale technological systems. Clearly the boundary between public and private necessarily becomes blurred. Critics of technology have written whole volumes on how the "R & D cult," to use H.C. Nieburg's words, bypasses the checks and balances of the democratic system to erode democratic pluralism itself. Writers like Seymour Melman, Ralph Lapp, Richard Barnett, Langdon Winner, Peter Freund, John Zerzan, Alice Carnes, Jerry Mander, and many others have documented the concentration and abuse of power in the high technology networks which bind together government agencies and many large American corporations. Technology is based on the concept of ownership of property. Corporations will only market a particular technology if it is cost-effective. A firm can certainly develop the technology that it wants, but it will market it only if there is some profit to be made from this developed product. In the final analysis, everything is predicated on its ownership of that technology. Government and the legal system naturally support that proprietorship. Marshall McLuhan has warned us how even the media and technology are an important theme in the PR of many image-conscious American enterprises.[8] Lewis Mumford has echoed the social pitfalls of Shelley's Frankenstein syndrome.[9]

It would be worthwhile to say that if something is true the opposite is also true. If science and technology are propelled solely by the desire for growth and efficiency, we may also regard efficiency as a reduction of needless waste. There is truly a dark side to growth, but without economic growth no economy could provide jobs for an expanding population, pay for imports, or compete on the world market; nor would any financial or charitable institution be able to survive. The whole idea of a Gross Domestic Product would be meaningless. As for the narcotic effect of TV and the computer (I have heard of them as the major cause of divorce), I know of friends who are similarly numbed with pleasure while jogging through the countryside and stopping for a day or two actually produces mental anguish. Or--for that matter--try telling a

Russian or Ukrainian immigrant to the West that excessive auto mobility is bad for the psyche, bad for the environment. He or she will immediately reply that things were far worse under the Soviet passport system, the *propiska*, which interdicted internal travel and forcibly bound Soviet peasants to their farms. Arguably, the advent of the automobile did much to alleviate the loneliness and alienation in rural America. Surely there must be a human face to technology. Even if the automobile has caused pollution, technology is already rising to the challenge of cleaning up the messes that technology has made. One day, perhaps in a decade or two, the world will witness hydrogen-fueled cars that are far more safe for the environment.

By the same token, while such ideas like teleworking might bind the working woman to her house, with very few fringe benefits, by a large firm that sub-contracts a lot of its work, computer conferencing, another wave of the future, might not be a bad mode of communication for women sensitive to sexual discrimination. Computer conferencing should enhance cyberdemocracy and cyberequality, offsetting the spreading systems of computerized surveillance, an unhappy spinoff of office automation. Computer conferencing is absolutely authorless and odorless; it can substitute for the gatherings of entire communities.[10] Charisma, personal appearance, gender, race, even rhetorical skills--all one has to do is type fast and soon even that will be passé with voice-activated computers--are of no importance; and given the temporal/spatial distance this offers, anyone should be able to introduce unpopular or eccentric points of view. Perhaps the greatest danger of the modern computer is bound up with the controversial issue of invasion of one's privacy. It would be quite enjoyable to see someone breaking into secret data and using classified information against a corrupt politician, but it would be equally distressing to have someone break into your personal file (the official employment record) at work and putting in incriminating files without anyone's knowledge or--for that matter--deleting vitally important documentation. This kind of cyberworld intrigue is graphically shown in the film *Disclosure*, starring Demi Moore and Michael Douglas and dealing with the subject of sexual harassment.

True, as a University professor, I am in a position to access a mine of information through INTERNET in the way of articles, statistics, and other colleagues' views about a country I happen to be studying. But no computer network can possibly substitute for actually going there, speaking that language, seeking out hidden repositories of information, organizing surveys, or backpacking through remote areas foraging for hard-to-find primary sources. How, for example, would one research on the Russian mafia solely by surfing the information superhighway which cannot be wired to everything there is on this topic? If there is a form of cyberinequality, the fact is that information machines are widening the gap between the haves and the have-nots of our society. This statement is more true of Eastern Europe, Russia, China, and the Third World, where the new capitalists can log on to, say, the INTERNET, and where the rest of the people live in poverty, mainly because the cost of that technology is so exorbitant. But in the West, computers are not the root cause of wage inequality; they simply reflect the wage differences that are either structural, the policy of new hiring procedures resulting from competition and corporate debt, or systemic pressures--not a worker's ability to tap into the INTERNET. Nevertheless, in the US, Vice President Al Gore "has appealed to the telecommunications industry to cut costs and wire all schools to the information highway."[11] Even Newt Gingrich, the spokesman for the New American Right, wants to give the poor a tax credit for laptops.[12] I am still impressed with the scenario in the U.S. where the South American immigrant could use his child's computer to e-mail the school principal in Spanish. The principal then uses his translation software and answers back. Partially, this would be a departure from the cultural bias of machines I discussed earlier in my conclusion.

The postmodernist or poststructuralist perspectives on modern technology are often the most poignant, except that this line of logic is too dependent on metaphors. Langdon Winner, one of the critics of technology admitted quite frankly: "I am suggesting that we use metaphors and rhetorical devices of political speech to unpack the meaning of various technologies for how we live."[13]

At quite another level, let us look at the notion of money from a postmodernist standpoint. Money has much in common with technology today, since money was and still is a precious metal, it is a piece of paper that is being used less and less; and is increasingly a computer blip. It is as sought after as technology itself. Marx, not himself a theorist of this particular school of critical thought, wrote a great deal of sophisticated nonsense about the nature and function of money. He loved using metaphors and images, quoting Feuerbach's descriptions of commodities as "fetishes." Marx called money the "alienated ability of mankind," "crystallized labor," and a "monster" which separates itself from man and comes to dominate him. These qualifications appealed to the Bolshevik intellectuals who wanted to implement a new fiscal policy that was designed to lead to a moneyless economy. Yet since time immemorial, some unit of measurement had to serve as (a) a medium of exchange, (b) a store of value, and (c) a unit of account. Gold had functioned as a medium of exchange and as a store of value. Gold represented money in view of its attribute as a scarce commodity. The German word for money is *Geld*, which is a variation on the German word *Gold* (gold) and *gelb* (yellow). We recall what Lenin said about the absurd notion of gold being used to build public lavatories in the world after the Revolution (see chapter 4). In time, money came to designate bank notes representing precious metals stored in state depositories. The bank notes had legal tender but were not precious themselves since they could be printed at random. As Mark Poster argues in this postmodernist vein focusing on a semiotic image of money (notice here how postmodernism likes to employ symbols, metaphors, signs, images, and representations):

The correspondence between word and thing was dropped in favor of a relation of representation. Later, checks, representing deposits of bank notes, came to serve as money and . . . were even less precious in themselves. At present bank cards are replacing checks, representing not deposits of bank notes, but electronic information in databases, which in turn are representations of deposits of bank notes. The word "money" now refers to a configuration of oxides on a tape stored in the computer department of a bank. The connection between the oxides and the function of exchange medium is arbitrary, revealing its socially constituted character, and the representational aspect of money is sustained through language.[14]

Here indeed is a graphic dialectic of concepts that Hegel would have applauded. The word, and the semiotic language itself, has come to mean everything and anything, and yet it ends up meaning nothing. Anyone familiar with economic history, would realize that some unit of measurement, whether or not called "money," had existed in every society practicing the division of labor and the exchange of goods and services, right down to the service economies of our post-industrial world. The postmodernists have made too much of words and of the art of deconstruction. Most postmodernists eventually arrive at some theory of post-Marxism via deconstruction. The postmodernist depiction weakens the argument in view of the fact that money has always been a hard social reality. On the other hand, I do admit that the semiotic approach to literature and art, to architecture and science fiction is a wonderful form of pictorial design and sheer entertainment.

There are other ways that signs and images can be turned into distorted meanings, especially in regard to computer technology and the celebrated Golem syndrome. Metaphorically speaking, computer networks are like living bodies, the argument goes. Like living bodies, computers are informationally interconnected. And, like living bodies, they may succumb to occasional "viruses" that could disable the entire computer network. The virus could even start a whole epidemic, just like in human communities. Now if the metaphor of the "virus" suggests anything, it is that these networks can form a new program (read: new body). Pursuing this line of argument a little farther, some are saying that if a computer network is tagged with a virus (as was the case in Soviet-American cold war rivalry when the protagonists used Trojan horse chips), this diseased new body could affect the body of the computer user by altering his DNA.[15] It is one thing to transfer a virus from computer to computer, from network to network, but it is quite another to assert that computer viruses can be switched to biological viruses. A computer may well be a "body," but it is a body without DNA, and therefore cannot transfer to a human what it does not have. Or how about the scenario of the symbiotic relationship described above, man and machine feeding off each other, where human beings create computers--or virtual reality[16] for that matter--and then these technologies create a new species of humans. We see this in films like *Robocop* and *The Lawnmower Man*. In the latter film, the transformed human actually begins to play God. Most of these applications are surely in the realm of the fantastical, of pure imagination.

One need not constantly deal in dystopias to frighten us with the horrors of technology. The technology that I personally like most of all is genetic engineering. I see it as a monumental feat, one not only with a human face but immensely capable of helping to feed the millions of starving people on our planet. Genetic engineering has made strides beyond the crude genetics of a Mendel and the ludicrous theories of the Soviet Trofim Lysenko. Ever since molecular biologists were able to cut and splice DNA, the prospects are mind-boggling: new hormones that boost milk production in cows; new genes that are disease and pest-resistant; the discovery of genes responsible for everything from cancer to Alzheimer's to fostering hair growth in balding men. More than anything else, genetic manipulation should improve crop yields, especially in staple foods like potatoes and rice, triggering a major breakthrough in agriculture. The manipulation of DNA should improve human health. We need not associate this with the kind of manipulation seen in Steven Spielberg's blockbuster *Jurassic Park.*

At the time the Russian Bolsheviks were consolidating their revolution, still in the industrial, not post-industrial, mold the theme of human perfectibility was the main topic of discussion by these naive Marxists. Part of man's bright future as a machine was influenced by the theories of an American efficiency expert named Frederick Winslow Taylor, who pioneered the time-and-motion studies that transformed workers into operators of machinery. The Bolsheviks absolutely venerated this "father of scientific management." Reduced to its most absurd terms, we could easily envision workers who behave as though they too become fail-safe pieces of hardware. Taking a cue from this, Yevgeny Zamyatin, an early Soviet dramatist, wrote a novel *We* (Russian "*Myi*") that eventually inspired Orwell's *1984* and Huxley's *Brave New World,* latter-day dystopias of the mind. As one reviewer of *We* has described the Russian novel: " . . . the more I thought of it, the more it seemed to me that *We,* and all similar dystopias, . . . truly deserve to be called postmodern. If 'modern' means what any reader in any conceivable 'today' regards as up-to-date opinion and style, then every imagined distant future will be irretrievably 'post' all such notions."[17] The problem with most postmodernist theory is that it will often rely on abstractions, a surreal language, frequently imposing a fantasy by means of which initiates of this theory can communicate with each other. I would not be surprised if in the very near future when "postmodernist" as an application of critical theory fails to delineate three-dimensional, artificial realities, it will begin calling such phenomena "hypermodernist." Where modern technology is concerned, perhaps the best thing to do would be to cease looking for utopias like the Soviets did and failed (and American culture is still blindly pursuing) and not let ourselves be frightened that such monumental achievements can only lead to a dystopian future. Modern technologies have become a fact of life. It should be enough that we have to cope with the downside of this reality--we need not imagine surrealities to interpret this new life.

## NOTES

1. See Norbert Wiener, *God and Golem Inc.: A Comment on Certain Points Where Cybernetics Impinges on Religion* (Cambridge, Mass.: The M.I.T. Press, 1964).

2. John Zerzan and Alice Carnes, ed., *Questioning Technology: Tool,*

*Toy, or Tyrant* (Philadelphia: New Society Publishers, 1991), p. 58.

3. Ibid., pp. 62-3. Benzodiazepines are a group of tranquilizer drugs, such as Prozac and Valium.

4. Marshall McLuhan, *Understanding Media*. (Boston: Mifflin, 1986), p. 51.

5. Peter Freund and George Martin, *The Ecology of the Automobile* (New York: Black Rose Books, 1993), p. 51.

6. See André Gorz, *Ecology as Politics* (Montreal: Black Rose Books, 1980).

7. Freund and Martin, p. 9.

8. Marshall McLuhan and Quentin Fiore, *The Medium is the Message* (New York: Bantam Books, 1967).

9. Lewis Mumford, *The Myth of the Machine: Technics and Human Development* (New York: Harcourt Brace Jovanovich, 1967).

10. Mark Poster, *The Mode of Information: Poststructuralism and Social Context* (Cambridge: Polity Press, 1990). See his chapter "Derrida and Electronic Writing," p. 121.

11. *Newsweek*, February 27, 1995, pp. 51-2.

12. Ibid., p. 52.

13. Langdon Winner, *Whole Earth Review*, Vol. 73: Winter 1991, p. 22.

14. Poster, pp. 12-3.

15. See Paul Brodeur, "Annals of Radiation: The Hazards of Electromagnetic Fields, III--Video Display Terminals," *New Yorker*, June 26, 1989, 39 pages.

16. Virtual reality involves use of a headset and fiber-optic gloves or data suits that permit a player to enter a three-dimensional, 360-degree computerized world to retrieve information, observe phenomena, or to interact with other players wearing similar gear and programmed to the same world. In *The Lawnmower Man*, the viewer gets a glimpse of cyberforms engaged in high-tech lovemaking. It has ramifications in areas like automotive design, medicine, and architecture, and is probably the leading videogame technology of the future.

17. See Professor Clarence Brown's introduction to *We* by Yevgeny Zamyatin (London: Penguin Books, 1993. First published in English by E. P. Dutton Inc. in 1924). Zamyatin perished in the purges in 1937.

# Glossary

| | |
|---|---|
| AAASS | American Association for the Advancement of Slavic Studies. |
| ABM | Anti-Ballistic Missile Treaty. |
| AGAT | One of the first Soviet commercial computers copied entirely from Western design. |
| *Apparatchik* | Soviet bureaucrat or official (not necessarily with decision-making powers). |
| ASAT | Anti-satellite system. |
| ASU | (*Avtomatizirovannaia Sistema Upravleniia*) Automated management system. See also OGAS. A crude form of management information services under a centrally planned economy. |
| *Aviatsiya Dal'nogo Deistviya* | Soviet Long-Range Aviation, or long-range strategic strike force. |
| BMD | Ballistic Missile Defense. Around the Moscow perimeter, it was called GALOSH. Also see SDI. |

C2                          Command and Control. It is a computer-assisted process of troop movement and tactical deployment of personnel.

C3                          Command, Control, and Communications using computer-based technology.

CARP                        Computerized Airborne Release Point.

CMEA                        The name given to the Eastern European Common Market (*Strany Ekonomicheskoi Vzaimopomoshchi*--Mutual Economic Assistance).

COCOM                       Coordinating Committee on Multilateral Export Control. Based in Paris at the U.S. Embassy, it is an American-run agency whose mandate is essentially to prevent the acquisition of sensitive technology that could be used for military purposes by hostile nations.

CSE                         Communications Security Establishment. A special department in the Canadian Department of Defense.

Directorate T              Scientific and Technical Branch of Soviet espionage. See KGB.

EASS                        Unified Automated Communications System.

ELINT                       Electronic Intelligence, also known as electronic surveillance, mainly via satellites.

ELORG                       (*Elektronorgtekhnika*) Organization of Electronic Technology.

ESPRIT                      European Strategic Research Program on Information Technology.

FOBS                        Fractional Orbital Bombardment System.

| | |
|---|---|
| GATT | General Agreement on Tariffs and Trade. This specialized agency is based in Geneva, Switzerland but, as an international institution, has generally excluded countries of the East Bloc until now. |
| GKNT | (*Gosudarstvennyi Komitet Nauki i Tekhniki*) Soviet State Committee for Science and Technology. |
| *Glasnost* | The buzzword associated with Gorbachev's reforms, implying openness and freedom of expression and criticism. |
| *Glavkosmos* | Soviet Space Agency. |
| GLAVNAUKA | Special department of the People's Commissariat of Education. |
| GOERLO | Electrification plan. |
| *Goskompriroda* | State Committee for the Protection of the Environment. |
| GOSPLAN | (*Gosudarstvennoe Planirovaniie*) State Planning Committee. |
| Great Terror | In reference to Stalin's purges and persecutions of the 1930s. |
| GRU | (*Gosudarstvennoe Razvedovatel'noe Upravleniie*) Chief Intelligence Directorate of the Soviet General Staff or Soviet Military Intelligence. |
| GSVT | All-Union State Network of Computers. |
| *Gulag* | Concentration camp system for political prisoners as popularized by Alexander Solzhenitsyn's books like *Arkhipelag Gulaga* (*The Gulag* |

*Archipelago*) and *Odin Den'v zhizni Ivana Denisovitcha* (*One Day in the Life of Ivan Denisovitch*).

Humint

Human-based Intelligence.

IKI

(*Instit Kosmicheskogo Issledovaniia*) Institute of Space Research.

KGB

(*Komitet Gosudarstvennoi Bezopasnosti*) Soviet Secret Police, literally the "Committee for State Security."

MCTL

Military Critical Technologies List. See also COCOM.

MNTK

Interbranch Scientific Technical Complexes.

NEP

(*Novaia Ekonomicheskaia Politika*) Lenin's new economic policy of the early 1920s. It was designed to introduce a temporary market and small business into all sectors of the Soviet economy excluding key strategic areas such as heavy industry, energy, transport, and so on.

OGAS

(*Obshchegosudarstvennaia avtomatizirovannaia sistema*) All-Union System for the Collection and Processing of Information for the Accounting, Planning and Management of the National Economy. See also ASU.

OGSPD

(*Obshchegosudarstvennaia Sistema Peredachi Dannykh*) All-Union System of Data Transmission.

*Perestroika*

A buzzword of the Gorbachev reforms denoting restructuring and reconstruction.

REC

Radio-Electronic Combat.

SDECE

(*Service de documentation extérieure et de contre-espionnage*) French Secret Service. Basically a counter-intelligence organization and by Soviet, British, and Israeli standards, one of the most porous among industrialized countries.

SDI

Strategic Defense Initiative, or the American "Star Wars" program.

*Sharashki*

Plural of *sharashka*, a prison cell, or group reserved for brilliant scientists working on secret projects in Stalin's Gulag.

Sigint

Signals Interception.

*Spetsnaz*

Diversionary units which make up the special forces of the GRU.

STR

Scientific Technological Revolution, a Soviet term signalling the advent of the Third Industrial Revolution.

Taylorism

Named after the American efficiency expert, Frederick Winslow Taylor (1856-1915), the father of scientific management. He pioneered the time-and-motion studies involving industrial workers and machines. Absolutely venerated by the early Russian Bolsheviks.

Techint

Technical Information Gathering.

*Techmashimport*

Technical Machinery Import. Part of the Soviet Foreign Trade Establishment.

TsBIRP

(*Tsentral'nyi Buro dlya Izucheniia Raketnykh Problem*) Central Bureau for the Study of the Problems of Rockets.

*Uskoreniie*

After *glasnost* and *perestroika*, this is the third buzzword of the Gorbachev reforms, denoting "acceleration."

*Valovaya Produktsiya*   Drive for gross output.

VHSIC                    Very High-Speed Integrated Circuits.

VNIIPAS                  All-Union Scientific Research Institute for Applied Automated Systems.

VPK                      (*Voenno-Promyshlennaia Kommissiya*) Military-Industrial Commission which was the main decision-making body of the Soviet military-industrial complex.

*Vychislitel'naia*       Computer technology.
*Tekhnika*

# Selected Bibliography

## BOOKS

Aganbegyan, Abel. *The Challenge: Economics of Perestroika*. Ed. Michael Barratt Brown. Trans. Pauline M. Tiffen. London: Hutchinson Educational, 1988.

Agranorsky, I., et al. *USSR: Questions and Answers*. Moscow: Novosti Press, 1967.

American Die Casting Institute, *Position Paper on Minerals and Metals*. ADCI, May 1981.

Andrew, Christopher, and Oleg Gordievsky. *KGB: The Inside Story of its Foreign Operations from Lenin to Gorbachev*. London: Hodder and Stoughton, 1990.

Arbatov, A. A., and A. F. Shakai. *Obostreniye Syr'evoi Problemy i Mezhdunarodniye Otnosheniya*. Moscow: Mezdunarodniye Otnosheniya, 1981.

Aslund, Anders. *Gorbachev's Struggle for Economic Reform*. London: Pinter Publishers, 1989.

Balzer, Harley D. *Soviet Science on the Edge of Reform*. Boulder, Colo.: Westview, 1989.

Barron, John. *The KGB*. New York: Reader's Digest Press, 1974.

Bullis, L. Harold, and James E. Mielke. *Strategic and Critical Materials*. Boulder, Colo.: Westview Press.

Capra, Fritjof. *The Turning Point: Science, Society and the Rising Culture*. New York: Bantam, 1983.

Caragata, Patrick James. *National Resources and International Bargaining Power*. Kingston, Ont.: Queen's University, Centre for Resource Studies, 1984.

Chernyshev, Vladimir. "The First Steps." In *Conversion: Goods Instead of*

*Weapons*. Moscow: Novosti Press Agency Publishing House, 1989.

Chizum, David G. *Soviet Radioelectronic Combat*. Boulder, Colo.: Westview Press, 1985.

CIA. *Soviet Acquisition of Western Technology*. Langley, Virginia: CIA, 1984.

"Constitution (Fundamental Law) of the Union of Soviet Socialist Republics." In *The Soviet Crucible: The Soviet System in Theory and Practice*, 5th edn. Ed. Samuel Hendel. North Scituate, Mass.: Duxbury Press, 1980.

*Conversion: Goods Instead of Weapons*. Moscow: Novosti Press Agency Publishing House, 1989.

Critchlow, James. *Nationalism in Uzbekistan: A Soviet Republic's Road to Sovereignty*. Boulder, Colo.: Westview, 1991.

Dallin, Alexander, and Condoleeza Rice, eds. *The Gorbachev Era*. Palo Alto, Cal.: Portable Stanford, 1986.

Daniels, Robert V. "Can Gorbachev Escape History?" In *Perestroika: How New is Gorbachev's New Thinking?* Eds. Ernest W. Lefever and Robert D. Vander Lugt. Washington, D.C.: Ethics and Public Policy Center, 1989.

De Bardeleben, Joan. *The Environment and Marxism-Leninism: The Soviet and East German Experience*. Boulder, Colo.: Westview, 1985.

---. *Soviet Politics in Transition*. Toronto: D.C. Heath, 1992.

---, ed. *Environmental Quality and Security after Communism: Eastern Europe and the Soviet Successor States*. Boulder, Colo.: Westview, 1994.

de Bressen, Chris. *Understanding Technological Change*. London: Black Rose Press, 1987.

Desai, Padma. *Perestroika in Perspective--The Design and Dilemmas of Soviet Reform*. Princeton: Princeton University Press, 1989.

Dizard, Wilson P., and S. Blake Swensrud. *Gorbachev's Information Revolution--Controlling Glasnost in a New Electronic Era*. Boulder, Colo.: Westview, 1987.

Dragadze, Peter. "Russia's Embryonic Capitalists," *Forbes*, October 16, 1989. Quoted in *Global Studies: The Soviet Union and Eastern Europe*. Ed. Minton Goldman. Guilford, Conn.: Dushkin Publishing, 1990.

Eklof, Ben. *Soviet Briefing: Gorbachev and the Reform Period*. Boulder, Colo.: Westview Press, 1989.

Ericson, Richard E. "Economics." In *After the Soviet Union: From Empire to Nations*. Ed. Timothy J. Colton and Robert Legvold. New York: W. W. Norton, 1992.

Feshbach, Murray, and Alfred Friendly, Jr. *Ecocide in the USSR: Health and Nature Under Siege*. New York: Basic Books, 1992.

Fine, Daniel I. "Mineral Resource Dependency Crisis: Soviet Union and United States." In *The Resource War in 3-D: Dependency, Diplomacy, Defense*. Eds. James A. Miller, Daniel I. Fine, and R. Daniel McMichael. Pittsburgh: World Affairs Council of Pittsburgh, 1980.

Freund, Peter, and George Martin. *The Ecology of the Automobile*. New York:

Black Rose Books, 1993.

Gleason, Gregory. "Uzbekistan: From Statehood to Nationhood." In *Nation and Politics in the Soviet Successor States*. Eds. Ian Bremner and Ray Taras. Cambridge, England: Cambridge University Press, 1993.

Goldman, Marshall I. *The Spoils of Progress: Environmental Pollution in the Soviet Union*. Cambridge, Mass.: MIT Press, 1972.

---. *Gorbachev's Challenge--Economic Reform in the Age of High Technology*. New York: W. W. Norton, 1987.

---. "The Consumer." In *The Soviet Union Today*, 2nd edn. Ed. James Cracraft. Chicago: University of Chicago Press, 1988.

Goodman, S. E. "Advanced Technology: How Will the USSR Adjust?" In *Soviet Politics in the 1980s*. Ed. Helmut Sonnenfeldt. Boulder, Colo.: Westview Press, 1985.

Gorbachev, Mikhail. *Perestroika: New Thinking for Our Country and the World*. New York: Harper and Row, 1987.

Gorz, André. *Ecology as Politics*. Montreal: Black Rose Books, 1980.

Graham, Loren. "Science Policy and Organization." In *The Soviet Union Today*, 2nd edn. Ed. James Cracraft. Chicago: University of Chicago Press, 1988.

---. *The Ghost of the Executed Engineer: Technology and the Fall of the Soviet Union*. Cambridge, Mass.: Harvard University Press, 1993.

---. *Science in Russia and the Soviet Union: A Short History*. Cambridge, England: Cambridge University Press, 1993.

Grigorov, Viktor. *Eksperty v sisteme upravleniia obshchest'vennym proizvod stvom*. Moscow: Mysl', 1977.

Grigoryev, Vasili. *The Soviet Union: Facts, Problems, Appraisals*. Moscow: Novosti Press Agency Publishing House, 1987.

Grozier, Brian. *Strategy of Survival*. London: Temple Smith, 1978.

Haglund, David. "The West's Dependence on Imported Strategic Minerals: Implications for Canada" Working Paper. Vancouver: University of British Columbia, June 1983.

Hanson, Philip. "Soviet Assimiliation of Western Technology." In *Trade, Technology and Soviet-American Relations*. Ed. Bruce Parrott. Bloomington, Ind.: Indiana University Press, 1985.

Hardt, John P., and Jean F. Boone. "Computer-Assisted Third Industrial Revolution in the USSR: Policy Implications for the Soviet Union and the United States." In *The Future Information Revolution in the USSR*. Ed. Richard F. Staar. New York: Crane Russak, 1988.

Havlik, Peter. "Gorbachev's Reform Course Confirmed." In *Economic Reforms in Eastern Europe and the Soviet Union*. Ed. Hubert Gabrisch. Boulder, Colo.: Westview, 1989.

Hewett, Ed A., ed. *Reforming the Soviet Economy--Equality Versus Efficiency*. Washington, D.C.: Brookings Institution, 1988.

Hiltunen, Rudolf. "Transferring to a Peaceful Footing." In *Conversion: Goods instead of Weapons.* Moscow: Novosti Press Agency Publishing House, 1989.

Hoffman, Erik P., and Robbin F. Laird. *The Scientific-Technological Revolution and Soviet Foreign Policy.* New York: Pergamon, 1982.

Ivanov, Vladimir, and Alexander Kollontai. *A Pacific-Oriented Economy: Development of the Soviet Far Eastern Areas and Economic Cooperation in the Asia-Pacific Region.* Moscow: Novosti Press Agency Publishing House, 1989.

Jasani, Bhupendra, and Christopher Lee. *Countdown to Space War.* London: Taylor and Francis, 1984.

Johnson, Nicholas L. *Soviet Space Programs 1980-1985* (Science and Technology Series, Vol. 66). San Diego: American Astronautical Society, 1987.

Judy, Richard W. "Computer-Integrated Manufacturing." In *The Future Information Revolution in the USSR.* Ed. Richard F. Staar. New York: Crane Russak, 1988.

Kaiser, Robert G. *Russia: The People and the Power* (New York: Pocket Books, 1976.

Kanaev, E. M. et al. *Promysclennye raboty dlia obsluzhivaniia oborudovaniia razlichnogo tekhnologicheskogo naznacheniia.* Moscow: Vysshaia shkola, 1987.

Kaser, Michael. "The Soviet Impact on World Trade in Gold and Platinum." In *The Soviet Impact on Commodity Markets.* Ed. M. M. Kostecki. Toronto: Macmillan, 1984.

Kelley, Donald R., Kenneth R. Stunkel, and Richard R. Wescott. *The Economic Superpowers and the Environment: The United States, the Soviet Union, and Japan.* San Francisco: W. H. Freeman, 1976.

Kireyev, Alexei. "Economic Aspects of Conversion." In *Conversion: Goods Instead of Weapons.* Moscow: Novosti Press Agency Publishing House, 1989.

Kir'yan, M. M., ed. *Voyennotekhnicheskiy Progress i Vooruzhennyie Sily SSSR.* Moscow: Voyenizdat, 1982.

Kolbanovski, Yurii, *Filosofskie Voprosy Kibernetiki* (Moscow: Nauka, 1960).

Komarov, Boris. *The Destruction of Nature in the Soviet Union.* New York: M. E. Sharpe, 1980.

Kondratyev, Miroslav. *Cooperatives: Work and Initiative.* Moscow: Novosti Press Agency Publishing House, 1989.

Koslov, Igor. *Socialism and Energy Resources.* Moscow: Progress Publishers, 1981.

Kostecki, M. M. "The Soviet Impact on International Trade in Asbestos." In *The Soviet Impact on Commodity Markets.* Ed. M. M. Kostecki. Toronto: Macmillan, 1984.

Kotkin, Stephen. *Steeltown U.S.S.R.* Los Angeles: University of California Press, 1991.

Lenin, V. I. "The Tax in Kind (June 1921)." In *Lenin on Politics and Revolution*. Ed. J. Conmer. New York: Pegasus, 1968.

Lovell, Sir Bernard. *The Origins and International Economics of Space Exploration*. Edinburgh: University of Edinburgh Press, 1973.

MacKay, Louis, and Mark Thompson. "Introduction: Chernobyl and Beyond." In *Something in the Wind: Politics after Chernobyl*. Eds. Louis MacKay and Mark Thompson. London: Pluto Press, 1988.

Makarov, I. M., ed. *Robototekhnika i gibkie avtomatizirovannye prozvodstva*. Moscow: Vysshaia skhola, 1986, 9 vols.

Mandel, Ernest. *Beyond Perestroika: The Future of Gorbachev's USSR*. Trans. Gus Fagan. New York: Verso, 1989.

Marchuk, Guri. *Science Will Help Speed Production*. Moscow: Novosti Press Agency Publishing House, 1986.

Mark, Hans. "Introduction." In *International Security Dimensions of Space*. Eds. Uri Ra'anan and Robert L. Pfaltzgraff Jr. Hamden, Conn.: Archon Books, 1984.

McCougall, Walter. . . . *The Heavens and the Earth: A Political History of the Space Race*. New York: Basic Books, 1985.

McHenry, William K. "Computer Networks and the Soviet-Style Information Society." In *The Future Information Revolution in the USSR*. Ed. Richard F. Starr. New York: Crane Russak, 1988.

McLuhan, Marshall. *Understanding Media*. Boston: Mifflin, 1986.

McLuhan, Marshall, and Quentin Fiore. *The Medium is the Message*. New York: Bantam Books, 1967.

McNeill, William H. *The Pursuit of Power*. Oxford: Basil Blackwell, 1983.

Medish, Vadim. *The Soviet Union*, 2nd edn. Englewood Cliffs, N.J.: Prentice-Hall, 1984.

Medvedev, Roy A. *Let History Judge: The Origins and Consequences of Stalinism*. Trans. Colleen Taylor. Eds. David Joravsky and Georges Haupt. New York: Vintage Books, 1971.

Medvedev, Zhores. *Soviet Science*. New York: W. W. Norton, 1978.

Melvern, Linda, Nick Anning, and David Hebditch. *Techno-Bandits: How the Soviets are Stealing America's High-Tech Future*. Boston: Houghton Mifflin, 1984.

*Mineral Commodity Summaries*. Washington, D.C.: Department of the Interior, Bureau of Mines, 1983.

Molodchik, A. V. and V. N. Kobelev. *EVM na stole: Personal'nyi kompiuter*. Perm': Knizhnoe izdatel'stvo, 1987.

Mose, Harvey, Leon Goure, and Vladimir Prokofieff. *Science and Technology as an Instrument of Soviet Policy*. Miami: University of Miami Press.

Mumford, Lewis. *The Myth of the Machine: Technics and Human Development*. New York: Harcourt Brace Jovanovich, 1967.

Nove, Alec. *Stalinism and After: The Road to Socialism*, 3rd edn. Boston:

Unwin Hyman, 1989.

---. "An Economy in Transition." In *Chronicle of a Revolution: A Western-Soviet Inquiry into Perestroika.* Ed. Abraham Brumberg. New York: Pantheon Books, 1990.

Oberg, James. *Red Star in Orbit.* New York: Random House, 1981.

---. *Uncovering Soviet Disasters: Exploring the Limits of Glasnost.* New York: Random House, 1988.

Office of Technology Assessment. *Technology and East-West Trade.* Montclair, N.J.: Osmun/Gower, 1981.

Ogarkov, N. V. *Vsegda V Gotovnosti K Zashchite Otechestva.* Moscow: Voyenizdat, 1982.

Ornstein, Robert, and Paul Ehrlich. *New World, New Mind: Moving Toward Conscious Evolution.* New York: Doubleday, 1989.

Otani, Tadao. *Komp'iutery.* Baku: Azerneshr, 1987.

Parrott, Bruce. *Politics and Technology in the Soviet Union.* Cambridge, Mass.: MIT Press, 1983.

---. *The Soviet Union and Ballistic Missile Defense.* Boulder, Colo.: Westview, 1987.

Peebles, Curtis. *Battle for Space.* New York: Beaufort Books, 1983.

Polmar, Norman. *Strategic Weapons.* Washington, D.C.: National Strategy Information Center, 1982.

Popovsky, Mark. *Manipulated Science--The Crises of Science and Scientists in the Soviet Union Today.* Trans. Paul S. Falla. New York: Doubleday, 1979.

Poster, Mark. *The Mode of Information: Poststructuralism and Social Context.* Cambridge: Polity Press, 1990.

Rumer, Boris Z. *Soviet Central Asia: "A Tragic Experiment."* Boston: Unwin Hyman, 1989.

Sagdeyev, Roald. *Deep Space and Terrestrial Problems.* Moscow: Novosti Press Agency Publishing House, 1987.

Schauer, William I. *The Politics of Space--A Comparison of the Soviet and American Space Programs.* New York: Holmes and Meier Publishers, 1976.

Selivanov, Arnold. "Rescue from Outer Space." In *Soviet Science and Technology--87.* Ed. Vitali Goldansky. Moscow: Novosti Press Agency Publishing House, 1988.

Shaffer, Harry G. "Soviet Economic Performance in Historical Perspective." In *The Soviet Crucible: The Soviet System in Theory and Practice,* 5th edn. North Scituate, Mass.: Duxbury Press, 1980.

Sheldon II, Charles S. *Peaceful Applications in Outer Space Prospects for Man and Society.* Ed. Lincoln P. Bloomfield. New York: Praeger Press, 1968.

Shelton, Judy. *The Coming Soviet Crash: Gorbachev's Desperate Pursuit of Credit in Western Financial Markets.* New York: Free Press, 1989.

Shevchenko, Arkady. *Breaking with Moscow.* New York: Ballantine Books,

1985.

Smith, Alan H. "Soviet Economic Prospects: Can the Soviet Economic System Survive?" In *The Soviet Union After Brezhnev*. Ed. Martin McCauley. London: Heinemann Educational Books, 1983.

---. "Gorbachev and the World: The Economic Side." In *The Soviet Union under Gorbachev: Prospects for Reform*. Ed. David A. Dyker. London: Croom Helm, 1987.

Smith, Hedrick. *The Russians*. New York: New York Times Book Company, 1976.

*Soviet Military Power*. Washington, D.C.: U.S. Department of Defense, 1983 and 1985.

Spooner, J., et al. *Mining Annual Review 1983*. London: Mining Journal Limited, 1984.

Stalin, I. V. *Sochineniya*. Moscow: Politizdat, 1951.

Stapleton, Ross A., and Seymour E. Goodman. "The Soviet Union and the Personal Computer Revolution." In *The Future Information Revolution in the USSR*. Ed. Richard F. Starr. New York: Crane Russak, 1988.

Stares, Paul B. *Space and National Security*. Washington, D.C.: The Brookings Institution, 1987.

*Statistical Yearbook, Member Countries of the Council of Mutual Economic Assistance*. Moscow: Statistika, 1986.

Stent, Angela. "Technology Transfer to Eastern Europe: Paradoxes, Policies, Prospects." In *Central and Eastern Europe: The Opening Curtain?* Ed. William E. Griffith. Boulder, Colo.: Westview, 1989.

Strishkov, Vasili V. *The Soviet Copper Industry of the USSR: Problems, Issues, and Outlook*. Washington, D.C.: Department of the Interior, Bureau of Mines, 1984.

Strong, Anna Louise. *The Stalin Era*. New York: Soviet Russia Today, 1956.

Sutton, Antony C. *Western Technology and Soviet Economic Development, 1917 to 1930*. Stanford, Calif.: Hoover Institute on War, Revolution and Peace, 1968.

Suvorov, Viktor. *Soviet Military Intelligence*. London: Hamish Hamilton, 1984.

Suzuki, David. *Inventing the Future*. Toronto: Stoddart Publishing, 1989.

Szuprowicz, Bohdan. *How to Avoid Strategic Minerals Shortages*. New York: John Wiley and Sons, 1981.

Thomas, John R. "Soviet Scientific-Technical Performance: A Framework for the USSR's Information Revolution." In *The Future Information Revolution in the USSR*. Ed. Richard F. Starr. New York: Crane Russak, 1988.

Tikhonov, N. A. *Sovietskaia Ekonomika: Dostizhenia, Problemy, Perspektivy*. Moscow: Novosti Press, 1984.

Tilton, J. E. *The Future of Non-Fuel Minerals*. Washington, D.C.: Brookings Institution, 1977.

U.S. Bureau of Mines. *Asbestos, Minerals Yearbook*. Washington, D.C.: Bureau of Mines, 1985.

U.S. Congress, Hearings of the Senate Committee on Foreign Relations. *Transfer of United States High Technology to the Soviet Union and Soviet Bloc Nations*. U.S. Congress, 2nd session, May 1982.

*United States Congressional Code and Administrative News*, Volume 3, 1981. St. Paul: West Publishing Company, 1983.

*USSR Yearbook '89*. Moscow: Novosti Press Agency Publishing House, 1989.

Vagt, G. O. *Asbestos, MR. 155*. Ottawa, Canada: Energy, Mines and Resources, 1976.

Vander Elst, Philip. *Capitalist Technology for Soviet Survival*. Washington, D.C.: Institute of Economic Affairs, 1981.

Vlasov, V. A. *Yaponskaya Promyshlennost: Nauchno-Teknicheskiy Progress i Yego Posledstviya*. Moscow: Nauka, 1979.

Volkova, Valentina, et al. *Teoriya Sistem i metody sistemnovo analiza v upravlenii i svyazi*. Moscow: Akademia Nauka, 1983.

Wellman, David A. *A Chip in the Curtain--Computer Technology in the Soviet Union*. Washington, D.C.: National Defense University Press, 1989.

*Who's Who in the Soviet Government*. Moscow: Novosti Press Agency Publishing House, 1990.

Wiener, Norbert. *God and Golem Inc.: A Comment on Certain Points Where Cybernetics Impinges on Religion*. Cambridge, Mass.: The M.I.T. Press, 1964.

Winner, Langdon. *Autonomous Technology: Technics-Out-of-Control as a Theme in Political Thought*. Cambridge, Mass.: The M.I.T. Press, 1977.

Wojciechowski, M. J., ed. *Structural Changes in the World Mineral Industry: Implications for Canada*. Ottawa, Canada: Centre for Resource Studies, 1986.

World Resources Institute. *The 1993 Information Please Environmental Almanac*. Boston: Houghton Mifflin, 1993.

Wynne, Greville. *The Man from Odessa*. London: Robert Hale, 1981.

*Yaponiya Yezhegodnik*. Moscow, 1985.

Zamyatin, Yeygeny. *We*. London: Penguin Books, 1993.

Zerzan, John and Alice Carnes, eds. *Questioning Technology: Tool, Toy, or Tyrant*. Philadelphia: New Society Publishers, 1991.

Ziegler, Charles. *Environmental Policy in the U.S.S.R.* Boston: University of Massachusetts Press, 1987.

## *MAGAZINE AND JOURNAL ARTICLES*

Adams, Mark B. "Biology After Stalin: A Case History," *Survey*, Winter 1977.

"Aggressive Soviet Space Program Threatened by Budget, Policy Changes." *Aviation Week and Space Technology*, 134 (11): March 18, 1991.

"Azerbaijan: The Bear Pauses." *The Economist*, 329 (7841): December 11,

1993.

"Baltic States: Kroons, Lats, Litas." *The Economist*, 328 (78-18): July 3, 1993.

Besher, Alexander. *Infoworld*, 12 November 1984.

"Bessarabian Homesick Blues." *The Economist*, 329 (7835): October 30, 1993.

Bieliavskas, Diana B. "U.S. Soviet Discussions on Energy Conservation." *American Association for the Advancement of Slavic Studies Newsletter*, 27 (5): November 1987.

Bores, Leo. "AGAT." *Byte*, November 1984.

Brodeur, Paul, "Annals of Radiation: The Hazards of Electromagnetic Fields, III--Video Display Terminals," *New Yorker*, June 26, 1989.

Browne, Malcolm W. "The Star Wars Spinoff." *The New York Times Magazine*, August 24, 1986.

Bruder, Eric T. and Kathleen A. Scanlan. "Central Asia: A New Business Frontier." *Business America*, 114 (18): September 6, 1993.

Bush, Keith. "Environmental Problems in the USSR." *Problems of Communism*, 21 (4): July-August 1972.

"CIS Environmental Rules Growing Tougher." *Oil and Gas Journal*, 91 (38): September 29, 1993.

Cooper, Andrew Fenton, and Ashok Kapur. "La Vulnerabilite strategique des Mineraux: Le Case de la Republique federale allemande face a l'Afrique de Sud et a l'Union Sovietique." *Etudes Internationales*, 15 (1): March 1984.

Covault, Craig. "Russians Reveal Secrets of Mir, Buran, Lunar Landing Craft," *Aviation Week and Space Technology*, 136 (6): February 10, 1992.

---. "Russian Military Space Maintains Aggressive Pace." *Aviation Week and Space Technology*, 138 (18): May 3, 1993.

---. "Russians Locked in Struggle for Space Program Control." *Aviation Week and Space Technology*, 138 (5) February 1, 1993.

"The Dangers of Sharing American Technology." *Business Week*, March 14, 1983.

"A Defector Warns: What Fools," *Time*, May 27, 1985.

"Diamonds--Flawed Monopoly." *The Economist*, January 17, 1981.

Dickson, David. "Shake-Up Announced for Soviet Academy." *Science*, 27 March 1987.

Dragadze, Peter. "Russia's Embryonic Capitalists." *Forbes*, October 16, 1989.

Edwards, Mike. "Chernobyl--One Year After." *National Geographic*, 171 (5): May 1987.

---. "A Broken Empire: Kazakhstan: Facing the Nightmare." *National Geographic*, 183 (3): March 1993.

---. "A Broken Empire: Ukraine: Running on Empty." *National Geographic*, 183 (3): March 1993.

*Ekonomika izhizn'*, 6, 1992.

Elson, John. "On the Front Line." *Time*, April 10, 1989.

Epstein, E. J. "Have You Ever Tried to Sell a Diamond?" *The Atlantic Monthly*,

February 1982.

Erickson, John. "Soviet Cybermen: Men and Machines in the System." *Signal*, 3 (8), 1983.

Feodoroff, Pamela. "Central Asia Trade Channels are Opening." *Business America*, 114 (8): April 1993.

Fine, D. "Moscow's Ominous Shift Towards Buying Minerals." *Business Week*, September 8, 1980.

Fletcher, W., and K. Oldenburg, "Strategic Minerals: How Technology Can Reduce U.S. Import Vulnerability." *Issues in Science and Technology*, 2 (4): Summer 1986.

Galuszka, Peter. "Is Russia 'Trying to Recapture Lost Lands'?" *Business Week*, issue 3334, August 30, 1993.

Gardner, H. Stephen. "Restructuring the Soviet Foreign Trade System." *The Columbia Journal of World Business*, 23 (2): Summer 1988.

Garelik, Glenn. "The Chernobyl Syndrome." *New York Times Book Review*.

Goldman, Marshall I. "To Russia, with Cash." *Business Month*, November 1988.

Graham, Loren. "Science in the Brezhnev Era." *The Bulletin of the Atomic Scientists*, February 1982.

Grange, Judith K. "Cybernetics and Automation in Soviet Troop Control." *Signal*, 3 (8): 1983.

"Great Siberia in the Sky, The." *The Economist*, October 3, 1987.

Henderson, Breck W. "U.S. Buying Soviet Topaz 2 to Boost Space Nuclear Power Program." *Aviation Week and Space Technology*, 134 (2): January 14, 1991.

Hoffmann, Erik. "Soviet Views of the Scientific Technological Revolution." *World Politics*, July 1978.

Hofheinz, Paul. "The New Soviet Threat: Pollution." *Fortune*, 126 (2): July 27, 1992.

"How DeBeers Dominates the Diamonds." *The Economist*, February 23, 1980.

"Huddled for Comfort." *Banker*, 143 (805): March 1993.

Iaroshevski, M. G. "Kibernetika--Nauka Mrakobesov." *Literaturnaia Gazeta*, 5 April 1952.

Jaroff, Leon. "Onward to Mars." *Time*, July 18, 1988.

Kerschner, Lee. "Cybernetics: Key to the Future?" *Problems of Communism*, November/December 1965.

Kincade, William H., and T. Keith Thomson. "Economic Conversion in the USSR: Its Role in Perestroyka." *Problems of Communism*, January-February, 1990.

Kireyev, Alexei. "Contrasts of Conversion." *Perestroika: A Soviet Monthly Digest*, 5: May 1990.

Kowalski, Adam. "Swords into Chocolate Truffles," *New Scientist*, 11 November 1989.

Lacayo, Richard. "Racing to Win the Heavens," *Time*, October 15, 1984.

Lawther, William. "Operation Exodus Nets a Catch," *MacLeans*, January 17, 1983.

Lenorovitz, Jeffrey M. "Russia to Expand Role in Manned Space Flight." *Aviation Week and Space Technology*, 139 (5): August 2, 1993.

Lenorovitz, Jeffrey M., and Boris Rybak. "Feeble Russian Economy Hinders Space Efforts," *Aviation Week and Space Technology*, 138 (11): March 15, 1993.

Levin, M. Sh., and D. B. Magidson. "Vybor kanalov sviazi pri proektirovanii otraslevoi avtomatizirovannoi sistemy nauchno-tekhnicheskoi informatsii." *Nauchno-tekhnicheskaia informatsiia, Seriia 2: Informatsionnye protsessy is sistemy*, 3: March 1985.

Linville, Lt. Col. Ray P. "Emerging Soviet Space Programs: Prospects for Military Application." *Armed Forces Journal International*, January 1987.

Mally, Gerhard. "Technology Transfer Controls." *Atlantic Community Quarterly*, Fall 1982.

Marshal, R. Scott. "Caucasus, Moldova--Future Depends on Reform." *Business America*, 114 (8): April 8, 1993.

Mattews, David B. "Controlling the Exportation of Strategically-Sensitive Technology: The Extraterritorial Jurisdiction of the Multilateral Export Control Enhancement Amendments Act of 1988." *Columbia Journal of Transnational Law*, 28 (747): 1990.

Meyer, Herbert. "Russia's Sudden Reach for Raw Materials." *Fortune*, July 28, 1980.

Meyer, Stephen M. "Soviet Military Programmes and the New High Ground." *Survival*, 25 (5): September/October 1983.

Nehra, Rashmi. "Kazakhstan Has an Abundance of Oil and Other Resources." *Business America*, 114 (18): September 6, 1993.

"New Push for Gold Standard." *Financial Times*, November 20, 1981.

"Nickel--Downhill Battle." *The Economist*, November 22, 1980.

Nodwell, Jack. "Doing Business Soviet-Style." *Report on Business Magazine*, November 1988.

Painton, Frederick. "Crackdown on Spies," *Time*, April 18, 1983.

Parker, Richard. "Inside the 'Collapsing' Soviet Economy." *The Atlantic*, 265 (6): June 1990.

Pratt, Susan. "Perestroika: More Food for Thought than for Grocery Shelves." *Bloc*, premiere issue, 1989.

*Pravitel'stvennyi vestnik*, 13: March 1991.

Reich, Robert. Review of *The Soviet Economy: Problems and Prospects* by Padma Desai and *Gorbachev's Challenge: Economic Reform in the Age of High Technology* by Marshall Goldman. *The New Republic*, August 3, 1987.

Renner, Michael. "The Drain of a Permanent War Economy." *USA Today Magazine*, July 1989.

"Return to the Gold Standard." *The Economist*, April 20, 1985.

Rezun, Miron. "The Politics of Computers in the USSR." *Queen's Quarterly*, 93 (4): Winter 1986.

Rogers, Michael, with Carroll Bogert. "Red Hackers, Arise!" *Newsweek*, March 20, 1989.

Rumer, Boris."Structural Imbalance in the Soviet Economy." *Problems of Communism*, July-August 1984.

"Russia Under Gorbachev." *The Economist*, November 16, 1985.

"Russian Management--Perestroika in the Factory." *The Economist*, June 9, 1990.

"Russia's Greens--The Poisoned Giant Wakes Up." *The Economist*, November 4, 1989.

Sagan, Carl. Review of *Science, Philosophy and Human Behavior in the Soviet Union* by Loren Graham. *New York Times Book Review*, September 27, 1987.

Schoenfeld, Gabriel. "Rad Storm Rising." *The Atlantic*, 266 (6): December 1990.

Seeger, Murray. "Tightening up the High-Tech Trade." *Fortune*, December 28, 1981.

Severin, William K. "Soviet Nonfuel Minerals: Resource War or Business as Usual?" *Materials and Society*, 7 (1): 1983.

Stares, Paul. "U.S. and Soviet Military Space Programs: A Comparative Assessment." *Daedalus*, 114: 1985.

"Staying On?" *The Economist*, April 28, 1990.

Szulc, Tad. "Why the Russians Are Trying Harder to Steal Our Secrets." *Washington Post Parade Magazine*, November 7, 1982.

Thomas, John, and Ursula Kruse-Vaucienne. "Soviet Science and Technology." *Survey*, Winter 1977.

Thompson, Dick. "The Greening of the USSR." *Time*, January 2, 1989.

"The Transcaucasus: Fiery Food, Fiery Tempers." *The Economist*, 328 (7821), July 24, 1993.

"Ukraine Over the Brink," *The Economist*, 328 (7827): September 4, 1993.

Ulsamer, Edgar. *Air Force Magazine*, December 1984.

Velikhov, Ye. P. "Personal Computers, Current Practise and Prospects." *Vestnik Akademii Nauk SSSR*, 8: August 1984.

Vid, Leonid. "Guns into Butter, Soviet Style." *Bulletin of the Atomic Scientists*, January/February 1990.

Winner, Langdon, *Whole Earth Review*, Vol. 73, Winter 1991.

Young, John P., and Jeanne P. Taylor. "Science and Technology Policy in the USSR: Impact of the Changing Character of Soviet Science and Technology in its Administration." *Policy Studies Journal*, December 1976.

## *NEWSPAPER ARTICLES*

Brusov, Pavel. "Rabota Kovalenka." *Pravda*, February 2, 1984.

Knapp, Bill. "Space University Coming to Canada." *Globe and Mail*, August 12, 1989.

Penny, Louise. "Where Even the Air Is a Sewer." *Globe and Mail*, July 11, 1990.

Rakitov, A. "Informatizatsiia  obshchestva i  strategiia uskoreniia." *Pravda*, January 23, 1987.

Sallot, Jeff. "Ottawa Tries to Protect Computers Against Spies with Sensitive Radios." *Globe and Mail*, October 14, 1984.

# Index

## About the Author

MIRON REZUN is a Professor of Political Science at the University of New Brunswick. He has published widely on Soviet and Mideastern affairs and has recently completed *Europe and War in the Balkans* (Praeger, 1995), detailing the many perspectives of the war in the former Yugoslavia.

ISBN 0-275-95383-1